MUHAMMAD AT MECCA

MUHAMMAD AT MECCA

BY

W. MONTGOMERY WATT

OXFORD
UNIVERSITY PRESS

OXFORD
UNIVERSITY PRESS

Great Clarendon Street, Oxford OX2 6DP

Oxford University Press is a department of the University of Oxford.
It furthers the University's objective of excellence in research, scholarship,
and education by publishing worldwide in

Oxford New York

Auckland Cape Town Dar es Salaam Hong Kong Karachi
Kuala Lumpur Madrid Melbourne Mexico City Nairobi
New Delhi Shanghai Taipei Toronto

with offices in

Argentina Austria Brazil Chile Czech Republic France Greece
Guatemala Hungary Italy Japan South Korea Poland Portugal
Singapore Switzerland Turkey Ukraine Vietnam

Oxford is a registered trade mark of Oxford University Press
in the UK and in certain other countries

First published in Great Britain, 1953

ISBN-13: 978-0-19-577278-4
ISBN-10: 0-19-577278-4

Reprinted in Pakistan, 1979,
by permission of Oxford University Press, Oxford

Sixth Impression 2006

Printed in Pakistan by
Times Press, Karachi.
Published by
Ameena Saiyid, Oxford University Press
No. 38, Sector 15, Korangi Industrial Area, PO Box 8214
Karachi-74900, Pakistan.

PREFACE

It would not be fitting to allow this book to appear without a tribute to the memory of my teacher and friend, Richard Bell, formerly Reader in Arabic in Edinburgh. It was he who first guided my study of Islam, and in recent years he gave freely of his time, scholarship, and wisdom, whenever consulted on particular questions. He read the first draft of this book and, though he could not altogether accept its standpoint, made many helpful suggestions, besides allowing me to see some unpublished writings of his own. Most of my Qur'anic quotations are from his translation, by kind permission of the publishers, Messrs. T. & T. Clark.

I have to thank Professor H. A. R. Gibb for much generous help. I am also indebted to colleagues at Edinburgh, especially to Dr. Pierre Cachia for the compilation of the index, and to Mr. J. R. Walsh for useful comments and references.

W. M. W.

EDINBURGH
December 1952

CONTENTS

BIBLIOGRAPHY

THE following is merely a list of the abbreviations used for the works most frequently referred to. For further bibliographical details see G. P. Pfannmüller, *Handbuch der Islam-Literatur* (Berlin, 1923), 115–98, and J. Sauvaget, *Introduction à l'Histoire de l'Orient Musulmane* (Paris, 1943, &c.), 111–14.

Ahrens, *Muhammed* = Karl Ahrens, *Muhammed als Religionsstifter*, Leipzig, 1935.

Azraqī = al-Azraqī, *Kitāb Akhbār Makkah* (in F. Wüstenfeld, *Mekka*, vol. i, Leipzig, 1858).

Bell, *Origin* = Richard Bell, *The Origin of Islam in its Christian Environment*, London, 1926.

Bell, *Translation of Q.* = Richard Bell, *The Qur'ān, translated with a critical re-arrangement of the surahs* (2 vols.), Edinburgh, 1937–9. (See also under Q.)

Bukhārī = al-Bukhārī, *Al-Jāmi' aṣ-Ṣaḥīḥ*, ed. Krehl et Juynboll, Leyden, 1862–1908. French translation by O. Houdas and W. Marçais: El-Bokhari, *Les Traditions Islamiques* (4 vols.), Paris, 1903–14. The primary reference is by *Kitāb* (= *titre*) and *Bāb* (= *chapitre*).

Buhl, *Muhammed* = Frants Buhl, *Das Leben Muhammeds* (German tr. by H. H. Schaeder), Leipzig, 1930.

Caetani, *Ann.* = Leone Caetani, *Annali dell' Islam*, vol. i, Milan, 1905.

Caetani, *Studi* = —— *Studi di Storia Orientale*, vols. i and iii, Milan, 1911–14.

EI = *Encyclopaedia of Islam* (4 vols. and supplement), Leyden, 1913, &c.

Goldziher, *MS.* = Ignaz Goldziher, *Muhammedanische Studien* (2 vols.), Halle, 1888–90.

IH = Ibn Hishām, *Kitāb Sīrat Rasūl Allāh* (*Das Leben Muhammed's nach . . . Ibn Ishāk bearbeitet von . . . Ibn Hischām*), ed. F. Wüstenfeld (2 vols.), Göttingen, 1859–60.

IS (or ISa'd) = Ibn Sa'd, *Ṭabaqāt* (Ibn Saad, *Biographien . . .*), ed. E. Sachau (9 vols.), Leyden, 1905, &c.

Islam = *Der Islam*.

Jeffery, *Vocabulary* = Arthur Jeffery, *The Foreign Vocabulary of the Qur'ān*, Baroda, 1938.

JRAS = *Journal of the Royal Asiatic Society*.

Lammens, *Arabie* = H. Lammens, *L'Arabie Occidentale avant l'Hégire*, Beirut, 1928.

—— *Berceau* = —— *Le Berceau de l'Islam: l'Arabie Occidentale a la Veille de l'Hégire*, Rome, 1914.

—— *Mecque* = —— *La Mecque à la Veille de l'Hégire*, in Mélanges de l'Univ. S. Joseph, IX; also separately, Beirut, 1924. (Both pagings usually given.)

Lammens, *Ṭā'if* = H. Lammens, *La Cité Arabe de Ṭāif à la Veille de l'Hégire*, Mél. Univ. S. Joseph, VIII; also separately, Beirut, 1922.

MW = *The Moslem World.*

Nicholson, *Lit. Hist.* = R. A. Nicholson, *A Literary History of the Arabs* (2nd edn.), Cambridge, 1930.

Nöldeke–Schwally = Theodor Nöldeke, *Geschichte des Qorāns* (2nd edn., vols. i and ii), ed. F. Schwally, Leipzig, 1909–19.

Q = *Qur'ān* (with Flügel's numbering of the verses); the translation is normally that of Richard Bell, but occasionally, for the sake of harmonizing with the context, this has been modified or replaced by some other rendering. In certain places an attempt has been made to indicate by letters Bell's provisional dating of passages, as follows:

A = very early.
B = early, early Meccan, early Qur'ān period.
C = Meccan.
D = late Meccan.
E = early Medinan.
E+ = Medinan.
F = connected with Badr.
G = connected with Uḥud.
H = up to Ḥudaybiyah.
I = after Ḥudaybiyah.
— = revised.

Sale and Wherry = E. M. Wherry, *A Comprehensive Commentary on the Qurān: comprising Sale's Translation and Preliminary Discourse with Additional Notes and Emendations* (4 vols.), Boston, 1882–6.

Ṭab. (or Ṭab. *Ann.*) = aṭ-Ṭabarī, *Ta'rīkh ar-Rusul wa 'l-Mulūk* ('*Annales*'), ed. M. de Goeje (15 vols.), Leyden, 1879–1901. All references are to the page of the Prima Series; the third volume of this contains the life of Muḥammad up to 8 A.H. (pp. 1073–1686).

Torrey, *Jewish Foundation* = C. C. Torrey, *The Jewish Foundation of Islam*, New York, 1933.

Wellhausen, *Reste* = J. Wellhausen, *Reste Arabischen Heidentums*, 2nd edn., Berlin, 1897.

WK = al-Wāqidī, *Kitāb al-Maghāzī*, ed. von Kremer, Calcutta, 1856.

Wüst. (or Wüstenfeld), *Mekka* = F. Wüstenfeld, *Die Chroniken der Stadt Mekka* (collection of texts with a German 'Bearbeitung') (4 vols.), Leipzig, 1858–61.

WW = al-Wāqidī, *Kitāb al-Maghāzī*, tr. J. Wellhausen (*Muhammed in Medina; das ist Vakidi's Kitab alMaghazi in verkürzter deutscher Wiedergabe*), Berlin, 1882.

ZDMG = *Zeitschrift der Deutschen Morgenländischen Gesellschaft.*

Particulars of other works are mostly given at the first occurrence.

INTRODUCTION

I. STANDPOINT

THIS book will be considered by at least three classes of readers: those who are concerned with the subject as historians, and those who approach it primarily as Muslims or Christians. It has been addressed, however, first and foremost to the historian. On the theological questions at issue between Christianity and Islam an attempt has been made to preserve neutrality. For example, in order to avoid deciding whether the Qur'ān is or is not the Word of God, I have refrained from using the expressions 'God says' and 'Muḥammad says' when referring to the Qur'ān, and have simply said 'the Qur'ān says'. I do not, however, regard the adoption of a materialistic outlook as implicit in historical impartiality, but write as a professing monotheist.

This academic attitude is, of course, in a sense incomplete. In so far as Christianity is in contact with Islam Christians must adopt some attitude towards Muḥammad, and that attitude ought to be based on theological principles. I would readily admit that my book is incomplete in this respect, but would claim that it presents Christians with the historical material which must be taken into account in forming the theological judgement.

To my Muslim readers I would say something similar. I have endeavoured, while remaining faithful to the standards of Western historical scholarship, to say nothing that would entail the rejection of any of the fundamental doctrines of Islam. There need be no unbridgeable gulf between Western scholarship and Islamic faith; if some of the conclusions of Western scholars have been unacceptable to Muslims, it may be that the scholars have not always been faithful to their own principles of scholarship and that, even from the purely historical point of view, their conclusion requires to be revised. On the other hand, it is probably also true that there is room, without any change in essentials, for some reformulation of Islamic doctrine.

The need for a fresh life of Muḥammad has been felt for some time by students of Islam, especially the more historically minded. This is not because of the discovery of fresh material—though Leone Caetani, for instance, writing about Muhammad in his

Annali dell' Islam (published 1905, &c.), did not have access to Ibn Sa'd's collection of biographies of early Muslims—but because in the last half-century or so historians' interests and attitudes have altered, and in particular because they have become more conscious of the material factors underlying history. This means that the historian of the mid-twentieth century, while not neglecting or belittling the religious and ideological aspects of the movement initiated by Muḥammad, wants to ask many questions about the economic, social and political background. Even those who deny (as I do) that such factors entirely determine the course of events have to admit their importance. The special feature of this biography of Muḥammad is thus not that it combs available sources more minutely but that it pays fuller attention to these material factors, and attempts to answer many questions that have hardly been raised in the past.

2. NOTE ON THE SOURCES

The main sources for the life of Muḥammad are firstly the Qur'ān or record of the revelations which (as he believed) he received from God, and secondly historical works by writers of the third and fourth centuries of the Muslim era. In the second group the works accessible to us are:

1. the *Sīrah* or life of Muḥammad by Ibn Hishām (d. 833/218);
2. the section of the *Annals* of aṭ-Ṭabarī (d. 922/310) dealing with the life of Muḥammad (Series I, vols. 2–4);
3. the *Maghāzī* or History of Muḥammad's Campaigns by al-Wāqidī (d. 822/207)—one recension was published in the Bibliotheca Indica, while Wellhausen gave an abbreviated translation of another recension in his *Muhammad in Medina*; an edition of the latter recension is in preparation;
4. the *Ṭabaqāt* of Ibn Sa'd (d. 845/230), the secretary of al-Wāqidī, a vast compilation containing, besides much material about Muḥammad, biographies of his chief Companions and of later 'bearers of Islam'.

Mention should also be made of the collections of Traditions (or anecdotes about the sayings and doings of Muḥammad) such as the *Ṣaḥīḥ* of al-Bukhārī and that of Muslim and the *Musnad* of Aḥmad b. Ḥanbal; these contain some material of importance for the historian, although the interests of the compilers were chiefly legal. The later biographical dictionaries of the Companions of

Muḥammad—*Usd al-Ghābah* by Ibn al-Athīr (1234/631) and the *Iṣābah* by Ibn Ḥajar (1447/851)—contain additional background material. There are later Muslim biographers of Muḥammad but none appears to have had access to any important primary sources other than those used by the above-mentioned writers.

These extant works were themselves based on earlier written sources. Indeed the *Sīrah* of Ibn Hishām is perhaps best described as an edition of the *Sīrah* of Ibn Isḥāq (d. 768/151). Ibn Isḥāq himself had predecessors, but his contribution to the biography of Muḥammad is the most considerable and has been the most influential. Ibn Isḥāq collected nearly all the available information, including old poems, and so ordered and selected his material that he produced a coherent story. Frequently he gives references to his sources in the usual Islamic manner. Ibn Hishām added a few explanatory notes. Some passages that are missing in his edition are found elsewhere, but it is not clear whether he is responsible for the omissions.

Aṭ-Ṭabarī also quotes Ibn Isḥāq, but not nearly so fully as Ibn Hishām. His importance is that he does not attempt to produce a smooth narrative of events, but gives variants. Thus he has a large number of separate authorities who made statements about the first male Muslim after Muḥammad, and some said it was ʿAlī, some Zayd b. Ḥārithah, and some Abū Bakr; Ibn Isḥāq mentions only one view, namely, that it was ʿAlī. Among his general authorities aṭ-Ṭabarī has a very early one, ʿUrwah b. az-Zubayr (d. 712/94), who left written material which has not been preserved elsewhere.

The *Campaigns* of al-Wāqidī are a valuable check on Ibn Isḥāq, since they come from an independent line of authorities, and they are usually fuller, but they refer only to the Medinan period. His secretary, Ibn Saʿd, gives variants on many points, but he admits much material of little historical value, and it is only occasionally that he is the sole source for anything of importance. On the other hand, his biographies of Muḥammad's Companions are a mine of useful information about the background of Muḥammad's life. The biographical dictionaries of persons who had known Muḥammad compiled by Ibn al-Athīr and Ibn Ḥajar are on a vaster scale —some 20,000 articles—and have many facts not in Ibn Saʿd; but little of this material affects the life of Muḥammad.

The Traditions collected by Muslim, al-Bukhārī, and others

include among their historical anecdotes some variants from the forms in Ibn Hishām and aṭ-Ṭabarī.

Much has been written by Western scholars in criticism of these sources, and especially of the Traditions. Sir William Muir's remarks on the sources in his *Life* are still a useful introduction. The most detailed study is that of Caetani in *Annali dell' Islam*; it is not difficult to correct his occasional excess of scepticism. The studies of Henri Lammens led him to almost complete rejection of the accounts of the Meccan period, but later scholars have generally held that he went too far; Theodor Nöldeke's remarks in his article *Die Tradition über das Leben Muhammeds*[1] may absolve one from further discussion of Lammens' more extreme views.

The important and well-founded conclusions about Islamic Traditions in J. Schacht's *Origins of Muhammadan Jurisprudence*[2] seem to force upon us a distinction between legal and historical traditions, and indeed Goldziher's epoch-making investigations in *Muhammedanischen Studien*, ii, are mainly applicable to legal traditions, though by no means entirely so. In the legal sphere there may be some sheer invention of traditions, it would seem. But in the historical sphere, in so far as the two may be separated, and apart from some exceptional cases, the nearest to such invention in the best early historians appears to be a 'tendential shaping' of material.[3] As Frants Buhl puts it, 'in dealing with the traditional material one must always be on one's guard, where a definite party-interest may be supposed, not to be led astray by its sometimes innocent-looking appearance'.[4]

Once the modern student is aware of the tendencies of the early historians and their sources, however, it ought to be possible for him to some extent to make allowance for the distortion and to present the data in an unbiased form; and the admission of 'tendential shaping' should have as its corollary the acceptance of the general soundness of the material. Moreover, inasmuch as many of the questions in which the historian of the mid-twentieth century is interested are not affected by the process of shaping, there should be little difficulty in obtaining answers to his questions from the sources.

[1] *Islam*, v, 1914, pp. 160–70. Cf. also C. Becker, *Prinzipielles zu Lammens' Sirastudien* in *Islam*, iv. 263 ff., reprinted in Becker's *Islamstudien*, i. 520–7; G. Levi della Vida, art. *Sīra* in EI.

[2] Oxford, 1950.

[3] Cf. Nöldeke, ZDMG, lii, 1898, pp. 16 ff.

[4] *Muhammed*, 374.

It should also be noticed that one of the simplest ways in which 'tendential shaping' takes place is by the attributing of motives for external acts. The distinction between external acts and alleged motives should therefore be kept firmly in mind. The actor himself and his friends will suggest the most praiseworthy motives; his enemies will assert that the motives were dishonourable. But there can be little dispute about the external acts except within narrow limits, e.g. on the relative dating of two events. Thus nobody denies that 'Ā'ishah left Medina shortly before the murder of the caliph 'Uthmān, but whether her motives were honourable, dishonourable, or neutral is vigorously debated. The modern historian will therefore largely discount allegations of motives in his sources and will suggest his own motives in the light of what he knows of the total pattern of the external actions of a man.

This distinction between act and motive is most important in the period after the Hijrah, but it also applies to Muḥammad's Meccan period and to pre-Islamic times. Before the Hijrah, however, the history was shadowy and it is always possible that events have been invented. Probably the train of reasoning was somewhat as follows: *A* did *X*; his motive cannot have been *L* or *M*, which are not creditable to him; therefore it must have been *N*; therefore he must also have done *Y*.

In dealing, then, with the background of Muḥammad's career and his Meccan period, I have proceeded on the view that the traditional accounts are in general to be accepted, are to be received with care and as far as possible corrected where 'tendential shaping' is suspected, and are only to be rejected outright where there is internal contradiction. It is barely conceivable, for instance, that the genealogical material in Ibn Sa'd is a sheer fabrication. Who would have taken the trouble to invent all this intricate network, and for what reason? Besides, if we who are not interested in genealogy know something about our ancestors for two or three generations, is it fanciful to suppose that the Arabs who were intensely concerned with descent should have known their ancestry for six or eight or ten generations? John Van Ess met a boy of ten who apparently knew fifteen of his ancestors.[1] Moreover, Ibn Sa'd gives the impression of being a careful scholar in genealogical matters, aware of the difficulties of disputed points; and he is therefore worthy of credence in his genealogies back to about the

[1] *Meet the Arab*, London, 1947, p. 77.

time of Quṣayy in Mecca. Earlier genealogical and historical material must, of course, be handled with greater care; and there are special difficulties in Medina owing to the remnants of a matrilineal system.

The procedure here described involves a fresh view of the relation of the traditional historical material to the Qur'ān. It has been fashionable for some time to assert that the Qur'ān was the fundamental source for the Meccan period. The Qur'ān is certainly in a sense contemporary, but quite apart from the difficulty of determining the chronological order of the various parts and the uncertainty of many of the results, the Qur'ān is partial and fragmentary. It does not give anything like a complete picture of the life of Muḥammad and the Muslims during the Meccan period. What in fact Western biographers have done is to assume the truth of the broad outlines of the picture of the Meccan period given by the *Sīrah*, and to use this as a framework into which to fit as much Qur'anic material as possible. The sounder methodology is to regard the Qur'ān and the early traditional accounts as complementary sources, each with a fundamental contribution to make to the history of the period. The Qur'ān presents mainly the ideological aspect of a great complex of changes which took place in and around Mecca, but the economic, social, and political aspects must also be considered if we are to have a balanced picture and indeed if we are to understand properly the ideological aspect itself.

This may sound in theory revolutionary—or reactionary—but it will be found that it does not indicate any startling change in practice, except for the pre-Islamic period. Indeed it may seem at times that in practice I sit rather more lightly to tradition than those who are in theory more sceptical. In particular the principle of distinguishing between public acts and alleged motives and of not accepting statements about motives except when they are in accordance with the results of an independent scrutiny of the acts leads to the rejection of many of the details of the traditional account, as, for example, in the case of the emigration to Abyssinia.

The traditions relating to the Meccan period are here considered mainly from the point of view of the *matn* or contents, and little attention is paid to the *isnād* or chain of authorities. In the Medinan period the study of *isnāds* helps towards assessing the value and authenticity of a tradition and estimating its bias. But in the case of events prior to the Hijrah, study of *isnāds* does not appear to lead to results of importance. The one authority whose contributions are worthy of investigation is ʿUrwah b. az-Zubayr, and his 'tendencies' are considered in Excursus F.

I

THE ARABIAN BACKGROUND

WITH the material now available, it would be possible to devote at least a volume to the description of the Arabian background of the life of Muḥammad. This chapter has therefore the limited aim of drawing attention to those features of the background which are most important for a proper understanding of his career and achievements. It is largely dependent on the works of others, both orientalists and travellers, and a complete acknowledgement of this indebtedness would be impossible.

While it is convenient to speak of 'Arabia', for the most part we are concerned only with one region of it, the district surrounding Mecca and Medina—the Ḥijāz in the wider sense[1]—and the adjoining steppe-land of the Najd.

I. THE ECONOMIC BASIS

To a Westerner the primary association of Arabia is with deserts and bedouin, and the economics of desert life is a useful starting-point. It is true that the desert played no creative part in the development of Muḥammad's monotheism;[2] none the less in the total phenomenon of Islam the desert has a role of first importance. Mecca and Medina were islands in a sea of desert, or rather steppe, still in close economic relations with the nomads, and inhabited by descendants of nomads who still retained many of the desert-born habits of their ancestors. Some consideration of the desert is thus unavoidable.

The nomadic life is based upon stock-breeding, especially the breeding of the camel. Within the Arabian steppes several different types of land are distinguished, of which we need only mention two. Firstly there are those lands which, though in summer a waterless, sandy waste, in winter after the rains—the season which the Arab calls *rabīʿ*—are covered, particularly in the hollows, with luscious green vegetation, a paradise for camels. Then there are those districts in which perennial trees and shrubs, mostly of an aromatic character, manage to maintain themselves. These two

[1] Cf. Nöldeke in *Islam*, v. 206, n. 1.

[2] Cf. H. A. R. Gibb, *Mohammedanism*, London, 1949, p. 1.

types of country explain the need for a migratory life. As soon as rain falls (though rainfall is somewhat erratic) the lands of the first type become the best pasture for camels; but when with the coming of summer that pasture deteriorates and vanishes, the nomads must retire to lands of the second type. In the lands of the first type the nomad is dependent on the camel for moisture as well as for sustenance; in the second there are wells, though these are often used more for watering the camels than for human consumption. In either case milk is the staple article of diet of the nomad along with dates which he obtains from the oases. Flesh he eats occasionally. Cereals are a luxury reserved for the rich and great.

The nomad is to some extent dependent on the settled lands. Robbery in his eyes is no crime, whether it be a raid on an oasis or on a caravan. As the nomad is usually the better fighter in the skirmishing involved in such brigandry, it frequently happens that agriculturists and merchants are ready to pay a desert tribe for the protection of their homesteads and herds and for the safe passage of their caravans. For many nomads such fees are a regular source of income. In these ways the nomad is able to enjoy some of the products of the civilization of the Sown

In the region with which we are concerned agriculture was practised at the oases and at certain favoured spots high in the mountains. The chief crop at the oases was dates, while in the mountains, as at aṭ-Ṭā'if, cereals were important. Yathrib (later known as Medina) was a large and flourishing oasis in the time of Muḥammad. There were several Jewish agricultural colonies such as Khaybar. At Mecca, on the other hand, no agriculture at all was possible—an important fact which should be kept in mind. Although it does not come within our present purview, the Yemen or Arabia Felix (it is worth remembering) was fertile agricultural country where artificial irrigation had been practised from early times. This is now thought to have been the original home of the Semites or at least their 'cradle-land' and 'first separate habitat'.[1] Reminiscences of a connexion with the fertile south certainly abound in the traditional Arabic accounts of pre-Islamic times. This connexion had doubtless made its contribution to the Arab culture of Muḥammad's day, but the study of such influence has not so far led to any assured results.

Mecca, Muḥammad's home for half a century, was entirely a

[1] G. A. Barton, *Semitic and Hamitic Origins*, 27 f.

commercial city, set amidst barren rocks. The growth of the city as a trading centre came about through the existence there of a *ḥaram* or sanctuary area, to which men could come without fear of molestation. Geographical conditions were also in its favour; it stood at the cross-roads of routes from the Yemen to Syria and from Abyssinia to 'Irāq. To Mecca, therefore, the nomad came for goods brought from the four points of the compass by caravan. Originally the Meccans themselves were probably only middlemen and retailers and not the importers and entrepreneurs who organized caravans. But by the end of the sixth century A.D. they had gained control of most of the trade from the Yemen to Syria—an important route by which the West got Indian luxury goods as well as South Arabian frankincense. Aṭ-Ṭā'if was a rival of Mecca in commercial matters, but Mecca clearly had the stronger position.

Mecca was more than a mere trading centre, it was a financial centre. Scholars as a whole may not be quite so certain about details as Lammens[1] appears to be, but it is clear that financial operations of considerable complexity were carried on at Mecca. The leading men of Mecca in Muḥammad's time were above all financiers, skilful in the manipulation of credit, shrewd in their speculations, and interested in any potentialities of lucrative investment from Aden to Gaza or Damascus. In the financial net that they had woven not merely were all the inhabitants of Mecca caught, but many notables of the surrounding tribes also. The Qur'ān appeared not in the atmosphere of the desert, but in that of high finance.[2]

There remains one further point. Was the rise of a new religion in the Ḥijāz and the subsequent Arab expansion into Persia, Syria, and North Africa linked up with any deep economic change? One answer that has been given is that it was due to increasing desiccation of the Arabian steppe, and that it was hunger that drove the Arabs along the road of conquest. Let us set aside for the moment the general question of economic change. Here it is sufficient to state that there is no good evidence of any significant deterioration in climatic conditions in the steppe.[3] Life there was still tolerable; we hear of followers of Muḥammad who turned back from the later conquests outside Arabia to the desert life they loved. The general impression one receives is that the nomads were no worse

[1] See esp. *Mecque*, 135/231 ff.

[2] Cf. the use of mercantile terms to express theological doctrines—C.C. Torrey, *The Commercial-Theological Terms of the Koran*, Leyden, 1892.

[3] But cf. A. J. Toynbee, *Study of History*, iii. 439, 445, 453–4.

off than they had previously been, but rather better in view of the benefits which came to them from the growing prosperity of Mecca. Later, with the emigration from Arabia in the period of conquests, the pressure of population upon food supplies must have decreased.

There were small local industries in the Ḥijāz, mostly to serve the needs of nomads and townsmen, though we hear, for example, of leather-work being exported from aṭ-Ṭā'if. From the perspective of a life of Muḥammad, however, they are not sufficiently important to be considered as a separate factor.

2. MECCAN POLITICS

Within the commercial community of Mecca there was a continuous struggle for power. The political groupings within Mecca to which this gave rise were in turn involved in relations with the Arab tribes with whom the Meccan caravans came into contact, and with the great powers to whose markets they carried their goods. Some of these matters are extremely complex, but, since from the first Muḥammad was something of a statesman, it is necessary to consider at least the chief points.

(a) *Political groupings within the Quraysh*

The Arabic sources give much information about the family and tribal feuds and alliances within the Quraysh. Some Western critics have overemphasized the legendary aspect of these stories and have concentrated too much on a discussion of whether the characters are historical individuals or merely personifications of tribes. There is probably more historical fact than the radical critics allowed, but it is not proposed to touch on this difficult problem here. It only diverts attention from the significant fact that these stories show us how Quraysh conceived their family and clan relationships about the time of Muḥammad. Certain points may have been modified by later events; e.g. the hostility between ʿAbbāsids and Umayyads may have affected the account of the relations of B. Hāshim and B. Umayyah. But on the whole the picture may be accepted as reliable.

The sanctuary of Mecca was of extreme antiquity. After being controlled for a long period by the tribe of Jurhum, it passed to the Khuzāʿah, with whom were associated B. Bakr b. ʿAbd Manāt b. Kinānah, though certain privileges, possibly of a sacral character, remained in the hands of the old families, as the Ijāzah in the hands of B. Ṣūfah. The Khuzā'ah and their allies lost power to Quṣayy, who gained his strength partly from an alliance with certain members of Kinānah and Quḍā'ah, and partly from bringing together various groups of Quraysh, hitherto disunited and uninfluential. Quṣayy is probably to be regarded as the founder of the city of Mecca as distinct from a mere encampment round the sanctuary.[1]

To Quṣayy is perhaps to be attributed the distinction between Quraysh al-Biṭāḥ (those who inhabited the district immediately round the Ka'bah) and Quraysh aẓ-Ẓawāhir (those whose quarters were in the outskirts). Certainly the distinction existed, and it is natural to suppose that it is due to the man who assigned districts at the original building of the city. All the descendants of Quṣayy and all those of his great-grandfather Ka'b are included in Quraysh al-Biṭāḥ. Details based on two lists of al-Mas'ūdī[2] are given in the table on page 7.

It is within Quraysh al-Biṭāḥ that we hear of further divisions. 'Abd ad-Dār at first succeeded to the position of Quṣayy, but in course of time his family, led by his great-grandson, was challenged by that of 'Abd Manāf, represented by his son 'Abd Shams. Mecca became divided into two hostile camps. 'Abd Manāf was supported by Asad, Zuhrah, Taym, and al-Ḥārith b. Fihr, while 'Abd ad-Dār had the help of Makhzūm, Sahm, Jumaḥ, and 'Adī. 'Āmir b. Lu'ayy and Muḥārib of Quraysh aẓ-Ẓawāhir are mentioned as neutral. The two groups were known as Muṭayyabūn and Aḥlāf respectively—the Perfumed and the Confederates. It is interesting to note that the alinement does not follow strictly family lines. The family of Quṣayy is divided, 'Abd ad-Dār being opposed by 'Abd al-'Uzzā (= Asad) and 'Abd Manāf; and similarly the rest of Murrah is opposed to Makhzūm. (This is an argument against the view that the genealogies are rationalizations of later events.) The quarrel nearly led to fighting, but a compromise was achieved in time, whereby 'Abd ad-Dār retained certain privileges, largely nominal, and 'Abd Manāf was given the substance of power. Both sides realized how much they had to gain from agreement and how much to lose from disagreement.

1 IH, 73–80, &c.

2 *Murūj adh-Dhahab*, iii. 119 ff.; iv. 121 f.; cf. Ibn Ẓuhayrah *ap.* Wüstenfeld, *Mekka*, ii. 339 f.

The Ḥilf al-Fuḍūl, or Confederation of the Virtuous (?), seems to be a later development of the Muṭayyabūn, and not a general league against injustice, as Caetani takes it to be.[1] Al-Masʿūdī[2] says it originated in an attempt to help a Yamanī to recover a debt from al-ʿĀṣ b. Wā'il of B. Sahm. The participants were the clans of Hāshim, al-Muṭṭalib, Asad, Zuhrah, Taym, and perhaps al-Ḥārith b. Fihr,[3] that is to say, the Muṭayyabūn without B. ʿAbd Shams and B. Nawfal. Now there had been a quarrel between Nawfal and ʿAbd al-Muṭṭalib b. Hāshim, in which al-Muṭṭalib had supported the latter.[4] Thus ʿAbd Shams and Nawfal may have grown sufficiently strong to do without the alliance, whereas Hāshim and al-Muṭṭalib, being weaker, would still be glad of its support.

The story told by Ibn Isḥāq of a later appeal to the 'Confederation of the Fuḍūl' confirms this interpretation. During Muʿāwiyah's caliphate the governor of Medina, his nephew al-Walīd, had a dispute about property with al-Ḥusayn b. ʿAlī, and settled this in his own favour. Al-Ḥusayn protested and said that he appealed to the 'Confederation of the Fuḍūl'. He received offers of support from ʿAbdallāh b. az-Zubayr, al-Miswar, and ʿAbd ar-Raḥmān b. ʿUthmān. Faced with this threat of the renewal of an old alliance—the men named are of Hāshim, Asad, Zuhrah, and Taym respectively—al-Walīd gave way. The later conversation between the caliph ʿAbd al-Malik (of B. Umayyah or ʿAbd Shams) and a member of B. Nawfal implies that these clans had left the confederation at an early date, if indeed they had ever been members of it.[5]

By the time of Muḥammad's mission further changes in political alinement seem to have taken place, but it is difficult to say, at least in the later stages, how far the changes were independent of the impact of Islam and how far the result of it. The position I take to have been as follows:

Group A	*Group B*	*Group C*
Hāshim	ʿAbd Shams	Makhzūm
al-Muṭṭalib	——	Sahm
Zuhrah	Nawfal	Jumaḥ
Taym	Asad	ʿAbd ad-Dār
al-Ḥārith b. Fihr	ʿĀmir	
ʿAdī		

[1] *Annali*, i. 164–6.
[2] *Murūj*, iv. 123 f.
[3] IH, 85–87.
[4] Ṭab. 1084 f.
[5] IH, 86 f.

Group A is the old Ḥilf al-Fuḍūl with the loss of Asad and the addition of ʿAdī; the latter change might partly be linked with the conversion of ʿUmar b. al-Khaṭṭāb, but is more likely the outcome of the entente between ʿAbd Shams and group C, since there had at one time been a bitter feud between ʿAdī and ʿAbd Shams;[1] economic factors may also have been present, of course. Groups B and C worked together for many purposes, and in particular ʿAbd Shams seems to have had close relations with group C, doubtless through common mercantile interests. Group C is the old Aḥlāf with the loss of ʿAdī.

THE CLANS OF QURAYSH

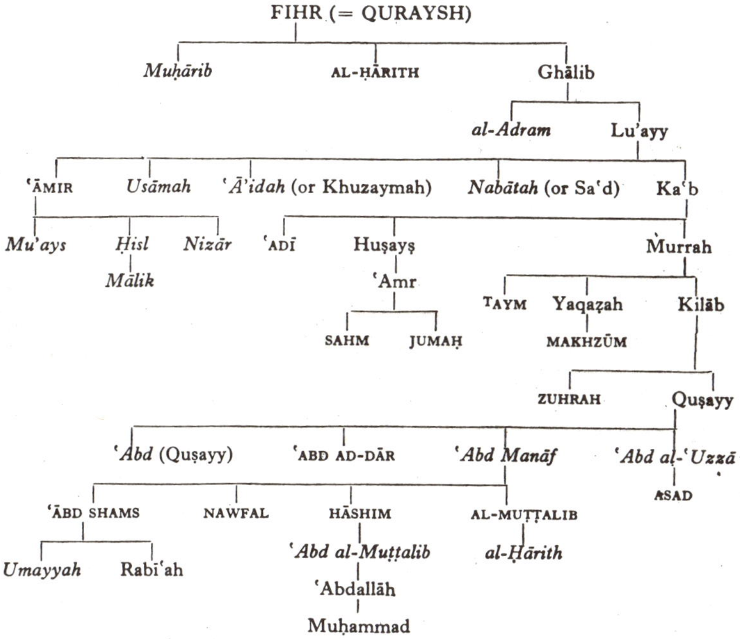

ʿADĪ—clans commonly mentioned in Muḥammad's time.
ʿAbd—clans mentioned occasionally as such. Quraysh al-Biṭāḥ were descendants of Kaʿb, sometimes with al-Ḥārith b. Fihr and ʿĀmir added.

The chief evidence for supposing that the clans were so divided is this.[2] (1) At the battle of Badr the main leaders on the Meccan side came from B and C; al-ʿAbbās (Hāshim) is the only exception, and his case is rather doubtful, since his name may have been

[1] Azraqī *ap.* Wüstenfeld, *Mekka*, i. 472 f. [2] See also ch. IV.

added to glorify his descendants, and it is recorded that members of the clan under Ṭālib b. Abī Ṭālib are said to have withdrawn. On the other hand, Zuhrah and ʿAdī gave no support to the Meccans at all, and the others of group A were weakly represented. (2) The men who broke the boycott of the B. Hāshim[1] were from ʿĀmir, Nawfal, and Asad; a Makhzūmī is also named, but he presumably acted against the main part of his clan because his mother was of B. Hāshim. (3) The men to whom Muḥammad appealed for protection on his return from aṭ-Ṭā'if were from Zuhrah, ʿĀmir, and Nawfal; none was from group C. (4) The early Muslims who did not go to Abyssinia were with two exceptions (whose circumstances were unusual) members or confederates of Hāshim, al-Muṭṭalib, Zuhrah, Taym, and ʿAdī; this fact is suggestive even if the interpretation of it is not quite certain.[2]

(b) *The control of affairs in Mecca*

Almost the only organ of government in Mecca was the senate or *mala'*. This was an assembly of the chiefs and leading men of the various clans. The council was merely deliberative and had no executive of its own. Each clan was theoretically independent and could go its own way, and therefore the only effective decisions of the *mala'* were unanimous ones. There were, of course, ways of dealing with recalcitrant minorities; the boycott of the clans of Hāshim and al-Muṭṭalib is an example of how economic and social pressure could be brought to bear.

A great part of the strength of Mecca lay in the ability of its leaders to form a common mind and to soft-pedal petty rivalries for the sake of the common good. The composition of the quarrel between the Aḥlāf and the Muṭayyabūn is one example of this, and the organization of the city for war after the defeat at Badr another. Besides this central council, there were doubtless also meetings of the separate clans, when necessary, to discuss matters; thus, Abū Ṭālib called together Hāshim and al-Muṭṭalib to get them to agree to the protection of Muḥammad.

The sources also mention certain traditional offices and functions. Among these are the *nasī* (the privilege of deciding when a month was to be intercalated into the lunar calendar to keep it in line with the solar year), the *siqāyah* (the superintendence of the water-supply, especially with a view to the needs of pilgrims), the

[1] Cf. V. 3 b, below. [2] Cf. V. 2 c.

rifādah (provisioning of pilgrims), and the *liwā'* (carrying the standard in war, or arranging for this). This is hardly a municipal administration as we now understand it, or even as the Greeks and Romans understood it. These offices are rather privileges, some of which at least offered opportunities for making money; in connexion with the *siqāyah*, there was some charge for the use of the well of Zamzam by pilgrims.[1] We also hear of taxes of various kinds levied from pilgrims and merchants, but it is not clear how these were collected.

The influence of the individual in the affairs of Mecca depended on two things, his clan and his personal qualifications. The power of a clan had come to be in proportion to its wealth, although wealth in a commercial community of this sort was largely in a fluid form and varied with the extent and success of the current undertakings of the individual and clan. Inherited wealth and business connexions could give a man a start, but in the end his influence depended chiefly on his personal qualities—his commercial and financial shrewdness, his diplomacy in dealing with other clans and tribes and with the representatives of the great powers, and his ability to get his equals in the clan and in wider circles to follow his lead. The domination of Meccan policy by Abū Sufyān during Muḥammad's prime was not due to the holding of any office carrying authority, but to the importance and wealth of his clan, 'Abd Shams or Umayyah, and to his possession of such qualities. The other leading clan at this time was Makhzūm, and its notable members like al-Walīd b. al-Mughīrah and Abū Jahl were also prominent in city affairs.

It would be interesting to compare the position of Abū Sufyān at Mecca with that of Pericles at Athens. Arab democracy was less egalitarian than Athenian. Every member of a Meccan clan counted for one and no one for more than one, but somehow or other the Arabs had found a way of deciding who were the notable members of a clan who should attend the meetings of the Senate. The Meccan *mala'* was a much wiser and more responsible body than the Athenian *ekklesia*, and consequently its decisions were more often made on the solid merit of men and their policies and not on specious rhetoric that could make the worse appear the better cause. On the other hand, while the Athenians at their best recognized moral principles and would approve of a man primarily

[1] Lammens, *Mecque*, 65.

because he was honest and upright, the Meccans were more anxious that a man should have practical skill and be an efficient leader. This leads us, however, to the subject of section 3.

(c) *Quraysh and the Arab tribes*

Among the desert Arabs nobility and prestige were largely a matter of military power. Primacy among the tribes belonged to those which were able to protect all their clients, and to avenge all insults, injuries, and deaths. Quraysh were later said to be the first of all the Arabs, and the caliphs could be taken only from their number. In its absolute form, however, this ascendancy of Quraysh is probably a reading back into the decade before the Hijrah of later conditions. But, even if there is some exaggeration about the statement, yet it remains true that Quraysh were recognized as foremost among the tribes of west and west-central Arabia—that is, among all those with whom they came into close contact. On what was this primacy based?

It is only by straining the evidence that Lammens was able to make a case for his hypothesis of a mercenary army of black slaves. Some reasons for regarding this theory as groundless are given briefly in Excursus A. It is true, however, that Quraysh had numbers of black slaves and used some of these for fighting when the occasion arose. It is true that they had attracted many Arabs of other tribes to Mecca as *ḥulafā'* (sing. *ḥalīf*) or confederates, some engaging in commerce, others being of the cavalier-brigand type; and the latter at least were always ready for a scrap. It is true that by the time of Badr the prosperous merchants among Quraysh were disinclined for warlike expeditions; yet they were not sheer cowards, and could probably give a good account of themselves in a fight; those Quraysh among the Muslims at Badr acquitted themselves creditably, even if the exploits of 'Alī and Ḥamzah are greatly exaggerated, and even if on the whole the Anṣār were the better all-round soldiers. For all that, it is clear that the primacy of Quraysh did not rest on their military prowess as individuals.

The secret of their prestige was the military strength they could bring to bear on any opponent. This was not their own military strength only, but that of a whole confederacy. This confederacy they had built up on the basis of their mercantile enterprises. The caravans to the Yemen, Syria, and elsewhere required the services of large numbers of nomads as guides, escorts, camelmen, &c.

They would pay a chief for safe-conduct through his territory, for water, and for other supplies. Thus the nomadic tribes shared in the trade of Mecca, and quickly recognized on which side their bread was buttered. Meccan prosperity meant their own prosperity; Meccan loss was their loss. This feeling of solidarity with Mecca was heightened by matrimonial alliances between leading men of Mecca and various tribes, and by the tribal chiefs receiving an allocation of shares in the Meccan 'joint stock companies'.

It is thus true in a sense that the Meccans paid men to fight for them. But these men were in no sense mercenaries. They are not to be compared to a Swiss Guard or a French Foreign Legion. They were all free Arabs who entered into alliances and compacts with Quraysh as equal with equal. The leaders of the mysterious Aḥābīsh are quite outspoken towards the Meccans.[1] When al-Barrād of B. Bakr b. 'Abd Manāt b. Kinānah attacked a caravan[2]—the incident which led to the war of the Fijār—he doubtless knew that this was in accordance with Meccan policy and that Quraysh would support him, but presumably the action was for him primarily the pursuance of his own ends and not obedience to Meccan orders.

In holding together a confederacy of this sort money was important, but it alone was not enough. Men of this touchy and headstrong character could only be managed by constant tact and diplomacy, and these presuppose a strict control of one's own feelings. It was this wise and patient statesmanship, the *ḥilm* of Quraysh, that enabled them to keep their confederacy in being. 'This political wisdom, in which shines out all the *ḥilm* of Quraysh, was to guarantee for many years the supremacy of pre-Islamic Mecca over its nomadic neighbours.'[3]

(d) *The foreign policy of Mecca*

Mecca was in the sphere of interest of two great powers, the Byzantine and Persian empires, and one lesser power, the kingdom of Abyssinia or Ethiopia. It was chiefly trade reasons that attracted the attention of the empires to Arabia. The Byzantines wanted all sorts of luxury articles from the East, but Persia sat astride nearly all the trade routes—both the overland routes from China and India (apart from that north of the Caspian Sea) and the sea routes

[1] Excursus A, passages A, D, H. [2] IH, 117.
[3] Lammens, *Mecque*, 81/177.

from India and Ceylon by the Persian Gulf—and Persia made the Byzantines pay dearly for their silks and spices in time of peace, while war disrupted the trade. There remained the overland route through western Arabia to Syria (which was also the route for incense from southern Arabia), and the Red Sea route; but the latter, for no obvious reason, was apparently not much used.[1]

Justinian, who directed Byzantine policy under Justin from 518 to 527, and then as Emperor until 565, was keen to recover the Roman domains in the West, and therefore followed a policy of appeasement with Persia, even paying an annual subsidy to ensure peace. He made the semi-independent Ghassanid prince on his Syrian frontier a phylarch of the Empire, whose duty it was to keep order among the nomadic Arabs of the border lands and to extend Roman influence where possible. He encouraged the use of Christianity as a unifying and Romanizing factor. And he had some sort of understanding with Abyssinia. Ibn Isḥāq[2] relates how, in the death-throes of the South Arabian kingdom, a man called Daws Dhū Thaʿlabān escaped from Dhū Nuwās and made his way to Caesar, who instead of helping directly gave him a letter to the king of Abyssinia. This is probably more or less true; at the very least it shows how the Arabs conceived the relations of the Byzantines and Abyssinians. Justinian certainly approved of the conquest of the Yemen and South Arabia by the Abyssinians about 525, and, despite his own Orthodoxy, preferred Monophysitism there to either Judaism or Nestorianism, both of which had Persian connexions.[3]

After the death of Justinian the relations between the two empires changed and their long struggle entered its final phase. In particular, about 570 or 575, the Persians drove the Abyssinians from Arabia and set up an administration favourable to Persia, though not strictly controlled from the metropolis. By means of the Lakhmid princes of al-Ḥīrah (whose role on the Persian side was similar to that of the Ghassanids on the Byzantine) the Persians tried to direct the overland trade from the Yemen to Persia. The war of the Fijār and the battle of Dhū Qār arose out of Persian caravans from al-Ḥīrah to the Yemen. Doubtless these carried frankincense and other local products (and perhaps goods from

[1] But see also G. F. Hourani, *Arab Seafaring in the Indian Ocean*, Princeton, 1951, pp. 43 f.

[2] IH, 25.

[3] Cf. A. Vasiliev, *Justin the First*, Cambridge, U.S.A., 1950, 283–99.

Abyssinia) rather than imports from India. Much trade, however, still passed up the west coast route, if we may judge from the continued prosperity of Mecca; thus the Persians cannot have been strong enough to dominate this route to the West.

What was the position of Mecca in this struggle of the giants? What policy should it adopt? There was probably a tradition of friendship with the Byzantines. Ibn Qutaybah has the surprising remark that 'Caesar' helped Quṣayy against the Khuzā'ah.[1] If this is interpreted to mean that Quṣayy received help from the Ghassanids or other allies of Rome, it may very well be true. Quṣayy certainly had connexions with the B. 'Udhrah, a Christian tribe living near the Syrian border and so presumably under Byzantine influence. Quṣayy's conquest of Mecca was probably bound up with the development of trade between Mecca and Syria. It would seem that for some time after Quṣayy the route from the Yemen to Mecca was mainly in the hands of the Yamanīs; a Yamanī merchant was bringing goods to Mecca at the formation of the confederacy of the Fuḍūl (*c.* 580). If Mecca was thus mainly concerned with the northward trade, it would be necessary to be on good terms with the Byzantines and their allies.

The conquest of the Yemen by the Abyssinians ought to have made things easier for the Meccans, in view of the friendly relations between the Abyssinians and the Byzantines. It was presumably during this period of comparative peace that the Meccans developed their trade on a large scale and sent their own caravans in all directions. The traditional account is that, of the four sons of 'Abd Manaf, 'Abd Shams cultivated relations with Abyssinia, Hāshim with Syria, al-Muṭṭalib with the Yemen, and Nawfal with 'Irāq. The clan of Makhzūm probably also took a share in the trade with South Arabia; at least they were concerned with it later.[2] Relations with the Abyssinians must have deteriorated, however, for towards the end of the occupation the viceroy Abrahah[3] led an expedition against Mecca for the ostensible purpose of destroying the Ka'bah, so that the Arabs would make pilgrimage instead to his new temple in the south. One may conjecture that commercial interests were here mixed up with religious. Abrahah was probably dismayed at the growing commercial success of the Meccans, who were presumably making handsome profits as

[1] *Ma'ārif*, 313. 4 from foot; cf. Lammens, *Mecque*, 269.
[2] Cf. WW, 61; also Lammens, *Mecque*, 201/297.
[3] Cf. EI (2), art. 'Abraha', where he is said to have been originally an independent king.

middlemen even between Abyssinians and nomads. Abrahah would realize the important part played by the sacred area round Mecca in what may be called the 'Meccan system'. There may also have been a temple treasure.[1] If the power and wealth of Mecca were to be reduced, the Meccan sanctuary would have to be destroyed and another put in its place, as a centre for retail trade among the Arabs of the desert.

Ibn Isḥāq has preserved an account of how ʿAbd al-Muṭṭalib negotiated with Abrahah during this expedition.[2] While certain features of the story (e.g. the statement that ʿAbd al-Muṭṭalib was then the *kabīr* and *sayyid* of Quraysh) are doubtless due to a desire to glorify the clan of Hāshim, it is probable that the fact of the negotiations is correctly stated, but ought to be interpreted as a party move of a small group of Quraysh (along with the tribes of Du'il and Hudhayl), from which the main body of the Quraysh stood aloof. If that is so, then ʿAbd al-Muṭṭalib was presumably trying to get support from the Abyssinians against his rivals among Quraysh, such as the clans of ʿAbd Shams, Nawfal, and Makhzūm. The two former of these had apparently by this time seized most of the trade with Syria and the Yemen which had formerly belonged to Hāshim and al-Muṭṭalib. Against the pro-Abyssinian policy of ʿAbd al-Muṭṭalib the wealthier clans would stand for a policy of neutrality, which was clearly in their best interests. We cannot be sure whether Abrahah accepted the overtures of ʿAbd al-Muṭṭalib or whether, judging him not strong enough, he rejected them. In any case the expedition came to nothing as the Abyssinian army was destroyed, apparently by plague.

Neutrality was still more necessary for Mecca after the Persian conquest of South Arabia. It should be kept in mind, however, that this conquest was the result of a sea-borne expedition, and that therefore the conquered province was not firmly held, while the remainder of Arabia was not controlled by the Persians. The Meccans appear to have made good use of this situation to consolidate their power. The war of the Fijār, which probably began some time after the expulsion of the Abyssinians, was the result of an unprovoked attack by an ally of Mecca on a caravan from al-Ḥīrah to the Yemen by way of aṭ-Ṭā'if.[3] This would mean, in economic terms, that the Meccans were trying either to close this route altogether or to ensure that they had some control over it. As they

[1] Cf. that at aṭ-Ṭā'if, WW, 384. [2] IH, 33 f. [3] IH, 118.

were apparently successful in the war, they presumably attained their object.

Against this background, the confederacy of the Fuḍūl, which has already been mentioned, takes on a new significance. The cause assigned, the refusal of a Sahmī to pay for goods received from a Yamanī merchant, and the extensive repercussions of this event, suggest that it marked a significant new trend in policy, in short that it was the climax of an attempt by the wealthier clans to exclude the Yamanīs from the southern trade, and to concentrate it in their own hands. The reaction of Hāshim and the other clans forming the confederacy would then be understandable. These clans were not sufficiently strong financially to run their own caravans to the Yemen, but made something out of dealings with Yamanī merchants in Mecca—so we may suppose. If the caravans to the Yemen were entirely controlled by clans like ʿAbd Shams and Makhzūm, then the lesser clans might lose a good deal of their trade and might have no goods to carry north to Syria; or else they would be admitted to share in caravans but only on the terms prescribed by the wealthier merchants, and these would certainly allow them no more than a meagre profit.

The incident of ʿUthmān b. al-Ḥuwayrith, as developed by Lammens,[1] helps to illustrate the Meccan policy of neutrality. ʿUthmān entered into negotiations with the Byzantines or their agents, and received some promise of support. The Byzantines doubtless had in mind something similar to the Ghassanid phylarchate, though the sources say that ʿUthmān aimed at being 'king' of Mecca. This was part of the Byzantine reaction to the Persian conquest of the south. ʿUthmān, of course, as Lammens points out, would not make such an aim public; he would say that the Byzantines were going to close the frontier unless certain 'gifts' were made to them, and that they had appointed him to collect these gifts. Lammens's further statement, however, that he won over the heads of the Umayyah and the Makhzūm to his plan appears to be an assumption of his own based on the fact that there is no mention of their opposition. It is clear that the overt act which led to the wreck of ʿUthmān's scheme was his denunciation, as aiming at kingship, by a member of his own clan of Asad, al-Aswad b. al-Muṭṭalib Abū Zamʿah. The wealthy financiers would naturally object to the position of special prominence to which ʿUthmān would attain

[1] *Mecque*, 270–9/366–75.

under this scheme; but they doubtless also regarded it as unwise to depart from the policy of neutrality, and they probably realized how strong their position was in view of the Byzantine demand for the goods they carried. (The rejection of the Byzantine overtures had no serious effects for Mecca apart from the temporary imprisonment of a few men.) In this situation, had Umayyah and Makhzūm come forward as leaders of the opposition to 'Uthmān, that might have given fresh life to the confederacy of the Fuḍūl, of which Asad was a member. Such repercussions were avoided by getting a member of Asad to take the lead. It is not sound to suppose, as Lammens does, that al-Aswad was moved by purely personal jealousy; he was apparently a fairly wealthy man, and therefore probably opposed on general grounds to a policy of forming closer links with the Byzantines.[1]

This incident took place after the war of the Fijār, since 'Uthmān b. al-Huwayrith had taken his part in that. We are therefore brought within twenty years or less of Muḥammad's call to prophethood—years in which the heavy fighting between the two great empires would emphasize the importance of neutrality for the Meccans. Owing to the scantiness of our materials there is much in this account of Meccan policies that is conjectural. But even if many of the details are incorrect, the general picture is, I believe, sound. Muḥammad grew to maturity in a world in which high finance and international politics were inextricably mixed up.

3. THE SOCIAL AND MORAL BACKGROUND

(a) *Tribal solidarity and individualism*

Tribal solidarity is an essential for survival in desert conditions. A man requires the help of others both against the forces of nature and against his human rivals. The tribal groupings doubtless existed before men took to the desert, and did not come into being there, but the importance of solidarity was certainly enhanced by desert conditions. Up to a point the larger the group, the more powerful it is and therefore the more successful; but beyond a certain point it is difficult for the group to act as a unit, and there is consequently a tendency for it to break up. Thus the tribes are not permanent entities, but are constantly either increasing and breaking up or else dwindling away. This may be illustrated from

[1] Cf. al-Fāsī *ap.* Wüst., *Mekka*, ii. 143 f.

the Meccan clans. The common Arabic appellation of tribe, clan, or family is 'Banū Fulān', that is, 'the sons of Fulān or so-and-so' ('Banū' is commonly contracted to 'B.'). At one period of Meccan history we hear much of the 'Banū 'Abd Manāf', but a little later this term is falling out of use, as the clan has prospered and split up, and we hear instead of 'Banū 'Abd Shams', 'Banū Hāshim', &c., where 'Abd Shams and Hāshim are sons of 'Abd Manāf. Some of the bloodiest wars in Arabia, too, were between related clans—doubtless because they had to share a limited *Lebensraum*.

Each main or first-class tribe was independent of every other and acknowledged no political superior. It might therefore conceivably, and often in fact did, find itself at war with any neighbouring tribe. In this situation in which a man's 'hand will be against every man and every man's hand against him',[1] the security of a tribe and even its mere existence depends on its military power. Only by force can herds be kept safely, for raiding is the 'national sport' of the Arabs.

The blood-feud illustrates the place of tribal solidarity. This is a primitive method—but perhaps the only method in the circumstances of desert life, apart from modern inventions—of ensuring that crime will not be committed lightly and irresponsibly. The tribe of the murderer is held responsible for his act, and the penalty is 'a life for a life'. Apart from the natural human tendency to exact a penalty larger than what is due, this is a simple method of maintaining tribes at the same comparative strength.[2]

The tribe is based on kinship either in the male or in the female line; prior to the rise of Islam the latter seems to have been the more widespread. There was also what might be called 'artificial solidarity' brought about through either *ḥilf* (confederacy, mutual oaths) or *jiwār* (the formal granting of protection). For many purposes the *ḥalīf* and the *jār*, the 'confederate' and the 'client', were treated as members of the tribe or clan. *Ḥilf* or *taḥāluf* might take place between equals; a weak group, however, would become the confederates of a strong tribe in order to maintain itself in existence.[3]

While the tribe or confederation of tribes was the highest political unit, there was also a realization of the fact that the Arabs were

[1] Gen. xvi. 12.

[2] Cf. Austin Kennett, *Bedouin Justice*, Cambridge, 1925, pp. 27, 75.

[3] Cf. Goldziher, *MS*, i. 63–69.

in some sense a unity. This unity was based on a common language (though with variations of dialect), a common poetical tradition, some common conventions and ideas, and a common descent. Language was possibly the original basis of the distinction between Arabs and 'foreigners', *'Arab* and *'Ajam*, as it was between Greeks and *barbaroi*. The Arabian and Syrian deserts were the geographical basis of the unity, and indeed the word *'Arab* often means 'nomads'. The common descent was, strictly speaking, from one of two ancestors, either 'Adnān or Qaḥṭān; but the two groups were intermingled. Even if, as some Western scholars have maintained (with perhaps excessive scepticism), the common descent is fictitious, yet the existence of the belief in it implies some recognition of unity. This conception of the Arabs as a single people, with the corollary of their distinctness from other peoples (and superiority to them), came to be of considerable importance during Muḥammad's Medinan period, as he came within sight of a greater degree of political unity among the Arabs than had been attained by any of the great leaders of pre-Islamic times.

The principles of tribal solidarity outlined above applied in general to the city community of Mecca. By Muḥammad's time, however, the effective unit there was not the tribe of Quraysh as a whole but the separate clans. Security of one's person and property still depended on the readiness of one's clan to avenge murder or theft. To lay hands on a man without the permission of the head of his clan might lead to a feud; the same was true of Medina during the first few years of Muḥammad's residence there. It was because of this that Muḥammad was able to continue preaching in Mecca despite opposition so long as the B. Hāshim were prepared to protect him. A member of some other tribe who wanted to live in Mecca—and there were many in this position—had to become the *ḥalīf* or confederate of a prominent individual or family of Quraysh. In view of the superiority of Quraysh, this implied some inferiority.

Tribal solidarity, however, was never absolute. The members of the tribe were not automatons, but human beings prone to selfishness—or what Lammens[1] calls 'individualisme'; it would only be natural if sometimes they put private interests above those of the tribe. Then there were always a few 'bounders', men who kept getting into trouble regardless of what it would cost the tribe,

[1] *Berceau*, 187 ff.

and who therefore had to be disowned. Such a person was known as *khalī'*.

While tribal solidarity continued to govern the actions of the best people, yet a certain individualism began to make its appearance in their thinking, if we may judge from the poets. Hitherto, so far as we can tell, a man had been content to reflect upon the glory of the tribe and upon his own share in that glory. Now there was a growing awareness of the existence of the individual in separateness from the tribe, with the consequent problem of the cessation of his individual existence at death. What was the ultimate destiny of a man? Was death the end?

The tendency to individualism and away from tribal solidarity was fostered in Mecca by the circumstances of commercial life. Though public order depended on the clan system, yet in general a single family, even an individual with his dependents, could constitute a viable unit. So we frequently find men acting in opposition to their clans. Abū Lahab adopted a different attitude towards Muḥammad from most of the rest of Hāshim. The opposition to 'Uthmān b. al-Ḥuwayrith came from within his own clan. Muḥammad's earliest followers became Muslims despite the disapproval of their clans, and even of their parents. Business partnerships seem sometimes to have cut across clan relationships.

At the same time there was an interesting new phenomenon in Mecca—the appearance of a sense of unity based on common material interests. It was this rather than the fact that they all belonged to Quraysh that led the Aḥlāf and the Muṭayyabūn to compose their quarrel. It was this again that led to the forgetting of rivalries and the formation of a 'coalition government' after the defeat at Badr. The significance of this is that it marks a weakening of the bond of kinship by blood, and reveals the opportunity for establishing a wider unity on a new basis.

If we are to look for an economic change correlated with the origin of Islam, then it is here that we must look. (By 'correlation' is to be understood something essentially different from the absolute dependence of religion and ideology on economic factors as maintained by the Marxist.) In the rise of Mecca to wealth and power we have a movement from a nomadic economy to a mercantile and capitalist economy. By the time of Muḥammad, however, there had been no readjustment of the social, moral, intellectual, and religious attitudes of the community. These were still the attitudes appropriate to a nomadic community, for the most part. The tension felt by Muḥammad and some of his contemporaries was doubtless due ultimately to this contrast between men's conscious attitudes and the economic basis of their life. Of this malaise in the body-politic we shall have to speak more fully later.

(b) *The moral ideal*

The moral ideal of the desert Arabs may be called, in accordance with Goldziher's usage, *murūwah* or manliness. It has been well described by R. A. Nicholson as 'bravery in battle, patience in misfortune, persistence in revenge, protection of the weak, defiance of the strong'. These virtues are in fact those required if a tribe is to be successful in the struggle for existence in the desert. Bravery is not conceived in quite the same way as we conceive it. The Arab did not believe in taking unnecessary risks; unless when his blood was up, he avoided such dangers and hardships as could be avoided; desert life in itself is sufficiently hard without adding to it. This perhaps explains why persistence in revenge is counted a virtue. In many cases it might be easier to let sleeping dogs lie, but it would be a sign of weakness and would lead to a relative decline in the numerical strength of the tribe. Defiance of the strong is a reflection of the fact that continued existence depends on military strength. The strong, however, is prepared to protect the weak where the weak acknowledges the superiority of the strong; it is partly a case of human co-operation against the forces of nature, and it serves to strengthen the strong tribe.

Generosity and hospitality were greatly admired in the desert and are still prominent virtues of the Arabs. A large heap of ashes outside his tent was a mark of high excellence in a chief, for it meant that he had entertained many guests. Such a tradition is partly due to man's need for help from his fellows in face of the severity of nature; but there is possibly more to it than that. Generosity was admired even when it went to the length of prodigality, as, for example, when a poor woman killed the camel which was her only means of support in order to give a meal to a passing stranger. Perhaps in this liberal and indeed lavish use of things that are very scarce there is something akin to the extravagant wine-drinking of the poets about which they boast. Should we see in these things aspects of the virtue of 'taking no thought for the morrow'? Probably in the desert if one thought about all the fearful possibilities of disaster and tried to guard against them all, one would become a nervous wreck and would either perish or leave the desert or become the dependent of a stronger tribe. There is much in the desert that cannot be achieved by 'taking thought', for conditions are often uncertain, unpredictable, and completely erratic. A measure of carefreeness in the midst of cares is the higher wisdom, and it was doubtless for that reason that it was so much admired.

Loyalty and fidelity were also important virtues. Ideally a man ought to be ready to spring to the aid of a fellow tribesman whenever he called for help; he should act at once without waiting to inquire into the merits of the case. Similarly the individual ought to act with the tribe even when he disagreed with the decisions of its leaders. Again, though men had no scruples about carrying off the property of other tribes, there was often great fidelity in the keeping of a trust. One of the celebrated examples is as-Samaw'al b. 'Ādiyā' who permitted a son to be killed by a besieging force rather than surrender some weapons entrusted to his safe-keeping by Imru' al-Qays. This is perhaps to be regarded as an extension of the loyalty expected within the tribe to those persons with whom as the result of a compact one had, as it were, artificial solidarity.

As a result of the sovereign independence of the tribes there was no supreme law in the desert. It was indeed impossible to maintain law and order over the vast expanses of the Arabian and Syrian steppe, except where there was an exceptionally strong and wise ruler or where the ruler had an overwhelming superiority in arms and equipment (such as aeroplane and armoured car against rifle and camel). Neither before Islam nor later did any abstract idea of law develop among the Arabs; even Greek influences did not introduce it into Islamic theology. Instead of a supreme law of the universe the Muslim thinks of the will of the Divine ruler of the universe, expressed in His revealed commands.

The place of law and of the abstract idea of right and wrong is to some extent taken by the conception of honour, the honour first of the tribe and then of the individual. Being hospitable and keeping trusts were signs of one's honourable condition; lack of generosity or bravery was a mark of dishonour. The custodian and registrar of honour was public opinion. As reflected and indeed formed by the poets this had a certain power, and responsible men would shrink from actions which would bring discredit on themselves or on their tribe. A large part of the older poems is occupied with praise of the virtues and merits of one's tribe, and satire of the vices and faults of other tribes.

The ideal of *murūwah* played an important part among the Arabs. They respected those who had to some extent realized it, and the families in which there was a habit of reaching it. Authority depended largely on the respect in which a man was held and that in turn depended on his personal qualities, the degree of his *murūwah*. There was no rule of succession by primogeniture among the Arabs for obvious reasons; if the eldest son of a chief was inexperienced when his father died (as would frequently happen), the tribe could not jeopardize its very existence by having such a man as leader. The chief must be a man of wisdom and sound judgement, and so was usually the most respected male in the leading family. In this respect for moral excellence, and in their capacity for agreement about where it lay, the Arabs had accomplished a combination of aristocracy with egalitarianism, the rule of the best fitted with the recognition of the equality of each person *qua* person.

As A. J. Toynbee says in his interesting account of nomadism, it is a *tour de force*. Nomadism follows upon agricultural life, since stock-breeding can only be learnt there.

> And now, when the rhythmic process of desiccation, in its next onset, has made life still more difficult in the oases, and more difficult on the Steppe *a fortiori*, the patriarchs of the Nomadic Civilization audaciously return to the Steppe in order to wring out of it, now, no mere subsidiary supply but their entire livelihood—and this under climatic conditions under which the hunter and the cultivator alike would find life in the Steppe quite impossible.[1]

In all this there is a natural process of selection. To begin with it is only certain individuals who attempt the nomadic way of life, presumably those distinguished by qualities such as adventurousness and love of freedom. Then the fierce struggle for existence leads to a selection on the basis not merely of physical but also of moral qualities. A high level of solidarity is needed for success in the life of the desert, and that is linked up with a high level of respect for personality and appreciation of human worth. In the furnace of the desert the dross of inferior attitudes and actions was burned out and the pure gold left of a high morality, a high code

[1] *Study of History*, iii. 7–22, esp. 13 f.

and tradition of human relationships, and a high level of human excellence. It is one of the theses of this book that the greatness of Islam is largely due to the fusion of this element with certain Judaeo-Christian theistic conceptions.

4. THE RELIGIOUS AND INTELLECTUAL BACKGROUND

(a) *The decadence of the archaic religion*

The best account of the old religion of Arabia in English is in the article by Nöldeke entitled 'Arabs (Ancient)' in the *Encyclopaedia of Religion and Ethics*. The standard account is J. Wellhausen's *Reste Arabischen Heidentums*, which is based mainly on *Kitāb al-Aṣnām* of Ibn al-Kalbī.[1] H. Lammens brings some additions and emendations in *Le Culte des Bétyles et les processions religieuses chez les Arabes Préislamites*.[2] The divergent theories of Dietlef Nielsen[3] are not generally accepted. These recount what is known about a large number of gods and goddesses and about the ceremonies connected with their worship. As our knowledge is fragmentary and, apart from inscriptions, comes from Islamic sources, there is ample scope for conjecture. These matters are not dealt with here in any detail as it is generally agreed that the archaic pagan religion was comparatively uninfluential in Muhammad's time.

This religion was the result of a long development. Prominent among the objects worshipped originally were stones and trees. These were sometimes regarded not as the divinities but as their house or dwelling. Latterly abstract characteristics were also associated with them, possibly under foreign influence, and they were thought of as having some connexion with heavenly bodies. The nomads appear to have had little serious belief in them, perhaps because they were originally the gods of agricultural communities.[4] In view of the opposition to Muḥammad at Mecca it is conceivable that some small groups there—perhaps those specially concerned with certain religious ceremonies—had a slightly higher degree of belief. On the other hand, certain practices continued, such as pilgrimages to sacred spots in and around Mecca; the *ḥaram* or sacred area of Mecca was respected, but the violations during the

[1] Ibn al-Kalbī is further discussed by H. S. Nyberg in *ΔΡΑΓΜΑ Martino P. Nilsson Dedicatum*, Lund, 1939, pp. 346–66.
[2] *Arabie*, 101–79.
[3] See his *Handbuch der altarabischen Altertumskunde*, i.
[4] Cf. Barton, *Semitic and Hamitic Origins*.

war of the Fijār are probably signs of declining belief. In the crisis of the Meccan state Abū Sufyān took the goddesses al-Lāt and Al-ʿUzzā into battle against the Muslims at Uḥud; this recalls how the Israelites took the ark into battle with them, and suggests that the remnants of pagan belief in Arabia were now at the level of magic. In this sense many old ceremonies seem to have remained, but they are to be reckoned as superstition rather than religion.

(b) '*Tribal humanism*'

In contrast to the archaic religion stands what may be called 'tribal humanism'. This was the effective religion of the Arabs of Muḥammad's day, though it, too, was declining. This is the religion we find in the poets of the Jāhilīyah. For the poets what gives life a meaning is to belong to a tribe which can boast notable deeds of bravery and generosity, and to have some share in these oneself. From this standpoint the realization of human excellence in action is an end in itself, and at the same time usually contributes to the survival of the tribe, which is the other great end of life. This is humanism in the sense that it is primarily in human values, in virtuous or manly conduct, that it finds significance. But it differs from most modern humanism in that it thinks of the tribe rather than the individual as the locus of these values. We shall see (in ch. III) that while in its earliest passages the Qur'ān does not attack the old paganism, it does counter this humanism in its religious aspect; from this, however, is to be distinguished the ethical aspect of humanism, the moral ideal, which in general the Qur'ān respects.

While belief in the honour and excellence of the tribe was the mainspring of nomadic life, there was an intellectual background to this belief that is worth noticing. The fatalism of the Arabs is notorious, but it appears that it was a limited fatalism. They do not seem to have held that *all* a man's acts were predetermined by fate, but only that certain aspects of his life were thus fixed. I have suggested elsewhere[1] that in some of the canonical Traditions of Islam we have pre-Islamic ideas in an Islamic dress, and in particular that what was previously attributed to Time or Fate came to be ascribed directly or indirectly to God. If this is so, then the four main points in which human life was constricted within narrow limits by Fate were *rizq* or man's sustenance, *ajal* or the term of his life, the sex of the child, and happiness or misery. This was not

[1] *Free Will and Predestination in Early Islam*, London, 1949, p. 25, &c.

a religion, for Fate was not worshipped. It was rather a form of science, for it was essentially the recognition of facts. In desert conditions the matters named are beyond the control of human wit and wisdom. Sustenance is very precarious; one tribe may have copious rainfall and abundant pasture, and the neighbouring tribe may have neither. Expectation of life is low, and death often comes suddenly and unexpectedly as the result of a chance encounter. Even now, with all our science we cannot foretell, far less determine the sex of a baby. In the desert great vicissitudes of fortune are common, so that for the nomad the experience of Job would contain nothing improbable.

Thus the realization of the ideal of *murūwah* took place, as it were, within a fixed frame. To have noble blood in one's veins was probably regarded as making it easier to perform noble actions, though a man's moral qualities never depended on noble ancestry alone. Because of the tribal solidarity of the Arabs the question of individual freedom could hardly occur to them. The growth of individualism probably led, about the time of Muḥammad's youth, to a decline in this tribal humanism as a vital religious force. Hitherto men had not been greatly concerned with the fate of the individual so long as the tribe endured, but now they were beginning to wonder about the ultimate destiny of the individual. There was no way of passing from tribal humanism to individual humanism, since in the absence of a belief in personal immortality there was in the case of the individual nothing enduring; in the case of tribal humanism men could see that the tribe endured, and above all the blood, which they probably regarded as the source of the noble qualities of the tribe. In the sphere of religion the main problem of Muhammad's time seems to have been this breakdown of tribal humanism in face of the more individualistic organization of society.

(c) *The appearance of monotheistic tendencies*

The relation of Islamic teachings to Judaeo-Christian 'sources' has been discussed *ad nauseam*, and it is not proposed to deal with the question here at any length. It is desirable, however, to say something about the angle from which it ought to be approached, since the attitude of Western scholars has often been unfortunate in that it implied or seemed to imply a denial of Muslim theological doctrines. Even from the standpoint of the best Western scholarship the Western studies in the Qur'ān have often been unfortunate. They have made a fetish of literary dependence, and have forgotten that literary dependence is never more than one side of the picture; there is also the creative work of the poet, or dramatist, or novelist; and the fact of literary dependence never proves the absence of creative originality. The religious sphere is similar, though there are also differences. You may show that Amos or Ezekiel took over many conceptions from their predecessors; but, if you study *only* this dependence, you miss their originality and the uniqueness of the Divine revelation made through them.

In the eyes of orthodox Muslims the Qur'ān is a Divine revelation, the speech of God. The Qur'ān, however, makes explicit statements about the beliefs of the pagan Arabs and about certain ideas which have been passing through the mind of Muḥammad and the Muslims; there are also other passages from which inferences about the outlook of Muhammad and his contemporaries can be drawn with a high degree of certainty. These facts suggest a method of dealing with the question of Judaeo-Christian influences which would be satisfactory to Western scholarship and to which orthodox Muslims could hardly take exception. The first stage would be to ask what the Qur'ān stated or implied about the beliefs of the Arabs of Muḥammad's time, both the enlightened progressives and the conservatives. Then it would be possible to ask to what extent Judaeo-Christian influences could be traced there.

The impression given by the earliest passages of the Qur'ān[1] is that these were addressed to people who already believed in God, although perhaps with much vagueness and confusion. The Qur'ān explains certain strange words which were apparently not properly understood by those who heard them: Saqar (74), al-Qāriʿah (101), al-Ḥuṭamah (104), &c. But it does not require to explain the meaning of 'thy Lord' or 'God'. The phrase 'Lord of this House (*sc.* the Kaʿbah)' in Sūrat Quraysh (106) suggests that the more enlightened Meccans regarded themselves as worshipping God there. The Arabic word for 'God', *Allāh*, is a contraction of *al-ilāh*, which like the Greek *ho theos* simply means 'the god' but was commonly understood as 'the supreme god' or 'God'. It is possible that before the time of Muḥammad the Meccan pagans used *Allāh*

[1] See ch. III. 2

to indicate the principal deity of the Kaʿbah, in the same way in which the deity worshipped at aṭ-Ṭā'if was known simply as *al-Lāt*, the goddess. If the word *Allāh* was also used for God as acknowledged by Jews and Christians, the opportunities for confusion would be great. The probability therefore is that while some Meccans acknowledged God, they did not see that their old polytheistic beliefs were incompatible with belief in God and reject them.

These premonitions of monotheism among the Arabs must have been due mainly to Christian and Jewish influences.[1] The Arabs had many opportunities of contact with Christians and Jews. The Byzantine empire, whose power and higher civilization they greatly admired, was Christian, and so was Abyssinia. Even in the Persian empire Christianity was strong, and al-Ḥīrah, the Persian vassal-state with which the Arabs were much in contact, was an outpost of the East Syrian or Nestorian Church. This combination of monotheism with military and political strength and a higher level of material civilization must have impressed the Arabs greatly. The nomadic tribes and settled communities in closest contact with these states were indeed being gradually Christianized; and even some of the Meccan merchants were not uninfluenced by what they saw when they travelled to the border market-towns on business. There were also Christians in Mecca, traders and slaves,[2] but the influence of isolated individuals was probably not so important.

The opportunities for contact with Jews were not so extensive as those with Christians, but some were probably more intimate. This was especially so in Medina where Jews and pagan Arabs were settled side by side. There were also quite a number of Jewish tribes settled at oases in Arabia and in the fertile parts of southern Arabia, either refugees of Hebrew race or Arab tribes which had adopted Judaism. There were apparently practically no Jews in Mecca.[3]

When one turns to questions of detail, one finds that the particular Jewish and Christian groups which influenced the Arabs must have had many strange ideas. By this is not meant the technical heterodoxy of the East Syrians (Nestorians) and the Syrian and

[1] See Excursus B.

[2] Cf. Lammens, *Arabie*, 1–49.

[3] Cf. ibid., 51–99, esp. 68: contrast Torrey, *Jewish Foundations*, 13, &c.

Abyssinian Monophysites; the expressions of the leading doctors of these churches were sober compared with many of the extraordinary ideas, derived from apocryphal gospels and the like, that seem to have been floating about Arabia. The passage of the Qur'ān which suggests that the Trinity consists of Father, Son, and Virgin Mary is doubtless a criticism of some nominally Christian Arabs who held this view. On the Jewish side, too, much of the detail came not from the sacred Scriptures but from secondary sources of various types.

The possibility of influence from monotheistic groups other than Jews and Christians cannot be entirely excluded, but at most it must have been slight. There may possibly have been small communities professing a monotheism based mainly on Greek philosophy, like the Sabians. Such is a possible interpretation of some uses of the word *ḥanīf.*[1] Here I shall simply say that there is no good evidence of any concerted movement towards monotheism. If there had been such a movement, it would almost certainly have had political implications, just as the Christianity of 'Uthmān b. al-Ḥuwayrith is to be connected with his aspiration to become sole ruler of Mecca with Byzantine help. There is, however, a measure of truth in the traditional account of the *ḥanīfs* as seekers for a new faith. In the religious situation of Arabia, and particularly of Mecca, as it was at the end of the sixth century, there must have been many serious-minded men who were aware of a vacuum and eager to find something to satisfy their deepest needs.

Finally, it should be noticed that there was some modification of Judaeo-Christian ideas to assimilate them to the Arab outlook. We have already noticed how old ideas connected with Fate or *dahr* came to be attached to God. The idea of God had permeated Arab thought to such an extent that pagans maintained that their superstitious rites were the command of *Allāh*: 'When they commit an indecency they say, We found our fathers doing this and God (or the god) hath so commanded us' (7. 27). The theistic interpretation of the retreat of Abrahah from Mecca may be prior to the Qur'ān and (even if the Qur'ān developed the material) the idea that Hūd and Ṣāliḥ were prophets to 'Ād and Thamūd was probably a pre-Qur'anic instance of the application of the Judaeo-Christian conception of prophethood. If *per improbabile* it were

[1] Cf. Excursus C.

the case, as has been suggested,[1] that Musaylimah of B. Ḥanīfah set up as a prophet *before* Muḥammad, that would illustrate how the conception of prophet had taken root. Assimilation to the Arab outlook is also reflected in the selection or rejection of Judaeo-Christian ideas, though it is usually difficult to show that Arabs *must* have been aware of an idea which is not mentioned, and therefore must have rejected it.

For the study of the life of Muḥammad it is hardly necessary to decide the relative importance of Jewish and Christian influences, especially since many details are disputed. The main necessity is to realize that such things were 'in the air' before the Qur'ān came to Muḥammad and were part of the preparation of himself and of his environment for his mission.

[1] D. S. Margoliouth, in JRAS, 1903, 467 ff., but cf. C. J. Lyall, ibid., 771 ff., and Buhl, *Muhammed*, p. 99, n. 278.

II

MUHAMMAD'S EARLY LIFE AND PROPHETIC CALL

I. MUḤAMMAD'S ANCESTRY

MUḤAMMAD was the son of ʿAbdallāh, the son of ʿAbd al-Muṭṭalib, the son of Hāshim, the son of ʿAbd Manāf, the son of Quṣayy, the son of Kilāb, &c. Quṣayy, as we have seen, was the effective ruler of Mecca during his lifetime, and his descendants inherited much of his power, although gradually it became divided among them as their numbers increased. The chief question to be considered in a life of Muḥammad is whether his ancestors were as important in the politics of Mecca as the sources suggest, or whether (as some Western scholars have thought) their importance has been exaggerated. The later ʿAbbāsid dynasty claimed descent from Hāshim, whereas the rivals whom they ousted, the Umayyads, traced their lineage to his brother ʿAbd Shams. In view of the unsympathetic way in which the Umayyads have been treated by later historians who wrote under the ʿAbbāsids, it would not be surprising if Hāshim and his sons and grandsons had been given greater prominence in extant histories than they really possessed. Scrutiny of the sources, however, suggests that this has not happened to any appreciable extent Whatever incidents tradition related have doubtless been presented in the most favourable light, but there are no grounds for supposing serious falsification or large-scale invention.

The four principal sons of ʿAbd Manāf appear to have done much to develop the trade of Mecca. ʿAbd Shams went to the Yemen, Nawfal to Persia, al-Muṭṭalib to Abyssinia, and Hāshim to Syria. This may very well be the source of their prosperity, though, of course, others were engaged in trade too. The story that ʿAbd Shams yielded to Hāshim the rights of supplying food and water to the pilgrims because Hāshim was less occupied in commercial journeys may have a foundation in fact. ʿAbd Shams may have realized that there were greater potential gains in long-distance trading than in petty dealings with pilgrims. Whatever was the relative importance and prosperity of the two, the comparatively early death of Hāshim at Gaza weakened his descendants and their associates, the clan of al-Muṭṭalib. Hāshim's brother, al-Muṭṭalib, was now head of the whole group, but it does not seem to have had any prominence in Meccan affairs until Hāshim's son, ʿAbd al-Muṭṭalib, who had been brought up in Medina with his mother, was brought to Mecca by his uncle al-Muṭṭalib.

With ʿAbd al-Muṭṭalib the position of the clan appears to have improved once more. His digging of the well of Zamzam beside the Kaʿbah shows him to have been a man of energy and initiative. Although Zamzam afterwards became the central well of Mecca and shared in the prestige of the sanctuary, ʿAbd al-Muṭṭalib's action does not show that he was the leading man in Mecca, though it links up with the right of providing water for the pilgrims which he had inherited from his father through his uncle.

The best evidence we have for his standing in the community is the record of the marriages of his daughters. Ṣafīyah (whose mother was from Zuhrah) married first a son of Ḥarb b. Umayyah (chief of ʿAbd Shams) and secondly al-ʿAwwām b. Khuwaylid (Asad). Of the others ʿĀtikah (whose mother was from Makhzūm) married Abū Umayyah b. al-Mughīrah (Makhzūm), Umaymah married Jaḥsh, a confederate of Ḥarb b. Umayyah, Arwā married first ʿUmayr b. Wahb (ʿAbd) and then a man of the clan of ʿAbd ad-Dār, Barrah married first Abū Ruhm (ʿĀmir) and then Abū 'l-Asad b. Hilāl (Makhzūm), Umm Ḥakīm married Kurayz (ʿAbd Shams). That is to say, ʿAbd al-Muṭṭalib was able to marry his daughters into some of the best and most powerful families of Mecca.[1]

The suggestion that he and Ḥarb b. Umayyah were rivals for supreme power in Mecca is suspect, since it is not described in detail, and sounds like a reflection of later rivalries; the marriage connexions show that, to begin with at least, they were on good terms. The account of ʿAbd al-Muṭṭalib's meeting with Abrahah during the expedition of the Elephant is probably to be accepted in outline, but to be regarded as a negotiation on behalf not of all Mecca but of a minority there. Many of the details in the different versions are probably attempts to supply motives for ʿAbd al-Muṭṭalib's policy, since whatever justification it may originally have had would be forgotten when the policy came to nought upon

[1] Cf. ISaʿd, viii. 27–31.

the catastrophic withdrawal of the Abyssinians. Whether this affected ʿAbd al-Muṭṭalib's influence in Mecca we cannot tell, since he died shortly afterwards. That he should have adopted such a policy at all suggests that his clan was becoming relatively worse off.

For a short time the leadership of the B. Hāshim (doubtless together with B. al-Muṭṭalib) passed to az-Zubayr b. ʿAbd al-Muṭṭalib. This was the period of the war of the Fijār and the Ḥilf al-Fuḍūl. But az-Zubayr seems to have been in no way outstanding. The Ḥilf al-Fuḍūl was a union of the weaker clans, and the leading part was played by ʿAbdallāh b. Judʿān (Taym), since the critical meeting took place in his house; he had been one of the chief men of Mecca at the beginning of the war of the Fijār.[1]

Less shadowy than az-Zubayr is his brother Abū Ṭālib, who was apparently head of the double clan from some time after the Ḥilf al-Fuḍūl until his death three years before the Hijrah. While he was respected as head of the clan, the clan's affairs were clearly not prospering, even if a contemptuous reference to him pasturing camels in the desert[2] is inspired mainly by the jealousy of the descendants of al-ʿAbbās. Owing to Abū Ṭālib's impoverished circumstances Muḥammad took his son ʿAlī to live with him. This state of affairs was doubtless due partly to the lack of any outstanding qualities in Abū Ṭālib and partly to the decline in the fortunes of the clan which had set in before the death of ʿAbd al-Muṭṭalib and was connected with his appeal to Abrahah and its failure.

Muḥammad's father, ʿAbdallāh, was a full brother of az-Zubayr and Abū Ṭālib. Like the rest of the family he was engaged in trade with Syria. He died at a comparatively early age at Medina on his way back from a trading expedition to Gaza.[3] This probably happened shortly before the birth of Muḥammad.

Muḥammad's mother was Āminah bint Wahb of the clan of Zuhrah of Quraysh; her mother was of the clan of ʿAbd ad-Dār and her maternal grandmother of that of Asad. Thus Muḥammad was connected with several of the principal families of Mecca.

On the whole the impression we get is that Muḥammad's clan had once been in the forefront of Meccan affairs, but that in the third of a century before his mission its influence had been on

[1] A. P. Caussin de Perceval, *Essai sur l'histoire des Arabes avant l'Islamisme* Paris, 1847–8, i. 300, 305, from *Aghānī*.

[2] Azraqī, *ap.* Wüst., *Mekka*, i. 71. 4.

[3] IS, i. 1. 61.

the wane, so that it was now no more than a prominent member of the group of weaker and poorer clans. Although members of the clan continued to be interested in the Syrian trade they probably did not share (or at least not to any important extent) in the large-scale operations of ʿAbd Shams and Makhzūm, and for business reasons the clan as a whole was probably ready to be unfriendly towards these clans, though there are perhaps traces of an approach to them by Muḥammad and Abū Lahab; thus, Muḥammad's daughter Zaynab married a man of ʿAbd Shams (her cousin on her mother's side).

2. MUḤAMMAD'S BIRTH AND EARLY YEARS

Muḥammad was born in the Year of the Elephant, the year of Abrahah's unsuccessful expedition against Mecca. This is usually held to be about A.D. 570. He was probably a posthumous child, and was under the care of his grandfather ʿAbd al-Muṭṭalib. It was the custom in Mecca for the upper classes to give their children to wet-nurses of the nomadic tribes, so that the children would grow up in the healthy air of the desert and develop a strong constitution. This was done with Muḥammad for two years or longer. His wet-nurse was Ḥalīmah, a woman of the clan of Saʿd b. Bakr of the great tribe or tribal group of Hawāzin.

Misfortune was piled upon misfortune for the orphan. When he was six his mother died, and two years later his grandfather. He was now under the charge of his uncle Abū Ṭālib, and with him is said to have made a journey to Syria. The war of the Fijār took place when Muḥammad was between fifteen and twenty, and he is said to have played a small part in the fighting at the side of his uncles. He was probably also present at the formation of the Ḥilf al-Fuḍūl, and in later years is said to have expressed approbation of it; its aim was to uphold principles of justice against the malpractices of the stronger and richer tribes, and that was an aim very close to certain aspects of Qur'ānic teaching.

These are the main facts about the life of Muḥammad prior to his marriage from the point of view of the secular historian, and arguments have been brought against even some of these. There is also, however, a large number of stories of what might be called a theological character. It is almost certain that they are not true in the realistic sense of the secular historian, for they purport to describe facts to which we might reasonably have expected some reference at later periods of Muḥammad's life; but there is no such reference. Yet they certainly express something of the significance of Muḥammad for believing Muslims, and in that sense are true for them and a fitting prologue to the life of their prophet. Perhaps they might also be regarded as expressing what anyone 'with eyes to see' might have seen had he been there. It will suffice to give the best-known of the stories in the words of Ibn Isḥāq.

Ḥalīmah bint Abī Dhu'ayb of the clan of Saʿd, the wet-nurse of the Messenger of God (God bless and preserve him) used to tell how, with her husband and a small son she was suckling, she set out from her country along with some women of the clan of Saʿd b. Bakr in quest of children to suckle. It was a year of drought, she said, which left nothing; I set out on a tawny she-ass I had, and with us was an old she-camel—by God, it gave us not a drop of milk; none of us slept at night for the little boy's crying because he was hungry; there was not enough milk in my breasts for him and the she-camel had nothing to satisfy him. . . . We kept hoping for rain and an end of misery. So I set out on that ass of mine; it was weak and emaciated and moved so slowly that it made things hard for the others. At length we reached Mecca looking for children to suckle. Not a woman of us but had the Messenger of God (God bless and preserve him) offered to her; but when she heard he was an orphan she refused him. We were thinking of the present we would get from the child's father. We kept saying, An orphan! What are his mother and grandfather likely to do! So we did not want him. Every woman in our party found a baby except myself. So when we agreed to leave for home I said to my man, By God, I will go to that orphan and take him. By God, I do not like to go back with the other women without any baby. That will not do you any harm, he said; perhaps God will bless us through him. So I went and took him, she continued, and my only reason was that I had not found any other baby. After taking him, I returned with him to where my stuff was; then I placed him on my bosom and gave him my breasts with whatever milk he wanted. He drank till he had enough, and his brother (*sc.* her own baby) drank too; both had enough and then both slept, although we had got no sleep with the baby previously. My husband got up and went to that old she-camel of ours and to his surprise she had plenty of milk. He milked her, and he and I drank our fill and then had an excellent night. In the morning my husband would say, By God, Ḥalīmah, you know you have taken a blessed creature; and I replied, By God, I hope so. Then we set out, she continued, and I rode my she-ass carrying the baby, and she moved so quickly that none of their asses could keep up with me, so that my companions would say to me, Confound you, Bint Abī Dhu'ayb, wait for us. Is this not the ass you rode on the outward journey? Yes, by God, the very same, I would reply. By God, something has happened to her, they would say. She continued: Then we came to our encampments in the country of the clan of Sa'd, and of all God's earth I know no tract more barren. Well, after I brought him back there, the beasts used to come back to me in the evening satisfied and full of milk, and we used to milk them and drink. Yet nobody else found a single drop of milk in the udders (of their beasts). So those of our tribe who were settled there used to say to their herdsmen, Confound you, go to pasture where Bint Abī Dhu'ayb's herd goes; but their beasts came back hungry and gave not a drop of milk, and mine were satisfied and full of milk. So we continued to experience God's bounty and favour until the baby's two years were up and I weaned him. He was lustier than any other boy, quite sturdy by the time he was two. We took him to his mother but we were as keen as anything to have him stay among us for the blessing we saw he brought. We spoke to his mother and I said to her, Perhaps you would leave my son with me until he grows up, for I am afraid he may get the Meccan plague. We kept at her until she sent him back with us. We returned with him and some months after our coming, by God, he was among our lambs with his brother behind our tents, when his brother came to us hurrying and said to me and to his father. That brother of mine from Quraysh—two men with white clothes have taken him and laid him down and split his body open, and they are stirring him up inside. So I and his father went out to him and found him standing looking pale. I clasped him and so did his father, and we said to him, What is wrong with you, my son? Two men with white clothes came to me, he said, and split open my body and looked for something in it, I do not know what. We took him back to our tent, and his father said to me, Ḥalīmah, I am afraid something has happened to this boy; take him to his family before there is anything about him to be noticed. So we carried him and brought him to his mother. What has made you come, nurse, she said, seeing you were so eager to have him with you? God has made my son grow up, I answered; I have finished my job, and I am afraid he may have an accident, so I have brought him to you as you desire. That is not what is worrying you, she said; tell me the truth about it. She did not leave me alone until I told her the story. Then it is the devil you are afraid of for him, she asked. Yes, I said. No, by God, she replied; the devil has no hold on him; my son is going to be something; shall I tell you about him? Yes, I said. When I was carrying him, she went on, a light went out from me that lit up for me the palaces of Buṣrā in the land of Syria. I never saw a pregnancy that was lighter and easier for me than with him. At his birth when he was delivered, there he was placing his hands on the ground and lifting his head up. Leave him now; and a safe journey home!

Ibn Isḥāq said: Thawr b. Yazīd related to me from a learned man—I think it was none other than Khālid b. Maʿdān al-Kalāʿī—that a party of the Companions of the Messenger of God (God bless and preserve him) said, O Messenger of God, tell us about yourself. He said, I am him for whom Abraham prayed and whom ʿĪsā announced.[1] When my mother was carrying me, she saw that there went out a light from her that lit up for her the palaces of Syria. I was suckled among the clan of Saʿd b. Bakr; while I was with a brother behind our tents tending the lambs, two men in white clothes came to me with a golden basin full of snow. They took me and split open my body, then they took my heart and split it open and took out from it a black clot which they flung away. Then they washed my heart and my body with that snow until they made them pure. Then one of them said to his fellow, Weigh him against ten of his people; and he weighed me against them and I outweighed them. Then he said, Weigh him against a hundred of his people; and he weighed me against them, and I outweighed them. Then he said, Weigh him against a thousand of his people; and he weighed me and I outweighed them. Then he said, Let him be; if you weighed him against the entire people he would outweigh them.[2]

Ibn Isḥāq said: Later Abū Ṭālib set out with a party to trade in Syria. When the preparations were complete and the party assembled, the Messenger of God (God bless and preserve him) showed his affection for him, so they say, and Abū Ṭālib was moved to pity and said, By God I shall take him with me, and we shall never leave one another—or something like that. So he took him with him. (At last) the party camped at Buṣrā in Syria. There was a monk there in his cell called Baḥīrā, who was versed in the lore of the Christians. From time immemorial there had been in that cell a monk well versed in their lore from a book that was there, so the story goes; as one grew old he handed it on to another. So they camped near Baḥīrā that year. Now many times previously they had passed, and he had not spoken to them nor even showed himself to them; but this year when they camped near his cell, he got ready abundant food for them, because of something he had seen in his cell they say; for, so the story goes, while in his cell he had seen the Messenger of God (God bless and preserve him) among the party as they drew near, and a white cloud shading him alone among the people; then they came up and alighted in the shade of a tree near him and he observed the cloud overshadowing the tree, and the branches of it bending together over the Messenger of God (God bless and preserve him) so that he found shelter under them. When Baḥīrā saw

[1] Q. 2. 123; 61. 6. [2] IH, 103–6.

that, he went down from his cell, having already given orders for that food. When it was ready he sent to them saying, I have made ready food for you, O tribe of Quraysh, and I would like all of you to come, small and great, slave and free. One of them said to him, By God, O Baḥīrā, what is the matter with you today? You have never at any time treated us thus, although we have passed by you many times. What is the matter with you today? Baḥīrā said to him, True, it is as you say; but you are guests and it has pleased me to honour you and prepare food for you that you may all eat of it. So they went together to him; because of his youthful years, however, the Messenger of God (God bless and preserve him) was not with the party but stayed behind among their stuff beneath the tree. When Baḥīrā looked among the party, he did not see the mark he was familiar with and had found in his (book), so he said, O tribe of Quraysh, none of you is to stay away from my food. They said to him, O Baḥīrā, none of us has stayed away from you whom it befits to come to you, except a lad, the youngest of the party in years; he has stayed behind among the stuff. That is not right, he said; call him and let him join in this feast with you. Then a man of Quraysh in the party said, By al-Lāt and al-ʿUzzā, it is shameful that the son of ʿAbdallāh b. ʿAbd al-Muṭṭalib should not be with us but should stay away from the feast. So he went to him and embraced him and set him among the party. When Baḥīrā saw him he began to eye him keenly and to observe features of his body which he had already found present. Then when the party had finished eating and had broken up, Baḥīrā went up to him and said, Young man, I adjure you by al-Lāt and al-ʿUzzā to answer my questions. Baḥīrā said that to him only because he had heard his people swearing by these two. They say that the Messenger of God (God bless and preserve him) said to him, Do not ask me by al-Lāt and al-ʿUzzā, for by God there is absolutely nothing I detest so much as these two. So Baḥīrā said to him, Then, in God's name, answer what I ask you. Ask what seems good to you, he said. So Baḥīrā began to ask him about certain particulars of his condition in sleep, his outward appearance and his affairs. Then the Messenger of God (God bless and preserve him) set about answering him; and what he said agreed with the description of him in Baḥīrā's (book). Then Baḥīrā looked at his back and saw the seal of prophethood between his shoulders in the place where it was described as being in his (book). Ibn Hishām said: It was like the imprint of a cupping-glass. Ibn Isḥāq continued: When he was finished, he went up to his uncle, Abū Ṭālib, and said, How is this youth related to you? He said, He is my son. Baḥīrā said to him, He is not your son; this young man's father cannot be alive. He said, Indeed, he is my brother's son. What did his father do?, he said. He died, he said, while his mother was pregnant with him.

True, he said; return to your own country with your nephew, and take care of him against the Jews; for by God if they see him and know what I know about him, they will desire evil; for great importance is in store for this your nephew. So hurry to your country with him. So his uncle Abū Ṭālib set out with him quickly, and soon reached Mecca, on the completion of their trade with Syria.[1]

3. MUḤAMMAD'S MARRIAGE WITH KHADĪJAH

The turning-point in the early part of Muḥammad's career is his marriage with Khadījah bint Khuwaylid b. Asad. The traditional account is that when Khadījah heard of the honesty, trustworthiness, and high moral character of Muḥammad she invited him to act as her agent on a caravan journey to Syria. She had had two husbands, of whom the second had been of the clan of Makhzūm, but she now traded on her own account by means of agents. Khadījah was so pleased with the results of Muḥammad's stewardship and so impressed by his personality that she made an offer of marriage to him, which he accepted. She is said to have been forty at this time and Muḥammad twenty-five.

The age of Khadījah has perhaps been exaggerated. The names of seven children whom she bore to Muḥammad are mentioned in the sources—al-Qāsim, Ruqayyah, Zaynab, Umm Kulthūm, Fāṭimah, ʿAbdallāh (aṭ-Ṭayyib), and aṭ-Ṭāhir; of these the boys all died young.[2] Even if, as one of Ibn Saʿd's authorities says, they came at regular yearly intervals, that would make her forty-eight before the last was born. This is by no means impossible, but one would have thought it sufficiently unusual to merit comment; it is even the sort of thing that might well have been treated as miraculous. Yet no single word of comment occurs in the pages of Ibn Hishām, Ibn Saʿd, or aṭ-Ṭabarī.

From the point of view of Meccan society Muḥammad had now set his foot on at least the lowest rung of the ladder of worldly success. Khadījah may not have been so wealthy as is sometimes stated, but Muḥammad had presumably sufficient capital to take a moderate share in trading enterprises.[3] The fact that there is no record of his having travelled to Syria again does not mean that he did not do so, though it is always possible that he entrusted the oversight of his business to others. The possibility should also be kept in mind, however, that he was excluded from the inner circle

[1] IH, 115–17.

[2] IS, i/1. 85. Cf. IH, ii, scholion to p. 121, where aṭ-Ṭāhir is said to have been a name of ʿAbdallāh.

[3] Cf. Azraqī, 471. 2.

of traders and from the most profitable operations. It is unlikely, however, that he was altogether excluded, since he was able to marry his daughter Zaynab to a member of the clan of 'Abd Shams—actually a nephew of Khadījah's, who was doubtless prominent in the negotiations. The fact that two other daughters were betrothed to sons of Abū Lahab, perhaps already recognized as the coming man of the clan of Hāshim, suggests that Muḥammad, too, was regarded as one of the most promising youths of the clan.

While we cannot expect a woman merchant of sixth-century Mecca to have been unmindful of the material factors, there is much to suggest that Khadījah also realized something of Muḥammad's spiritual capacities, and was attracted by these. Certainly she seems to have played an important role at critical junctures of his life in encouraging him to proceed on his way as a prophet. Moreover Khadījah's cousin, Waraqah b. Nawfal b. Asad, was a religious-minded man who eventually became a Christian.[1] Khadījah had almost certainly come under his influence, and Muḥammad may have acquired something of the earnestness of his outlook.

The years that followed his marriage were for Muḥammad years of preparation for the work that lay ahead. Nothing has been preserved, however, to enable us to reconstruct the process of preparation; and the best we can do is to make some inferences from what happened later. Thus there is a passage in Sūrat aḍ-Ḍuḥā (93. 6–8) which seems to refer to Muḥammad's early experiences:

> Did He not find thee an orphan and give thee shelter?
> Did He not find thee erring and feed thee?
> Did He not find thee poor and enrich thee?

From this we might perhaps argue that one stage in his development was the realization that the hand of God had been supporting him despite his misfortunes. Other pointers to these hidden years will come to our notice as we proceed.

4. THE CALL TO BE A PROPHET

(a) *The account given by az-Zuhrī*

At the age of forty, according to the traditional accounts, God called Muhammad to be a prophet and began to send him revela-

[1] Cf. Excursus C.

tions. The best starting-point is the account of az-Zuhrī together with the same historian's material about the *fatrah* or gap in the revelation. This has not been rewritten, as has Ibn Hishām's version, in order to give a smooth sequence, but simply puts together scraps of source material as they have come to az-Zuhrī. There are no divisions in the text as it has come down to us; some of the divisions here introduced for convenience, come at breaks in az-Zuhrī's material, as indicated by the change of narrator.

A. '. . . I heard an-Nuʿmān b. Rashīd narrating from az-Zuhrī who had it from ʿUrwah, who had it from ʿĀ'ishah, that she said: The beginning of revelation for the Messenger of God (God bless and preserve him) was true vision (*ar-ru'yā 'ṣ-ṣādiqah*). It used to come like the breaking of dawn.

B. Afterwards solitude became dear to him, and he would go to a cave on Ḥirā' to engage in *taḥannuth* (? devotional exercises) there for a certain number of nights before returning to his family, and then he would return to them for provisions for a similar stay. At length unexpectedly the Truth came to him and said, O Muḥammad, thou art the Messenger of God.

C. The Messenger of God (God bless and preserve him) said, I had been standing, but I fell to my knees; then I crept away, my shoulders quaking; then I entered Khadījah's chamber and said, Cover me (*zammilūnī*), cover me, until the terror left me. Then he came to me and said, O Muḥammad, thou art the Messenger of God.

D. He (*sc.* Muḥammad) said, I had been meditating throwing myself from a mountain crag, but while I was so meditating, he appeared to me and said, O Muḥammad, I am Gabriel, and thou art the Messenger of God.

E. Then he said, Recite. I said, I cannot recite (or "What shall I recite"). He (*sc.* Muḥammad) said, Then he took me and squeezed me vehemently three times until exhaustion overcame me; then he said, *Recite in the name of thy Lord who created.* And I recited.

F. And I came to Khadījah and said, I am filled with anxiety for myself; and I told her my experience. She said, Rejoice; by God, never will God bring you to confusion; you do good to your kindred, you speak the truth, you restore what is entrusted to you, you endure fatigue, you entertain the guest, you succour the agents of the truth (?).

G. Then she took me to Waraqah b. Nawfal b. Asad. She said, Listen to the son of your brother. He asked me, and I told him my experience. He said, This is the *nāmūs* which was sent down (or "revealed") to Mūsā b. ʿImrān (*sc.* Moses). Would that I were young here! Would that I might be alive when your tribe expel you! I said, Will *they* expel me?

He said, No man ever brought what you bring without being treated as an enemy; if your day had reached me, I should have helped you valiantly.

H. The first part of the Qur'ān revealed to me after *Recite* (96) was *N. By the Pen and what they write, Thou by the bounty of thy Lord art not mad; Verily for thee is a reward rightfully thine; For thou art engaged in a mighty task; So thou wilt see and they will see* (68. 1–5); and, *O thou clothed in the dathār, Rise and warn* (74. 1–2); and, *By the morning brightness, By the night when it is still* (93. 1–2). . . .'[1]

I. 'Az-Zuhrī said: There was a gap for a time in the revelation to the Messenger of God (God bless and preserve him), and he was very sorrowful. He started going early to the tops of the mountains to throw himself down from them. But whenever he reached the summit of a mountain, Gabriel would appear to him and say, Thou art the Prophet of God. At that his restlessness would cease and his self would return to him.

J. The Prophet (God bless and preserve him) used to speak about that. He said, While I was walking one day, I saw the angel who used to come to me at Ḥirā' on a throne (*kursī*) between heaven and earth. I was stricken with fear of him, and returned to Khadījah, and said, Cover me (*zammilū-nī*).

K. So we covered him, that is, we put a *dathār* on him (*daththarnā-hu*), and God most high sent down, *O thou clothed in the dathār, Rise and warn, Thy Lord magnify, Thy garments purify* (74. 1–4).

L. Az-Zuhrī added, The first to be revealed to him was *Recite in the name of thy Lord who created* . . . up to *what he did not know* (96. 1–5).'[2]

Az-Zuhrī, who is also known as Ibn Shihāb, transmitted another version of J and K, which begins thus: 'Jābir b. 'Abdallāh al-Anṣārī said, The Messenger of God (God bless and preserve him) said, speaking about the gap in the revelation, While I was walking.' This version avoids the change of narrator from J to K by writing *daththarū-nī*, 'they put a *dathār* on me'. This is interesting since this is a form of the tradition from Jābir which makes Sūrat al-Muddaththir (74) the first revelation.[3]

Passages A to H were presumably continuous in az-Zuhrī, but they need not all have come from 'Ā'ishah. The fact that Ibn Isḥāq breaks off 'Ā'ishah's narrative after the first sentence of B is probably due to his having other versions of the remainder which he preferred, and does not necessarily indicate a break in the source at that point. Not much, however, is to be gained by

[1] Ṭab. *Ann.* 1147 f. [2] Ibid. 1155. [3] Ibid. 1155 f.

discussion of the *isnād*. I propose rather to consider the internal evidence of the passages, and in particular to study what may be called the various 'features' of the stories.

(b) *Muḥammad's visions*

There are no good grounds for doubting the main point of passage A, namely, that Muḥammad's prophetic experience began with 'true vision'. This is quite distinct from dreams. Visions are mentioned also in B and J (apart from the appearances of Gabriel in D and I). The statement in A confirms what we learn from Sūrat an-Najm, but may be derived independently from remarks of Muḥammad. Two visions are described in the Qur'ān:

> By the star when it falls,
> Your comrade has not gone astray, nor has he erred;
> Nor does he speak of his own inclination.
> It is nothing but a suggestion suggested,
> Taught him by One strong in power,
> Forceful; he stood straight,
> Upon the high horizon,
> Then he drew near, and let himself down,
> Till he was two bow-lengths off or nearer,
> And suggested to his servant what he suggested . . .
> He saw him, too, at a second descent,
> By the sidra-tree at the boundary,
> Near which is the garden of the abode,
> When the sidra-tree was strangely enveloped.
> The eye turned not aside, nor passed its limits.
> Verily, he saw one of the greatest signs of his Lord.[1]

The usual exegesis of this by Muslims is that these were visions of Gabriel; but there are grounds for thinking that Muḥammad originally interpreted these as visions of God Himself. There is no mention of Gabriel in the Qur'ān until the Medinan period. The words in v. 10, 'His servant', must mean God's servant, as is agreed by Muslims; but that makes the construction awkward unless God is also the implied subject of the verbs. The phrase at the end of passage B, 'the Truth came to him and said . . .', is similar in import, since 'the Truth' is a way of referring to God. Passage C can also be taken in this way, since the wording merely is 'then *he* came to me and said'; and likewise some versions of the

[1] 53. 1–18.

tradition about Sūrat al-Muddaththir from Jābir simply say, quoting Muhammad, 'I heard a voice calling me, and I looked all round but could see no one; then I looked above my head and there *he* was sitting upon the throne'.[1]

While this may well have been Muhammad's original interpretation of the vision, it can hardly have been his final one, for it contradicts 6. 103, 'sight reacheth not to Him'. Sūrat an-Najm, however, although capable of bearing that interpretation, can also be taken in other ways. Indeed, the words 'one of the greatest signs of his Lord' (or 'of the signs of his Lord, the greatest') do not apply naturally to a vision of God. But it seems possible that they might be taken to mean that what Muhammad had seen was a sign or symbol of the glory and majesty of God. Verse II, 'the heart did not falsify what it saw', which was perhaps added later,[2] suggests a further development of this theory, namely, that while the eyes perceived the sign or symbol, the heart perceived the thing symbolized. If Muhammad had originally interpreted the vision as a direct vision of God, this would then imply that, though his interpretation was not quite accurate, in essentials he was not mistaken. Perhaps the verse ought to be translated: 'the heart was not mistaken in respect of what he, the man, saw'. In this way it would be possible to avoid making it a vision of Gabriel, which would be unhistorical, and also to avoid contradicting the view of Islamic orthodoxy that Muhammad had not seen God.[3]

The formal interpretation of the vision, however, is not so important from the standpoint of the life of Muhammad as the significance of it for his religious development. This will be dealt with when we come to the words 'Thou art the Messenger of God'.

(Karl Ahrens[4] has suggested that the *rasūl karim* of 81. 19 was originally identified with *ar-Rūh*, the Spirit. His reasons are that in the Meccan passages there is no mention of Gabriel, but of 'angels' in the plural only; e.g. 'in it the angels and the spirit let themselves down' (? come down), 97. 4; cf. 26. 193: 'with which hath come down the Faithful Spirit'. This would fit in with the view here developed.)

1 Bukhāri, 65, on 74. 1; cf. Tab. *Ann.* 1153; quoted from R. Bell, *Mohammed's Call*, in MW, xxiv, 1934, pp. 13–19; cf. Nöldeke–Schwally, i. 23, and Ahrens, *Muhammed*, 39 f.

2 Bell, *Translation of Q., ad loc.*

3 Cf. the tradition from 'Ā'ishah, Bukhāri, 65, on 53. I.

4 *Muhammed*, 41.

(c) *The visit to Ḥirā'; taḥannuth*

There is no improbability in Muḥammad's going to Ḥirā', a hill a little way from Mecca, with or without his family. It might be a method of escaping from the heat of Mecca in an unpleasant season for those who could not afford to go to aṭ-Ṭā'if. Judaeo-Christian influence, such as the example of monks, or a little personal experience, would show the need and desirability of solitude.

The precise meaning and derivation of *taḥannuth* is uncertain, though it is evidently some sort of devotional practice. The best suggestion is perhaps that of H. Hirschfeld[1] that it comes from the Hebrew *teḥinnōt* or *teḥinnōth*, meaning prayers for God's favour. The meaning may have been influenced by the Arabic root, however. *Ḥinth* is properly the violation of or failure to perform an oath, and so more generally sin; and *taḥannuth* is accordingly said to mean 'doing some work so as to escape from sin or crime'. The use of the word *taḥannuth* here is probably a mark that the material is old and in this respect genuine.[2]

We can perhaps fill out hypothetically this brief account of what preceded Muḥammad's call and first revelation. Muḥammad must have been aware from an early age of some of the social and religious problems of Mecca. His position as an orphan doubtless made him more aware of the malaise in the community. In religion his outlook was presumably the vague monotheism found among the most enlightened Meccans, but in addition he must have looked for some kind of reform in Mecca, and everything in his environment would conspire to suggest that this reform must be primarily religious. In this frame of mind Muḥammad apparently deliberately sought solitude to reflect on Divine things and to perform some acts of worship, perhaps an expiation for sins. Some religious experiences may have preceded this 'going into retreat', but of that we know nothing. The traditional accounts suggest that the visions came during the retreat, but in general the comparative dates of the different features of Muḥammad's call are uncertain. Sometimes the appearance is said to be unexpected, and sometimes Khadījah seems to have been not far away.

[1] *New Researches into the Composition and Exegesis of the Qoran*, London, 1902, p. 10 n.; supported by C. J. Lyall in JRAS, 1903, p. 780.

[2] But contrast Caetani, *Ann.* i, p. 222, n. 2.

(d) '*Thou art the Messenger of God*'

The words 'Thou art the Messenger of God' occur four times in the passages from az-Zuhrī, in B, C, D, I. In the last two Gabriel speaks, in the first 'the Truth', in the second merely 'he'. The circumstances are different in the four. Are these simply four versions of one event, that somehow or other have developed different features? The mention of Gabriel is suspicious at this early stage, since he is not mentioned in the Qur'ān until much later. Superficially the experiences belong to two types at least. B, perhaps together with C, describes his original call to be a Messenger, whereas D and I appear to be a reaffirmation of this to reassure him in a time of anxiety.

If B refers to the original call, what is its relation to the visions? The description of the first vision in Sūrat an-Najm occurs in a passage refuting certain objections raised by the Meccans to the authenticity of the revelations which Muḥammad transmitted to them; he must therefore have publicly proclaimed at least one revelation, and presumably several. The narration of the vision in this context shows that the vision must have something to do with the receiving of the revelations. Yet there is nothing to show that the receiving of specific passages accompanied the vision; indeed, if more than two passages were in question, it would be impossible. The practical outcome of the vision would seem to be something more general, such as the conviction that these passages were messages from God, and perhaps also that Muḥammad was called to proclaim them publicly. This would presuppose that Muḥammad had already received some revelations, but was not sure of the true nature of these words that came to him; now he is informed or given an assurance about that. Alternatively, the vision might be taken as a call to seek revelations, and Muḥammad may have known something about methods of inducing them. On the whole, the former of the alternatives is more probable. In line with this is the view[1] that what was inspired or suggested to him was 'the practical line of conduct' which he in fact followed. If then the purport of the vision was something general, that would fit in well with passage B. It is probable that the words 'Thou art the Messenger of God' were not an exterior locution, possible that they were not even an imaginative locution, but an

[1] R. Bell, *Muhammad's Visions*, in MW, xxiv, 1934, pp. 145–54, esp. 148.

intellectual locution, that is, that he did not hear with his ears nor even imagine himself hearing, but that these words formulate a communication which came to him without words.[1] The form of words may even be much later than the actual vision.

Could such an experience be repeated? It is not altogether impossible, and the conjunction of the two visions in Sūrat an-Najm perhaps implies some similarity in content. On the other hand, there is no mention of inspiration in the description of the second vision, and it is usually taken as referring to Paradise. Passages C, D, and I do not help much. The two latter are not so much a call to Muḥammad as a reassurance to him, reminding him of his original call. It would be natural to suppose that Muḥammad would remember his first vision in times of despair. Perhaps the thought of it flashed into his mind at critical moments and he ascribed this to supernatural agency. Whatever may be the facts about such remembrances, they are not so important as the original experience.

(e) '*Recite*'

There are numerous versions of the tradition about the revelation of Sūrat al-ʿAlaq (96), of which one occurs in passage E from az-Zuhrī. In the later versions the words *mā aqra'u* with which Muḥammad replies to the *iqra'* of the angel must be translated 'I cannot read (or recite)'; this is made clear by the existence of a variant *mā anā bi-qārin* ('I am not a reader or reciter'),[2] and by the distinction in Ibn Hishām between *mā aqra'u* and *mādhā aqra'u*, of which the second can only mean, 'What shall I recite?' This latter is also the more natural meaning for *mā aqra'u*. It is almost certain that the later traditionists avoided the natural meaning of these words in order to find support for the dogma that Muḥammad could not write, which was an important part of the proof of the miraculous nature of the Qur'ān. The form of the tradition from ʿAbdallāh b. Shaddād in aṭ-Ṭabarī's Commentary,[3] if the text is correct, requires that the *mā* be taken as 'what', since it is preceded by 'and'.

The words *qara'a* and *qur'ān* 'belong to that religious vocabulary which Christianity had introduced into Arabia; *qara'a* means to

[1] See section 5 and A. Poulain, *Graces of Interior Prayer*, London, 1928, 299 f.
[2] Bukhārī, 65, to Q. 96.
[3] xxx. 139; it differs a little from that in *Ann*. i. 1148.

read or solemnly recite sacred texts, while *qur'ān* is the Syriac *qeryāna* used to denote the "reading" or Scripture lesson'.[1] While the verb later came to mean 'read', in this sūrah it presumably means 'recite from memory', namely, from the memory of what had been supernaturally communicated to him. To whom and on what occasions was Muḥammad to recite? This question is not clearly discussed in the traditions. The most natural interpretation is that Muḥammad was to recite what followed as part of the formal worship of God. This is in accordance with the Syriac usage, and with the fact that Muslims still call the recitation of a sūrah or sūrahs in their *ṣalāt* or Worship the *qirā'ah*. It is noteworthy that in the tradition from ʿAbdallāh b. Shaddād referred to above, the answer to the question 'What shall I recite?' is not, as in most other forms, 'Recite in the name of . . .' but simply 'In the name of . . .'. Could this be a premonition of the Bismillah?

There are no effective objections to the almost universal view of Muslim scholars that this is the first part of the Qur'ān to be revealed. No other passage can contest the claim of Sūrat al-ʿAlaq with any chance of success.[2] A command to worship is just what we should expect to come first in view of the general tenour of the primary message of the Qur'ān.[3] The word 'recite' is addressed to Muḥammad alone, and, although there is no difficulty in extending it to his followers in imitation of him, it is conceivable that the very thought of having followers had not occurred to him when it was revealed; that is, it may very well belong to a stage before he began to preach to others. The possibility cannot be excluded, of course, that Muḥammad had already received other messages which he did not regard as part of the Qur'ān; one example would be the words in the traditions 'Thou art the Messenger of God'.

(f) *Sūrat al-Muddaththir; the Fatrah*

There is a tradition from Jābir b. ʿAbdallāh al-Anṣārī that the opening verses of Sūrat al-Muddaththir were the first revelation. This is fitting in that it contains the words 'Rise and warn', which seem to be a command to enter upon the work of an apostle or messenger. This can only be the first revelation, however, if Muḥammad entered abruptly on his public ministry without any

[1] Bell, *Origin*, 90 f.; cf. Nöldeke–Schwally, i. 82.
[2] Cf. ibid. 78.
[3] Cf. ch. III.

period of preparation. If, however, there was such a preparatory period, and if there were revelations in that, then this would not be the first revelation; and we have seen that *iqra'* does not necessarily imply a public ministry. The persistence of this tradition, despite the general agreement at an early period that Sūrat al-ʿAlaq was the first revelation, suggests that there is a grain of truth in it; the most probable view is that it marks the beginning of the public ministry.

There is in tradition good evidence for a distinction between a public ministry and a non-public ministry. Ibn Isḥāq,[1] writes: 'Then God ordered His prophet, three years after his commission, to declare publicly what had come to him from Him, to confront the people with God's word and to summon them to it.' Elsewhere we are told that prior to the ten years at Mecca when revelation was mediated to Muḥammad by Gabriel, there were three years when it was mediated by Asrāfīl.[2] The beginning of the three years is sometimes described as the coming of the *nubūwah* or commission to be a prophet, and the beginning of the ten years as the coming of the *risālah* or the commission to be a messenger or apostle.[3] In view of the wide consensus in tradition and the inherent likelihood we may take it that there was a difference between the two phases of Muḥammad's activity, and that the usual dates are roughly correct. What the precise nature of the difference was is more difficult to say, since the first converts are said to have been made during the first period.

The matter is complicated by the *fatrah* or gap in the revelation, as described in I. When the account in passages J and K, together with az-Zuhrī's version of the tradition from Jābir[4] is compared with the version of the tradition from Jābir transmitted by Yaḥyā b. Abī Kathīr,[5] it seems clear that az-Zuhrī introduces the *fatrah* in order to reconcile this tradition with the view that Sūrat al-ʿAlaq came first. There is other evidence for the *fatrah*, however; Ibn Isḥāq makes it precede the revelation of Sūrat aḍ-Ḍuḥā.[6] In itself, too, such an experience is highly probable. It is unlikely, however, that it should have lasted three years as is sometimes suggested; this figure is possibly due to confusion with the duration of the non-public ministry. These considerations suggest that there probably was some gap in Muḥammad's religious experi-

[1] IH, 166; also in Ṭab. *Ann.* 1169.
[2] Ṭab. *Ann.* 1248 f.
[3] Cf. Caetani, *Ann.* i. 218–20.
[4] Ṭab. 1155 f.
[5] Ibid., 1153.
[6] IH, 156.

ence; az-Zuhrī's conjecture (for such I take it to be) that it came immediately before the beginning of the public ministry is not strong evidence but is quite probable.

The word *muddaththir* is commonly taken to mean 'wrapped in a *dithār* (or *dathār*), that is, a cloak'. If this is correct, then the action has some connexion with the receiving of revelations; it may either be to induce revelations, or, more probably, to protect the human recipient from the danger of the Divine appearance.[1] On the other hand, certain cognate words develop metaphorically the idea of being covered over or hidden, and so are applied to a man who is obscure and of no reputation. This would be appropriate here if Muḥammad's reason for hesitating was that, according to the standards by which the rich Meccans judged, he was a comparatively unimportant person.

The picture which is formed when these uncertain details are fitted together is somewhat as follows. There was what we might call a preparatory stage in Muḥammad's career as prophet, lasting three years. In this he apparently began to receive revelations of some sort; in the Asrāfīl traditions it says that Muḥammad 'heard his voice but did not see his figure'. The first part of Sūrat al-ʿAlaq and Sūrat aḍ-Ḍuḥā may belong here; there may also have been revelations of a more private character which Muḥammad did not consider to form part of the Qur'ān. Towards the end of the three years one might place the *fatrah*. The transition from the non-public to the public ministry would also be the most natural place for the visions, or at least the first, with the giving of the title 'Messenger of God', and also for Sūrat al-Muddaththir (though the connexion of that with a vision in the traditional account is not good evidence owing to the disjunctions betraying its composite character). One would expect Muḥammad to speak about religious matters to his close friends during the preparatory period, but it is strange to have conversions before Muḥammad publicly claimed to be God's Messenger to the people of Mecca. There is therefore the suspicion that too much is ascribed to the preparatory stage in the traditional accounts.

(g) *Muḥammad's fear and despair*

In the passages from az-Zuhrī there are frequent references to

[1] See Nöldeke–Schwally, i. 87; and Wellhausen, *Reste*, 135, n. 2.
[2] Ṭab. 1249. 5.

emotions of fear and the like in Muḥammad. Two types of experience can be distinguished. Firstly, fear because of the appearance or presence of the Divine (C, F, J); and secondly, despair which led to thoughts of suicide (D, I).

The fear of the near approach of the Divine has deep roots in the Semitic consciousness, as the Old Testament bears witness. The traditions which mention this (see C and J) seem to be mainly derived from explanations of the word *al-muzzammil* (73. 1), and this suggests that the later exegetes were merely inferring the presence of fear from the Qur'ān, and had no information about it apart from the Qur'ān. The awkward transition from *zammilū-nī* to *muddaththir* shows that the interpretation of *muzzammil* was originally not connected with the story of Muḥammad's call, and that that connexion also is inference. On the other hand, if it seemed natural to these later exegetes to take *muzzammil* in this way, this fear at the onset of the Divine must have been widespread, and Muḥammad may well have shared in it. That is all we can say.

Feelings of despair can be roughly paralleled among the Old Testament prophets and from the lives of the Christian saints. St. Teresa of Avila writes:

> The words, their effects, and the assurance they carried with them convinced the soul at the moment that they came from God; that time, however, is now past; doubts afterwards arise whether the locutions come from the devil or from the imagination, although, while hearing them, the person had no doubt of their truth, which she would have died to defend.'[1]

The thought of suicide, however, could hardly have been attributed to Muḥammad, one would think, unless he had said something which gave a basis for the attribution. It goes beyond the exegesis of Sūrat aḍ-Ḍuḥā. Moreover, such a period of despair would fit in with the accounts of the *fatrah*. This does, therefore, seem to give us some real information about Muḥammad.

(h) *Encouragement from Khadījah and Waraqah*

There is no reason for rejecting the account of how Khadījah reassured Muḥammad. It is evidence that Muḥammad was lacking in self-confidence at this stage, and the general picture would

[1] *Interior Castle*, Sixth Mansion, iii. 12; quoted from Poulain, *Graces of Interior Prayer*, 304 f.

hardly have been invented, though details may have been added from inference or imagination.

The reassurance from Waraqah is important. There is no strong reason for doubting the authenticity of the phrase about the *nāmūs*. The use of the word, which is non-Qur'anic, instead of the Qur'anic *Tawrāh*, is an argument for its genuineness. On the other hand, the rest of the story seems to be an attempt to explain why Waraqah, though he approved of Muḥammad, did not become a Muslim. For a somewhat similar reason the version which makes Muḥammad meet Waraqah is preferable to that in which they do not meet. Moreover, some versions put his death two or three years after Muḥammad's commission, others as much as four.[1]

The word *nāmūs* is usually taken to be derived from the Greek *nomos*,[2] and thus to mean the law or revealed scriptures; this fits in well with the mention of Moses. Waraqah's remark would thus be made to Muḥammad after he had started to receive revelations, and would mean that what had come to Muḥammad was to be identified or at least classed with the Jewish and Christian scriptures. The suggestion may also have been present that Muḥammad should be the founder or legislator of a community. If, as seems likely, Muḥammad was of a hesitant nature, this encouragement to him to put the highest construction on his experiences must have been of great importance in his interior development.

There is a slight difficulty about dating. The concluding words of the first revelation, '. . . Who taught by the pen, Taught man what he did not know', almost certainly refer to previous revelations; Muslims usually take the former line to mean 'taught the use of the pen', but there is no point in this, especially if Muḥammad could neither read nor write. Now of the men with whom we know Muḥammad to have been in close contact Waraqah is outstanding for his study of the Christian scriptures.[3] The Qur'anic passage must, when Muḥammad repeated it, have reminded him of what he owed to Waraqah. It is tempting to think that it is subsequent to Waraqah's remark about the *nāmūs*, but that would require revelations prior to the *iqra'* passage to form the grounds for the remark. It is thus simpler to suppose that Muḥammad had frequent communication with Waraqah at an earlier date, and learnt much of a general character. Later Islamic conceptions may

[1] See Caetani, *Ann.* i, pp. 238, 260.
[2] Cf. ibid., p. 222, n. 6.
[3] IH, 143.

have been largely moulded by Waraqah's ideas, e.g. of the relation of Muḥammad's revelation to previous revelations.

(i) *Conclusion*

There is thus much uncertainty about the circumstances surrounding Muḥammad's call. Yet careful sifting of the earliest traditions leads to a general picture in which we may have a fair degree of confidence, even though many details, and especially the relative dates of the different features, must remain somewhat uncertain.

5. THE FORM OF MUḤAMMAD'S PROPHETIC CONSCIOUSNESS

Since Carlyle's lecture on Muḥammad in *Heroes and Hero-worship*, the West has been aware that there was a good case to be made out for believing in Muḥammad's sincerity.[1] His readiness to undergo persecution for his beliefs, the high moral character of the men who believed in him and looked up to him as leader, and the greatness of his ultimate achievement—all argue his fundamental integrity. To suppose Muḥammad an impostor raises more problems than it solves. Moreover, none of the great figures of history is so poorly appreciated in the West as Muḥammad. Western writers have mostly been prone to believe the worst of Muḥammad, and, wherever an objectionable interpretation of an act seemed plausible, have tended to accept it as fact. Thus, not merely must we credit Muḥammad with essential honesty and integrity of purpose, if we are to understand him at all; if we are to correct the errors we have inherited from the past, we must in every particular case hold firmly to the belief in his sincerity until the opposite is conclusively proved; and we must not forget that conclusive proof is a much stricter requirement than a show of plausibility, and in a matter such as this only to be attained with difficulty. Theories of Western authors which presuppose his insincerity will not be discussed as theories, though arguments against his sincerity will have to be considered.

If, then, we resolve to cling as far as possible to the belief in his sincerity, we must distinguish the Qur'ān from the normal consciousness of Muḥammad, since the distinction was fundamental

[1] Cf. Tor Andrae, *Mohammad, the Man and his Faith*, London, 1936, pp. 63, 69, 229, 233, 259, 268; W. Thomson in MW, xxxiv, 1944, pp. 129 f.

for him. From the first he must have distinguished carefully between what, as he believed, came to him from a supernatural source and the products of his own mind. Just how he made the distinction is not quite clear, but the fact that he made it is as certain as anything in history. We cannot with any plausibility imagine him inserting verses *of his own composition* among those which came to him from this source independent of his consciousness (as he believed). He may, however, have done some rearranging of revealed material, and he may have tried to induce emending revelations where he felt that a passage required emendation—it is part of orthodox Muslim theory that some revelations were abrogated by others.

The explanation and interpretation of the fact that Muḥammad made this distinction is another matter, and as it involves theological questions it will not be discussed here. The three main views are as follows. Orthodox Muslims hold that the Qur'ān is entirely supernatural in origin; it is the uncreated Word or Speech of God (though the material vehicle—the sounds, marks on paper, &c.—are created). The Western secularist holds (or should hold, if he allows for the distinction made by Muḥammad) that the Qur'ān is the work of some part of Muḥammad's personality other than his conscious mind. The third main view is that the Qur'ān is the work of Divine activity, but produced through the personality of Muḥammad, in such a way that certain features of the Qur'ān are to be ascribed primarily to the humanity of Muḥammad; this is presumably the view of those Christians who admit some Divine truth in Islam, though it has never been fully worked out. With regard to these three views I attempt to remain neutral, since they involve questions outside the province of the historian. Out of courtesy I have tried to speak so as not to deny any fundamental Islamic belief, and I have therefore always used the form of words 'the Qur'ān says' and not 'Muḥammad says'. On the other hand, when I speak of a passage being revealed to Muḥammad, for instance, that is not to be taken as implying an acceptance of the first of the above three views; I simply use the Muslim description leaving it to the reader to supply 'as the Muslims say' or some such phrase; this should not cause any confusion.

Once this rough distinction has been made between historical and theological matters, it is proper for the historian to consider the precise form in Muḥammad's consciousness of this experience of receiving revelations. How did it appear to him, and how did he describe it? These are objective historical facts, even though they deal with Muḥammad's consciousness and even though his descriptions are probably coloured by his previous views on such things. The first point to notice is that the visions described in Sūrat an-Najm are something exceptional; that is clear from the way in which they are described. We must therefore look elsewhere for the normal form or forms of Muḥammad's prophetic consciousness.

At this point it will be useful to introduce some technical terms. Those employed in *The Graces of Interior Prayer* by A. Poulain will be sufficient for the present purpose. In discussing those aspects of religious experience which he calls locutions and visions, Poulain distinguishes in both cases between exterior and interior types. Exterior locutions consist of words heard by the ear though not produced naturally; and similarly exterior (or ocular) visions are visions of material objects, or what seem to be such, perceived by the bodily eyes. The visions in Sūrat an-Najm are exterior visions. Interior locutions are divided by Poulain into imaginative and intellectual. The former are 'received directly without the assistance of the ear; they can be said to be received by the imaginative sense'; the latter is 'a simple communication of thought without words, and consequently without any definite language'.[1] Interior visions may similarly be either imaginative or intellectual. With this equipment we may now turn to the Qur'ān and the traditional accounts.

The 'manners' (*kayfīyāt*) of revelation was a subject of discussion among Muslim doctors. In the *Itqān*[2] as-Suyūṭī mentions five different manners; and from other sources scholars have collected as many as ten.[3] Most of these types, however, are found only in one or a few cases. The main types are doubtless those mentioned in Sūrat ash-Shūrā (42. 50–52): 'It belonged not to any human being that God should speak to him except by suggestion (*waḥyan*) or from behind a veil, Or by sending a messenger to suggest (*fa-yūḥiya*) by His permission what He pleaseth. . . . Thus We have suggested to thee a spirit belonging to Our affair' (*awḥaynā*).

The first 'manner' therefore is where God speaks by *waḥy*. The

[1] Op. cit. 299 ff.

[2] Cairo, 1354, pp. 44 f., *naw'* 16.

[3] Nöldeke–Schwally, i. 22 ff.

noun *waḥy* and the verb *awḥā* occur frequently in the Qur'ān in the contexts where the sense of 'reveal by direct verbal communication' is inappropriate. Richard Bell has studied these usages and concludes that 'at any rate in the early portions of the Qur'ān, *waḥy* does not mean the verbal communication of the text of a revelation, but is a "suggestion", "prompting", or "inspiration" coming into a person's mind apparently from outside himself'.[1] For most of the Meccan period this was apparently regarded as the work of the Spirit: 'Verily it is the revelation (*tanzīl*) of the Lord of the Worlds, With which hath come down (*nazala bi-hi*) the Faithful Spirit Upon thy heart, that thou mayest be of those who warn. . . .'[2] The mention of angels bearing a message (? to a prophet) is apparently later.[3] Moreover, during the Meccan period there is, so far as I have noticed, no mention of the prophet 'hearing' what is brought down to him. Perhaps, then, we ought to picture to ourselves the Spirit introducing the message into Muḥammad's heart or mind by some method other than speaking to him. This would certainly be an interior locution, and probably an intellectual one rather than imaginative; it was presumably not accompanied by any vision, not even intellectual, for the mention of the Spirit gives the impression of being a theory to explain the experience and not a description of an aspect of the experience.

Some of the accounts found in tradition are perhaps to be connected with this first 'manner'. Thus in the second tradition in the *Ṣaḥīḥ* of al-Bukhārī[4] it is reported on the authority of 'A'ishah 'that al-Ḥārith b. Hishām (may God be pleased with him) asked the Messenger of God (God bless and preserve him), saying, O Messenger of God, how does the revelation (*waḥy*) come to you? The Messenger of God (God bless and preserve him) said, Sometimes it comes to me like the reverberation of a bell, and that is the hardest on me; then it leaves me, and I have understood from it (or 'him') what He (or 'he') said. And sometimes the angel takes the form of a man for me, and addresses me, and I understand what he says. "Ā'ishah (may God be pleased with her) continued, I have actually seen him, at the coming down of the revelation upon him, on an extremely cold day, with his forehead running with perspiration.' There are some similar details towards the end

[1] '*Muhammad's Visions*, MW, xxiv, 1934, 145–54, esp. 148.

[2] 26. 192–4; cf. Ahrens, *Muhammed*, 41 f.

[3] 15. 8; 97. 4.

[4] i. 2.

of the tradition of the lie (*ḥadīth al-ifk*), the story of 'Ā'ishah's temporary disgrace:[1] 'a revelation came to him (*unzila 'alay-hi*), and the pain he usually felt gripped him, so that there ran down from him as it were pearls of perspiration on a cold day; and when it (*c.* the distress) passed away from the Messenger of God (God bless and preserve him)—he was laughing—the first word that he uttered was that he said to me, O 'Ā'ishah, praise God. . . .'

The various matters described here, apart from the angel in the form of a man, are quite compatible with the first 'manner'. The hearing of the bell is doubtless an imaginative experience, but there is no mention of hearing anyone speaking or of hearing words spoken, not even imaginatively. On the contrary, at the end of the experience he appears simply to find the words of the revelation in his heart. It is fairly clear that, in the terminology explained above, this is a description of an intellectual locution.

The second 'manner' is where God speaks from behind a veil. The primary reference of this is probably to certain early experiences of Muḥammad, such as that in paragraph B of the material from az-Zuhrī above, where 'the Truth came to him and said, O Muḥammad, thou art the Messenger of God'. The words 'from behind a veil' suggest that there is no vision of the speaker, but that fact together with the mention of speaking seem to imply that the words are heard, and that therefore this is an imaginative locution (or even an exterior locution). Some of the early sūrahs with strange expressions may have been revealed in this way, but, since we hear so little of this 'manner', it was presumably not common, and therefore presumably most of the early revelations were in the first 'manner'. It is conceivable that the second 'manner' is intended for a description of the experience of Moses.

The third 'manner' is where God sends a messenger to suggest (*fa-yūḥiya*) a message to the prophet. Later Muslim scholars adopted the view that the messenger was Jibrīl or Gabriel, and that this was the standard 'manner' of revelation from the first. Western scholars, on the other hand, have noted that Gabriel is not mentioned *by name* in the Qur'ān until the Medinan period,[2] and that both in the Qur'ān and in tradition there is much that is contrary to the common Muslim view; they therefore argue that the latter view reads back later conceptions into the earlier period. It may well be, however, that revelations by means of Gabriel

[1] Bukhārī, lii. 15.

[2] 2. 91; 66. 4.

were common throughout the Medinan period. In such cases the revelation was presumably an imaginative locution, but it was doubtless accompanied by either an intellectual or an imaginative vision of Gabriel; the words 'form of a man' in the tradition given above suggest an imaginative vision.

The precise form of such experiences, it must be insisted, is not of prime importance for the theologian, Islamic or Christian. To assert that Muḥammad's visions and locutions are hallucinations, as has sometimes been done, is to make theological judgements without being fully aware of what one is doing, and thereby to show a woeful ignorance of the science and sanity of writers like Poulain and the discipline of mystical theology which they represent. Whether visions and locutions are exterior, imaginative, or intellectual, is no criterion of their truth or validity. The 'exterior' experiences are doubtless more impressive to the recipient, but in a sense the intellectual ones are higher in that intellect is higher than sense. The question is chiefly of interest to students of religious psychology, and it would undoubtedly be profitable to make a full comparison of the phenomenal aspects of Muḥammad's experiences with those of Christian saints and mystics. For the theologian and historian, however, the main point is that, in general, Muḥammad made a distinction between revealed messages and his own thoughts.

Similarly, the physical accompaniments of the reception of revelation, though of historical interest, are of no theological importance. Opponents of Islam have often asserted that Muḥammad had epilepsy, and that therefore his religious experiences had no validity. As a matter of fact, the symptoms described are not identical with those of epilepsy, since that disease leads to physical and mental degeneration, whereas Muḥammad was in the fullest possession of his faculties to the very end. But, even if the allegation were true, the argument would be completely unsound and based on mere ignorance and prejudice; such physical concomitants neither validate nor invalidate religious experience.

It would be interesting to know whether Muḥammad had any method of inducing revelations.[1] We cannot be certain that he put on a *dithār* for this purpose. It is most likely that to begin with the revelations came unexpectedly; even that in the tradition of

[1] Cf. Ahrens, *Muhammed*, 37; J. C. Archer, *Mystical Elements in Mohammed*, New Haven, 1924, pp. 72, 76, &c.

the Lie came thus. Later, however, it is possible that he developed some technique of 'listening', perhaps while he recited the Qur'ān slowly at night. Especially where he doubted the completeness of a revelation, this might prove a method of discovering the missing verses. The details must remain conjectural, but it would seem to be certain that Muḥammad had some way of emending the Qur'ān, that is (in his view), of discovering the correct form of what had been revealed in incomplete or incorrect form. Once again, this fact, if it is a fact, that Muḥammad sometimes induced his experiences of revelation (by 'listening' or self-hypnotism or whatever we like to call it) is irrelevant to the theologian's judgement of validity.

6. THE CHRONOLOGY OF THE MECCAN PERIOD

At the time when these apparently trivial, but really momentous, events were taking place, nobody paid attention to precise dates. Years later, when men became interested in dates, various conflicting reports were in circulation, and the Muslim scholars had a difficult task to work out a coherent scheme. They managed to do so, however, for the main points, while admitting uncertainty and differing among themselves on others. The question of precise dating is not a vital one for an understanding of the life of Muḥammad, and little is to be gained by trying to go behind the scheme explicitly or implicitly present in the standard Muslim writers on the subject. No alternative can have more than a slight degree of probability, and it is therefore better to use the standard scheme.

Caetani, who went into the matter carefully, since his main work is in the form of Annals, says[1] that the Muslim writers are agreed in four points:

1. for three years Muḥammad expounded his message secretly to close friends, and only at the end of that period began to preach publicly;
2. the emigration to Abyssinia took place in the fifth year, that is, in the second year after the beginning of public preaching;
3. the boycott of the clan of Hāshim began *after* the emigration to Abyssinia and lasted two or three years;
4. Abū Ṭālib and Khadījah died after the ending of the boycott and three years before the Hijrah (in A.D. 622).

[1] *Ann.* i, p. 219.

Caetani further argues that, when we allow for the periods between the emigration and the boycott and between the boycott and the death of Abū Ṭālib, this implies a minimum time of twelve years. He therefore provisionally adopts the following scheme of dates, though he is inclined to think that the events may have taken place earlier:

610 first revelation;
613 beginning of public preaching;
614 entry into the House of al-Arqam:
615 emigration to Abyssinia;
616 commencement of the boycott of Hāshim;
619 end of the boycott; deaths of Khadījah and Abū Ṭālib; journey to aṭ-Ṭā'if;
620 first Medinan converts;
621 first convention of 'Aqabah;
622 second convention of 'Aqabah; Hijrah.

For most purposes these dates are a sufficiently accurate guide. Their chief importance is perhaps to make us realize that, despite the meagreness of the records which causes us to feel that things happened quickly, the development of Islam at Mecca was a slow process.

III

THE PRIMARY MESSAGE

I. THE DATING OF THE QUR'ĀN

As soon as we start to ask, 'What was the original message of the Qur'ān?', we are faced with the question which are the earliest parts of it. Our basis must naturally be the accounts given by the early Muslim scholars. A considerable amount of material is available about the occasions on which various passages were revealed. This material, however, suffers from two disadvantages: it is incomplete and it contains contradictions. The latter—of which we have already come across an example in the question of the first sūrah to be revealed—is perhaps not so serious as the former, especially in connexion with the Meccan sūrahs. The later Muslim scholars reached a measure of agreement as to which sūrahs and verses were revealed at Mecca and which at Medina. But for the great majority of Meccan passages there is no tradition about the occasion, and, moreover, many of the occasions are not events to which a precise year can be assigned. Thus while the traditional material about occasions is to be accepted as in general sound, it is unable by itself to provide answers to many questions which Western scholars ask.

The German scholar, Theodor Nöldeke, in his *History of the Qur'ān*, first published in 1860, put forward an additional criterion. He found that, if the length of verses was studied and compared with the traditional material about occasions, the admittedly early sūrahs had short verses and the admittedly late sūrahs had long verses—for the most part. He therefore put forward the hypothesis that passages were earlier or later according as their lines were longer or shorter. Relying on this criterion, Nöldeke arranged the sūrahs in four periods, three Meccan and one Medinan, and this scheme has been generally accepted by Western scholars as a rough guide.

The chief advance since Nöldeke is in the work of Richard Bell, contained in his *Translation of the Qur'ān*, published 1937–9.[1]

[1] Cf. R. Bell, *The Style of the Qur'ān*, in *Transactions of the Glasgow University Oriental Society*, xi. 9–15, esp. 14 f.

Muslim tradition has always admitted that most sūrahs contained passages revealed at different periods. In this *Translation* an attempt is made to split up the sūrahs into their original components and to date the separate passages. Whatever be the ultimate verdict on details, this work must undoubtedly be the starting-point for any further study of the dating of the Qur'ān. It accepts Nöldeke's criterion as roughly accurate, but holds that it requires to be modified in regard to particular passages by a consideration of their contents. This procedure appears to be sound, especially in the Medinan period; but many of the results so obtained, though highly probable, are not altogether certain, since alternative views are often possible.

In considering the original message of the Qur'ān, one has to be specially careful about the use of the criterion of contents. If one were to say, 'Sūrahs X, Y, Z, &c., cannot be early because they contain the idea of judgement after death', and then went on to say, 'the idea of judgement after death is not early because it is not found in any early sūrahs', one would be arguing in a circle. To obtain the greatest degree of objectivity, I have therefore taken those sūrahs or parts of sūrahs which are described both as 'first Meccan period' (Nöldeke) and as 'early' or 'early Meccan' (Bell). Within this group of early passages, I have left aside those where opposition to Muḥammad and the Qur'ān was expressed or implied, and concentrated on the remainder, namely, those where there was no suggestion of opposition. The principle here is that before opposition could arise some message which tended to arouse opposition must have been proclaimed.

The passages in question are: 96. 1–8; 74. 1–10; 106; 90. 1–11; 93; 86. 1–10; 80. 1–32 (omitting 23?); 87. 1–9, 14–15; 84. 1–12; 88. 17–20; 51. 1–6; 52, parts; 55.[1]

It is conceivable that some of these passages are to be dated after the first appearance of opposition, but, since they are logically prior to it, I have decided to disregard this possibility. The different aspects of the message contained in the early passages just listed appear to be coherent. I have therefore without more ado assumed that these passages present the primary message of the Qur'ān, the original prophetic *kerygma*, and now turn to give an account of the main notes of this *kerygma*.

[1] Verses are neglected which are shown as later additions in Bell, op. cit.

2. THE CONTENTS OF THE EARLY PASSAGES

(a) *God's goodness and power*

The theme of Sūrah 96. 1–5, which is the passage commonly regarded as earliest is God's creation of man—a manifestation of His power, and perhaps also of His goodness—and His revealing to man (*sc.* in the Jewish and Christian revelations) the mysteries of the Unseen.

> Recite in the name of thy Lord who created,
> Created man from clotted blood;
> Recite, for thy Lord is the most generous,
> Who taught by the pen,
> Taught man what he did not know.

Man's creation and guidance are referred to in several other passages. 'We have created man in trouble (i.e. subject to trouble). . . . Have we not given him two eyes, A tongue and two lips, And guided him the two paths?' (90. 4, 8–10). The theme of creation is expanded in 80. 17–22:

> From what kind of a thing did He create him (*sc.* man)?
> From a drop!
> He created him and assigned his power,
> Then the way He made easy.
> Then He caused him to die and buried him;
> Then when He willeth He raiseth him again.

The beginning of 87 is similar:

> Glorify the name of thy Lord the Most High,
> Who created and formed,
> Who assigned power and guided.

Sūrah 55. 1–3 also couples creation and guidance: 'The Merciful, Taught the Qur'ān, Created man, Taught him the Explanation.'

God's special goodness to Muḥammad is mentioned in 93. 3–8; the references are presumably to incidents in his early life:

> Thy Lord hath not taken leave of thee, nor despised thee.
> The last for thee is better than the first;
> Assuredly in the end thy Lord will give thee to thy satisfaction.
> Did He not find thee an orphan and give thee shelter?
> Did He not find thee erring and guide thee?
> Did He not find thee poor and enrich thee?

With this may be compared the assurance of 87. 6, 8:

> We shall cause thee to recite, without forgetting. . . .
> And we shall make it very easy for thee.

Sūrat Quraysh (106) urges the tribe to worship the Lord of the Ka'bah because He has 'given them provision against famine, and made them secure against fear'. Sūrah 80. 25–31 describes how God sends the rain which causes the earth to produce grain, pasturage, grapes, olives, palms, and so on; even if verses 24 and 32, which emphasize that this is food for man and his flocks, are a later addition,[1] that thought must have been implicit. It occurs explicitly in 55. 9–11:

> The earth hath He set for the cattle;
> In which are fruit, and palm-trees bearing spikes,
> And grain growing in the blade and fragrant herbs.

But just as God is the giver of death as well as life to men, so it is He 'Who brought forth the pasture, Then made it blackened drift' (87. 4 f.).

Finally, 88. 17–20 speak of God as creating camels, the sky, the mountains, the earth, while the early parts of 55[2] mention the heavenly bodies and the seas. The climax is the contrast between the transitoriness of created existence and the permanence of the Creator (55. 26 f.):

> Every one upon it (*sc.* the earth) passes away,
> But the face of thy Lord, full of glory and honour, endures.

There are thus quite a number of verses expounding this theme of God's goodness and power. Indeed, quantitatively this is by far the most prominent aspect of the message of the early passages. This is a most remarkable fact in several ways. The Qur'ān does not present the existence of God as something unknown either to Muḥammad or to those to whom he was to communicate the message. It appears to assume a vague belief in God, and makes this more precise and vigorous by asserting that various common events are to be attributed to Him. This tends to confirm the view that the conception of God had been seeping through to the Arabs from Judaeo-Christian monotheism. Since, however, the powers attributed by the pagan Arabs to their gods were presumably very limited, to think of Him as analogous to these gods but somewhat

[1] Bell, op. cit.

[2] As dated by Bell, op. cit.

greater was not to form an adequate conception of His significance in human affairs. We thus appreciate how important as a first step was the correction of this misconception.

What is perhaps even more surprising is that there is no mention of the unity of God. One apparent exception—'set not along with God another god' (51. 51)—is probably a later addition;[1] it certainly sounds like the repetition of a point already made; had it been a fresh point it would have received greater emphasis. There is, of course, in the early passages of our list nothing contrary to the doctrine of God's unity. What is interesting and important is that there is no stress laid on this doctrine and no denunciation of idolatry. In other words, the purpose of the early passages is limited. It is to develop positively certain aspects of the vague belief in God already found among thoughtful Meccans without bringing to consciousness the contrast between this belief, with its tolerance of secondary gods, and a strict monotheism.

(b) *The return to God for judgement*

Once again we may start with Sūrat al-ʿAlaq (96), for verse 8 states that 'to thy Lord is the return'; the implication is that this is 'for judgement after death'.[2] Sūrah 74 also speaks of the Judgement (vv. 8–10):

> When comes the trumpet-blast,
> That will then be a difficult day,
> For the unbelievers far from easy.

If *rujz* in v. 5 is from the Syriac *rugza* meaning 'wrath' (used in translating the phrase 'the wrath to come' in Matthew, iii. 7),[3] then that presumably originally had an eschatological connotation. Judgement on the last day is also implied by the mention of raising man to life again (80. 22) and by the verse, 'Over every soul is assuredly a watcher' (86. 4), whether the watcher be interpreted as God or as a recording angel.

The fullest description of the Last Judgement in these early passages is 84. 1–12:

> When the heaven shall be cleft,
> And shall give ear to its Lord and become amenable,
> When the earth shall be stretched out,
> Shall cast up what is in it (*sc.* the dead) and become empty
> And shall give ear to its Lord and become amenable,

[1] So Bell, op. cit. [2] Bell, op. cit. [3] Ibid.; cf. Bell, *Origin*, 88.

O man, lo then, thou art toiling heavily to thy Lord and art about to meet Him.
Then as for him who is given his book in his right hand,
He will be reckoned with easily,
And will turn back to his family well pleased;
But as for him who is given his book behind his back,
He will call for destruction,
And roast in a Blaze.

Apart from 51. 5 f. and 52. 7 f., which will be dealt with presently, there are no more direct references to the Last Judgement in the list of early passages, although the description of Muḥammad as a 'warner' might be taken to imply that.

The first point to notice is that there is here little more than a bare statement of the fact of Judgement, that man will be judged and either rewarded or punished. There is 'none of the lurid detail' which is found in later portrayals of the Last Day.[1] We may therefore without hesitation reject any view like that of Frants Buhl and Tor Andrae which sees in fear of the torments of the damned the prime motive in Muḥammad's religious life during the early Meccan period. If we regard all the sūrahs of Nöldeke's first and second Meccan periods, it may be plausible to say that 'above all it was the thought of the terrors of damnation which overpowered him and called forth the movement of spirit which was to have such great results.'[2] If, however, we restrict our view to the small group of passages which appear to be earliest of all, it ceases to be plausible.

On the other hand, it appears to be incorrect to say that the earliest references to judgement mean not anything eschatological, but temporal calamities. The group of early passages which we are studying contains several examples of eschatological ideas, but no verses which necessarily refer to 'calamity falling upon special unbelieving peoples'.[3] If 51. 6 and 52. 7 are translated respectively as 'the Judgement is about to fall' and 'the punishment of thy Lord is about to fall', they might have a temporal reference. From the context, however—'what ye are promised is true', 'of it there is no averter' (51. 5; 52. 8)—the word *wāqiʿ*, which could mean 'about to fall', would seem not to refer to the imminence of the

[1] Bell, *Origin*, 85.
[2] Buhl, *Muhammed*, 127.
[3] Bell, *Translation of Q*, p. 690.

judgement or punishment in the near future but to the reality and certainty of it at some unspecified future time.

There is certainly much in the Meccan sūrahs about a judgement of God in the form of a temporal calamity to come upon the Meccans, as it had come upon those who had opposed former prophets. But in so far as such a calamity is punishment for the rejection of a prophet's message, it would be more relevant to the situation at Mecca after opposition had developed than to the beginning of Muḥammad's mission. Indeed the verses just discussed, 51. 5 f. and 52. 7 f., with their insistence on the certainty and inevitability of judgement, seem to belong rather to the transition to the second stage when opposition was appearing and doubts about the reality of judgement had been expressed. It is perhaps worth remarking that it is mostly about temporal *calamities* that we hear, that is, only punishments, whereas eschatological judgement is followed by both reward and punishment, as in Sūrat al-Inshiqāq (84) above.

(c) *Man's response—gratitude and worship*

In view of God's goodness man ought to be grateful to Him and worship Him. Gratitude is the inner recognition of man's dependence on One who is powerful and good; worship is the formal expression of that dependence and of the goodness and power of God. The passage 80. 16 ff. mentions man's ingratitude with regard to God's goodness in creating him and ordering his life—'How ungrateful he is! (*mā akfara-hu*).' The simple active participle from this root, *kāfir*, came to mean unbeliever; it was those who were ungrateful towards God who rejected His messenger. Thus the phrase in 74. 10 that the day of judgement would be difficult 'for the *kāfirīn*' probably meant for its first audience that it would be difficult 'for the ungrateful'.

The opposite attitude to gratitude is represented by the words *ṭaghā* and *istaghnā*, as in 96. 6 f.:

> Nay, but verily man acts presumptuously (*yaṭghā*),
> Because he thinks himself independent (*istaghnā*).

The basic meaning of *ṭaghā* appears to be: 'it (*sc.* a torrent or water) rose high so as to exceed the ordinary limit in copiousness'.[1] Then, metaphorically, it comes to have the meaning of insolent,

[1] E. W. Lane, *Arabic-English Lexicon*, *s.v.*

exceeding the bounds; the thought appears to be of a man who presses on regardless of obstacles, and especially regardless of moral and religious considerations, who allows nothing to stop him and has unbounded confidence in his own powers. Thus in the Qur'ān it mostly can be aptly translated by 'to be presumptuous' or 'to act presumptuously'. It is the absence of a sense of creatureliness, a pride in the power of the creature, linked with disregard or denial of the Creator.

This is an attitude to which the wealthy Meccans would be prone, since, as the second of the verses quoted shows, it is based on trust in riches. The word *istaghnā* is difficult to translate because it connotes both wealth and independence. Lane gives as the basic meaning of the root 'free from want'. It comes thus in the Qur'ān to denote both the actual possession of wealth, and even more, the spiritual attitude prevalent among the wealthy. In 92. 8 it may be translated 'prides himself in wealth'.[1] Because of their financial strength the Meccans felt themselves independent of any higher power.

Gratitude finds expression in worship. Hence there are several commands to worship in the early passages. Some are addressed to Muḥammad himself: 'Thy Lord magnify, Thy garments purify' (74. 3 f.). One very early passage, Sūrat Quraysh (106), is an appeal to the Meccans as a whole:

> For the bringing together by Quraysh,
> For their bringing together the winter and the summer caravan,
> Let them serve the Lord of this House,
> Who hath given them provision against famine,
> And made them secure against fear.

Another passage, which may be a little later (87. 14 f.), makes the general statement: 'Prospered has he who . . . Makes mention of the name of his Lord and prays (*ṣallā*).'

Worship was a distinctive feature of Muḥammad's community from the first. He himself engaged in devotional exercises even before the first revelation, and the earliest Muslims observed the practice of night-prayer for a time.[2] Opposition was early directed against the performance of Worship—'Hast thou considered him who restrains A servant when he prays?' (96. 9 f.). On the other hand, in the traditional accounts of the 'satanic verses' interpolated

[1] Bell, op. cit.

[2] Cf. Sūrat al-Muzzammil (73).

in Sūrat an-Najm, 53, the sign of the acceptance of Muḥammad as prophet by the Meccans was that they joined in his acts of worship. In all this we must try to forget the idea of worship frequently found in the West, which regards the essence of it as a subjective feeling, perhaps described as a sense of the presence of God. The Arab is much more concerned with the objective aspects of worship, and especially its significance. For the Meccans to prostrate themselves to the Lord of the Ka'bah along with Muḥammad would be analogous to the act of an erstwhile staunch conservative who flaunted a red rosette on election day or of a quondam socialist who sported a blue one. Although the political illustration is here apt, it is not intended to suggest that Islam is not a religion; it may be rather that certain Western conceptions of religion are defective.

(d) *Man's response to God—generosity and purification*

It is not to worship only, however, that gratitude to God for His goodness should lead; it should also lead to certain types of ethical activity.[1] It is interesting and important to discover what morality the Qur'ān inculcates.

In some of these early passages we find a word *tazakkā*, which is a little mysterious. In Sūrat 'Abasa (80) Muḥammad is rebuked for paying more attention to an important rich man than to a blind man; perhaps the blind man 'will purify himself', and even if the rich man 'does not purify himself', it will not be counted against Muḥammad. Again, 'prospered has he who purifies himself'.[2]

The matter is somewhat complex and is discussed in Excursus D. Here only the conclusions need be presented. A useful clue is given by the remark of a commentator, Ibn Zayd,[3] that throughout the Qur'ān *at-tazakkı* means *islām*; that is to say, 'purifying oneself' in these passages is equivalent to 'surrendering oneself to God' or 'becoming a Muslim'. It would seem that in practice it amounts to this, but the exact point emphasized is slightly different. *Tazakkā* in the Meccan (and perhaps some early Medinan) passages of the Qur'ān is dependent on the similar use of the root in Hebrew, Aramaic, and Syriac. It thus designates the moral purity of which a vague idea had been formed in the Arab mind

[1] Cf. 80. 23.
[2] 87. 14; cf. 91. 9, perhaps a little later.
[3] In aṭ-Ṭabarī, *Tafsīr*, on 79. 18.

through Judaeo-Christian influence, as distinct from the ritual purity of Arab paganism and from physical purity. It has usually an eschatological reference, and makes one think of those qualities of life (mainly ethical) on account of which a man receives an eternal reward; it is almost what we mean by righteousness or uprightness. Sometimes, perhaps mostly, too, it means not so much the practice or attainment of righteousness as the adoption of righteousness as one's aim or principle of life. It is thus a comprehensive description of what is involved in the following of Muḥammad in the earliest period, with special emphasis on the ethical side.

What does this amount to in detail? What is the ethical content of the original *kerygma*? We do not find much to help us in the list of early passages. Apart from 'attempting the steep' (90. 11), there is only the injunction to Muḥammad himself (though applicable to others):

> So as for the orphan, be not thou overbearing;
> And as for the beggar, scold not;
> And as for the goodness of thy Lord, discourse of it. (93. 9–11.)

It is therefore necessary to go a little farther afield. The following are examples to be found in those sūrahs of Nöldeke's first period, which are also 'early Meccan' or 'Meccan' (Bell). As it is important to have the total impression of these passages, they are here quoted fairly fully.

The earliest in Nöldeke's order is Sūrat al-Humazah (104. 1–3):

> Woe to every maligner, scoffer,
> Who gathers wealth and counts it over,
> Thinking that his wealth will perpetuate him!

The next is also early and may be entitled 'The Two Ways':[1]

> So as for him who gives and shows piety,
> And counts true the best reward,
> We shall assist him to ease.
> But as for him who is niggardly, and prides himself in wealth,
> And counts false the best reward,
> We shall assist him to difficulty,
> Nor will his wealth profit him when he perishes. (92. 5–11.)

The 'parable of a blighted garden' (68. 17–33) is the story of a group of men who resolved to reap their garden on a certain day without

[1] Cf. Bell, op. cit.

permitting the poor to have any share in it; but when they came to it in the morning the crop had disappeared, and they bemoaned the fact that they had been presumptuous (*ṭāghin*). Sūrat an-Najm (53. 34 f.) mentions 'him who turns his back, Gives little and is mean', and suggests that he is ignorant and will be punished (eschatologically). Sūrat al-ʿĀdiyāt is similar:

Verily, man to his Lord is ungrateful. . . .
And verily he for the love of good (*sc.* wealth) is violent (*sc.* niggardly). . . .
Does he not know? . . .
Verily, their Lord that (*sc.* the Last) day will of them be well informed. (100. 6–11.)

In Sūrat al-Fajr (89. 18–21) man is reproached for his conduct:

> Ye do not honour the orphan,
> Nor urge to feed the destitute,
> Ye devour the inheritance indiscriminately,
> And ye love wealth ardently.

The following description occurs in Sūrat al-Ḥaqqah (69. 33–35) of the man who is condemned on the Last Day:

> He used not to believe in God the Mighty,
> Nor did he urge the feeding of the poor;
> So today he has not here a friend.

The pious, on the other hand, are described in Sūrat adh-Dhāriyāt:

Little of the night did they usually slumber,
And in the mornings they asked forgiveness,
And from their wealth was a share assigned to the beggar and the outcast. (51. 17–19.)

Likewise hell-fire

> . . . calls him who draws back and turns away,
> And gathers and hoards. (70. 17 f.)

If we set aside disbelief in God, His messengers and the message as not belonging to the ethical sphere, then the content of these passages amounts simply to this that it is good to feed the poor and destitute and bad to gather wealth for oneself. Moreover, this is the sole ethical content of the sūrahs examined, if we except the giving of false measure in 83. 1–3 and unchastity in 70. 29–31, which are probably late Meccan and Medinan respectively;[1] the

[1] Bell, op. cit.

reference to infanticide in 81. 8 f. is factual rather than normative. We have here, therefore, a surprising and puzzling fact, and one of the utmost importance for the understanding of the nature of the Qur'anic *kerygma*. The ethical part of the decalogue is almost entirely ignored. There is no mention of respect for parents, for life, for marriage, for property, or of truthfulness in witness; only to the avoidance of covetousness is there something analogous, but there are differences there too. The early Qur'anic ethic is entirely confined to matters of generosity and niggardliness or miserliness, to what the West would tend to call works of supererogation.

(e) *Muḥammad's own vocation*

Some of the passages already considered were commands addressed in the first place to Muḥammad himself—for example, 'thy Lord magnify'—but capable of being extended to apply to his followers also. But other passages indicate his unique and special vocation: 'Rise and warn'; 'So remind, if the Reminder profits' (74. 2; 87. 9). This point is not prominent in the early passages of our list, though it is present. It was only later that his position as prophet became one of the central matters.

The words for 'warn' and 'remind' here are *andhir* and *dhakkir*, and elsewhere we have the corresponding nouns *nadhīr* and *mudhakkir*. The word *andhara* corresponds closely to the English 'warn'; it describes the action of informing a person of something of a dangerous, harmful, or fearful nature, so as to put him on his guard against it or put him in fear of it. The use of the word in the above early passage shows that the conception of judgement in some form must have been present from the beginning. In view of the importance of both eschatological judgement and temporal punishment in the later Meccan periods, it is not surprising to find *nadhīr* more than forty times in the Qur'ān, as against a single occurrence of the form *mudhakkir*. For the special Qur'anic usage of *dhakkara*, Lane gives the following meaning: 'He exhorted; admonished; exhorted to obedience; gave good advice, and reminded of the results of affairs; reminded of what might soften the heart, by the mention of rewards and punishments.'[1] The implication of the English word 'remind' would be that the persons addressed already knew something about God and the Last Day; but the Arabic word has a wider series of uses, and the explana-

[1] *Arabic-English Lexicon, s.v.*

tions of the Arab lexicographers followed by Lane show that the implication of the English word should not be pressed.

In the early passages, then, the function of Muḥammad is confined to bringing to men's attention the matters mentioned in sub-sections (*a*) and (*b*) above.

3. THE RELEVANCE OF THE MESSAGE TO THE CONTEMPORARY SITUATION

What is here said by way of interpretation of the message of the earliest passages of the Qur'ān starts from the very reasonable assumption, that this message or *kerygma* was especially relevant to the Mecca of the time. The problem is therefore to explain how this is so. The studies of chapter I have thrown some light on conditions in Mecca, but what we learn from the traditional history of pre-Islamic times and from the poets must be supplemented by considering what diagnosis of the contemporary malaise is implied by the Qur'anic message itself. It is thus convenient to discuss the diagnosis and the remedy at the same time, under the four heads: social, moral, intellectual, religious.

(a) *Social*

The trend of the times, as noted in chapter I, was towards the weakening of social solidarity and the growth of individualism. In some respects tribal and clan organization was still strong, but in other respects men did not hesitate to disregard the ties of kinship. This was particularly so in Mecca where mercantile life fostered individualism and where financial and material interests were the basis of partnerships as often as blood-relationship. The amassing of large fortunes, which the Qur'ān shows to have been the preoccupation of many Meccans, is a sign of this individualism. The parable of the 'blighted garden' (68. 17 ff.) suggests the operations of a syndicate to gain a monopoly in some field and to shut out less successful rivals; there is nothing to show that the owners of the garden were kinsmen.

While it seems unlikely that there had been any increase in absolute poverty in Mecca, it is probable that the gap between rich and poor had widened in the last half-century. The Qur'ān implies an increasing awareness of the difference between rich and poor—or perhaps we should say between rich, not-so-rich, and poor. Apparently, too, the rich were showing less concern for the poor and uninfluential, even among their own kin. The references to orphans presumably imply that they were ill treated by their own relatives who acted as guardians. Sūrat ʿAbasa (80) depicts Muḥammad as for a moment being led astray and acting on the current principle that the rich and influential matter and the others do not.

All this must have meant a loss of the sense of community. Man is a social animal and is unhappy unless he has a group to which to belong. A possible new basis of community was presenting itself in material interests; but this was not a satisfactory substitute for kinship by blood. It could lead to a great confederation, as in the expedition to besiege Medina in A.H. 5; but the unity was always liable to disintegrate when an immediate party-interest was contrary to the permanent interest of the whole. And while it had some use in the larger questions of business and politics, it was less satisfactory in the daily lives of lesser men. In this sphere the sense of relative security which came from clan and family relationships was disappearing and leaving a void.

The early passages of the Qur'ān have no more than a premonition of the real remedy for this situation, namely, that a new basis for social solidarity is to be found in religion. The insistence on the duties of generosity would bring some alleviation of the troubles; the poor would be helped materially (though this was doubtless not the primary purpose of generosity), and money would cease to be so great a social divider in that the rich to some extent would admit or reaffirm that they were stewards of their wealth rather than absolute owners. The principle of stewardship, as it is sometimes called in the West, namely, that man is given wealth not simply for his own enjoyment but partly in trust for the community, is expressed in Sūrat al-Maʿārij (70. 24 f.) where the pious are described as 'those in whose wealth there is a recognized right for the beggar and the destitute'.

On the other hand, the Qur'ān makes no attempt to restore the old order. There was no possibility of return to the old tribal solidarity. Man's consciousness of himself as an individual had come to stay, and therefore had to be accepted and to be taken into account. This the Qur'ān does in the conception of the Last Judgement, for that is essentially a judgement on individuals. The Day of Judgement is 'the day when one shall have no influence on behalf of another at all' (82. 19). The isolation of the individual from his relatives is described in 35. 19 (though it may not have a reference to the Last Day): 'if a heavy-laden one call another to its load, no part of it will be borne, even though it were a near relative.' (It should be added that in the Medinan sūrahs, with the new community of Muslims in being, the special duties of a man to his kin are again emphasized, as in 2. 172.)

(b) *Moral*

The nomadic ideal of *murūwah* is inappropriate in a mercantile community. The qualities that make for success there are not 'bravery in battle, patience in misfortune, persistence in revenge, protection of the weak and defiance of the strong'; the first may have some connexion with the conduct of caravans and the second will not come amiss; but if persistence in revenge is translated into standing up for one's rights, there is a point beyond which it is not wise for a merchant to do so; while success in commerce and finance is linked up with disregard for the weak and cultivation of the friendship of the strong (ideally within the limits of straight dealing). The nomadic virtue of fidelity in the keeping of trusts is certainly important, for a certain minimum level of business integrity is necessary in order to inspire that confidence which oils the wheels of trade; the confederation of the Fuḍūl[1] seems to have originated in a protest against unscrupulously dishonest practices. Engaging in high finance, again, does not necessarily preclude generosity, but it militates against it, since the financier is always trying to increase his fortune (as the Qur'ān bears witness); on the other hand, the need for charity in a city like Mecca is perhaps just as great as in the desert.

The sanction of the ideal of *murūwah* was the conception of the honour of the tribe and, to a lesser extent, of the individual member of the tribe. The strength of this sanction lay in the public opinion in which it was rooted, and the forming and moulding of this public opinion was largely the work of the poets. In desert conditions the stronger tribes might be expected to be at least passable examples of *murūwah*; and these tribes would be able, if they did not produce their own poets, at least to induce other noted poets to sing their praises. But with the growth of large fortunes at Mecca public opinion apparently ceased to count for much there—even the public opinion of the Arabs in general.

[1] See I. 2 a above.

Wealth could always buy poetic praise, if necessary; but the impression one gets is that it was not necessary. Poetry was not held in high regard in Mecca. Probably the ramifications of the power of the rich Meccans were so wide that this created a strong public opinion to applaud them (or at least to refrain from criticizing them) though their praises were not brilliantly sung.

What has just been said is in part a deduction from the fact that the acts of generosity, which the Qur'ān accuses the Meccans of omitting, were acts regarded as virtuous by the nomadic Arabs. The virtue of generosity, which has for its opposite the vice of niggardliness, is part of the old Arab ideal. As Lammens put it, 'dans la conception bédouine... le riche apparaît comme un simple dépositaire, un détenteur momentané de sa propre fortune; sa mission est de la distribuer aux nécessiteux de la tribu, d'en user pour exercer l'hospitalité, pour racheter les prisonniers et payer le prix du sang.'[1] This might be criticized for omitting to mention that the position of the *sayyid* or chief in his tribe gave him special opportunities for increasing his wealth; but none the less there is a similarity to the teaching of the Qur'ān. Consequently the stress laid on these points in the Qur'ān argues a breakdown in the sanction of the old ideal. The conduct of the rich Meccans would have been looked on as dishonourable in the desert, but there was nothing in the atmosphere of Mecca to make them feel ashamed of it. The old ideal had been quietly abandoned.

The response of the Qur'ān to this situation had various aspects. In insisting on acts of generosity it was reviving one side of the old Arab ideal, and so building on foundations that were already present in the Arab soul. Acts of generosity, moreover, were relevant to the circumstances of Mecca. At the same time a new sanction was provided for these acts, eschatological reward and punishment. Those who are niggardly will be punished eternally. This sanction is not operative, of course, until men come to believe in the Last Day; but at any rate something has been produced capable of filling the gap caused by the breakdown of the old sanction, and of functioning in an individualistic society.

The problem, however, is not simply the restoration of the old nomadic ideal, but the production of a new moral ideal suited to the needs of settled life. To salvage what can be salvaged is one part of this task, but the smaller part of it. Much that is new will

[1] *Berceau*, 235; cf. 211, 239.

also be required; and this larger part of the task is dealt with in the early passages of the Qur'ān by the provision of a source or channel for the creation of the new morality, namely, the revealed commands of God and the prophet through whom they are revealed. The problem is solved in principle, though not in detail. The fact that the moral ideal is commanded by God is an additional sanction, reinforcing belief in the Day of Judgement and perhaps in some cases replacing it.

The difficulty of the task may be illustrated by looking at the fate of the conception of *tazakkī*. This originally meant, it would seem, something like righteousness; the word was perhaps applied to a man when he recognized the principle that one's eternal destiny depends on the ethical quality of one's life. This was not a native Arab conception, however, and gradually ceased to be mentioned in the Qur'ān, its place being taken by other conceptions, such as *islām* or surrender to God. Even if there is over-emphasis on the ethical aspect of *tazakkī* in saying it means righteousness, its fading out is an example of the difficulty of finding new conceptions which could be successfully grafted on deep-rooted native stocks.[1]

(c) *Intellectual*

The intellectual aspect of the problems confronting the Meccans of Muḥammad's day is the least important, but it should not be entirely neglected. There are two main points to be noted.

The first point is that the Meccans were coming to have too high an opinion of human powers and to forget man's creatureliness. The nomadic outlook also had a high opinion of human power, but it was tempered by the belief in fate. If we may take the Islamic traditions as giving some indication of the outlook of the Jāhilīyah,[2] then there were four things that were beyond man's control: his sustenance, the hour of his death, his happiness or misery (in this world), and the sex of a child. This provided a fixed framework for man's life within which he was free to practice *murūwah*. Whether he did so or not depended partly on the man himself, and partly on his heredity; but the latter was not so definite and fixed as the four things mentioned above; it might help or hinder the practice of virtue, but did not absolutely determine it. The limitations recognized by the nomadic outlook, however,

[1] Cf. Excursus D. [2] Cf. I. 4 b above.

were not so obvious in Mecca. Financial power could do much to alleviate any adverse effects of the fickle rainfall of Arabia; famine could be averted by imports. Again, for a generation or two it would be easy to identify the possession of a large fortune with happiness, and the fortune might even seem to be able to postpone the *ajal*, the term of a man's life. Thus an overestimate of human power and capacity would become the predominant intellectual assumption in Mecca.

The other main point is closely connected with this. It is that the fact that the leading men in Mecca, those who had the greatest political power, were not conspicuous examples of *murūwah*, must have raised intellectual doubts in thoughtful men—doubts about the ultimacy of *murūwah* as an ideal, and perhaps also doubts about the influence of heredity in transmitting *murūwah* or at least the capacity for a high degree of it. Thoughts of the latter kind would undermine the theoretical basis of tribal solidarity, and encourage the development of individualism.

About the latter point the early passages of the Qur'ān have little to say apart from connecting certain aspects of *murūwah*, notably generosity, with the decisions of God on the Last Day. There is more that has to do with the former. Those facts in human life that the pagans ascribed to Fate or Time (*dahr*) are ascribed to God. God's power and goodness are shown in causing plants to grow; that is precisely *rizq* or sustenance. God's power in creating man includes the determination of sex, though it is not explicitly mentioned. It is God who causes man to die, and on the Last Day decides his ultimate happiness or misery. Thus the purely intellectual problems are being dealt with.

(d) *Religious*

The religious aspect of the problems of pre-Islamic Mecca is concerned with that by which men live, that in which they find the meaning and significance of life. The old nomadic religion found the meaning of life in honour and, to a lesser degree in theory though perhaps greater in practice, in the maintenance of the tribe, for it is in the tribe that honour becomes incarnate. This religious attitude had broken down in Mecca because of the increasing individualism, because of the weakening of the public opinion which constituted, as it were, the register of honour, and because of the inadequacy of the ideal of *murūwah* which was the basis of honour. In Mecca there was a new ideal, supereminence in wealth instead of in honour, and to this ideal many besides the wealthy subscribed. This was an ideal and a religion which might satisfy a few people for a generation or two, but it is not likely to satisfy a large community for long. People soon discover that there are things which money cannot buy. At best they can only find meaning and significance in being wealthy by shutting their eyes to unpleasant facts such as disease and death, especially early death. In a community of any size some unpleasant facts are bound to thrust themselves forcibly even upon certain of the wealthy, quite apart from the poor who have difficulty in forgetting their financial inferiority. The tensions due to the inadequacy of this religion of wealth and material prosperity are perhaps felt most keenly by those who have some wealth, but are only on the fringes of the very wealthy; they have some leisure for reflection and some degree of awareness of the limitations of the power of money.

The Qur'ān in the early passages sees in this trust in wealth the besetting sin of the Quraysh, and regards it as in itself leading to condemnation. Trust in wealth brings with it an excess of self-confidence, and leads man to forget, and even to deny, his dependence on God. To recall man to a sense of his creatureliness, therefore, the Qur'ān tries to make him realize how many of the good things he actually enjoys are owed to God. It speaks of God's power in creating man and giving him all the conditions which make a happy life possible; and it reminds man that 'to Him is the return'. The exhortations to gratitude and worship are exhortations to acknowledge and to express man's dependence on God, and so to abandon the excessive trust in wealth. The mention of the Last Day is a warning that man's ultimate destiny is in God's hands, not man's, and that God determines it by His standards and not man's.

It is against all this background that we must try to understand the insistence on acts of generosity. Such acts had a social and economic effect, but that was almost certainly not the most important aspect. They were a reaffirmation of part of the ideal of *murūwah*, and that was important. But they were other things also. They were a practical exercise in detachment from wealth, an outward expression of the new inner attitude which should serve to strengthen it. This may have been all there was to it to begin with, but certainly as time went on these acts of generosity became associated with something deeply rooted in the Arab heart. They became a sort of sacrifice whereby man could propitiate the powers over him, warding off the consequences of their anger and doing something to gain their favour for the future, in just the same way as their forefathers had propitiated the pagan gods by the sacrifice of animals. It is difficult to be sure to what extent this idea was present among the early Muslims; it can hardly have been consciously present, yet in view of later developments, encouraged by the Qur'ān, we cannot say categorically that it was absent. If, then, these acts of generosity touched an impulse to offer sacrifice that lay deep in the hearts of the early Muslims, they would become a further expression of man's dependence on higher powers.

Be that as it may, the teaching of the early passages of the Qur'ān culminates in teaching God's goodness and power (as Creator and Judge) and in exhorting man to acknowledge and express his dependence on God.

4. FURTHER REFLECTIONS

(a) *Economic conditions and religion*

The diagnosis of the Meccan situation by the Qur'ān is that the troubles of the time were primarily religious. On the other hand, it has been suggested above that the rise of Islam is somehow connected with the change from a nomadic to a mercantile economy. Is there a contradiction here, or can the two views be reconciled?

This question raises very fundamental issues, but from the standpoint of theism the following points may be made. The economic change does not occur *in vacuo* but in a community which already has a certain social, moral, intellectual, and religious constitution. The malaise is due to the interaction of the economic change and these previously existing factors. In a word the trouble is the outcome of man's failure to adjust himself to the economic change because of certain pre-existing attitudes. The new economic circumstances lead to a heightening of man's confidence in himself without an awareness of his creatureliness to balance it, to an individualism in social affairs without a new moral ideal to balance it and without a new religious outlook to give the individual significance.

The problem is thus to bring about a readjustment of human beings to the changed economic circumstances. This requires the conscious co-operation of the human beings, and that presupposes that they are given an analysis of the situation, in the light of which they will make the necessary readjustments. The Qur'ān provides an analysis of the situation—not complete, but sufficient for practical purposes—and a guide to action. The immediately apparent troubles, such as the selfishness of some men which leads them to make use of the new conditions to improve their own position at the expense of their fellows, are traced back to pride in human power and failure to acknowledge God. The Qur'ān reminds man that, in the total situation in which he has to act, there are factors which he has neglected; there is the fact that for his life and the means of its support he is dependent on a higher power; there is the fact of death and eschatological judgement, or, if one likes, the existence of a sphere of significance beyond the sphere of space and time.

The Qur'ān thus envisages the troubles of the time as due primarily to religious causes, despite their economic, social, and moral undercurrents, and as capable of being remedied only by means that are primarily religious. In view of the success of Muḥammad's efforts, he would be a bold man who would question the wisdom of the Qur'ān.

(b) *The Originality of the Qur'ān*

Whatever our theological position, we must in my opinion regard the Qur'anic *kerygma* as a creative irruption into the Meccan situation. There were certainly problems to be solved, there were tensions from which men sought relief, but it was impossible by mere ratiocination, by logical thinking, to pass from these problems and tensions to the Qur'anic *kerygma*. From the average Western secular standpoint it might be said that when certain ideas came to the ears of Muḥammad by normal channels (e.g. the idea of the Last Judgement), he realized that they were answers to his problems; so by some such system of trial and error he gradually built up a system. But even from this secular standpoint that does not explain the course of events convincingly. The Qur'anic *kerygma* solves social, moral, and intellectual problems, but not all at once and not obviously. The secularist would have to say that it was by chance and for secondary reasons that Muḥammad stumbled across ideas that held the key to the solution of the fundamental problems of his day; and that is not plausible. Neither empirical groping nor hard and acute thinking adequately account for the Qur'anic *kerygma*. Muḥammad certainly did not enter upon an abstract analysis of the situation such as is attempted here. For the secularist the best description would be that it is an intuition of the creative imagination, or something like that. Between such a view and that of the Muslim that it is a Divine irruption into human life I am trying to remain neutral. I shall therefore try to compromise by speaking of it as a 'creative irruption'.

This irruption, however, was not unrelated to the milieu into which it came. As the previous section has shown, it was specially adapted to the circumstances of Mecca about A.D. 610. Not merely was it in the Arabic language, but in many respects it is typically Arab in its literary form, even though there is no other Arabic literature quite like it. Above all, it is in terms of the thought-forms and conceptions of the contemporary Arab and Meccan outlook. Who but an Arab would have singled out the camel for prominent mention among the works of God?[1] Other traits in the description of God's power are doubtless such as specially appealed to the Arabs. The acts of generosity which men are exhorted to perform are in line with old nomadic ideals.

It is indeed a truism that any reformer must to begin with address himself to people as they are. This may be illustrated negatively by considering that there is no criticism of usury in the Meccan sūrahs. If the financial system developed in Mecca was the main source of the troubles, why is criticism of it not in the forefront of the *kerygma*? But, even if we admit the protasis of this conditional sentence, we may parry by asking: how could usury have been criticized? How could any criticism have been 'got across' to the Meccans? One could not say that usury is wrong, for there was no abstract conception of right and wrong in the Arab outlook. The nearest would be the conception of honourable and dishonourable; but that was closely linked with traditional moral ideals, and according to these there was nothing dishonourable about usury in itself; and even if there had been, the old ideas of honour had lost much of their force in Mecca. There was thus no basis in the Meccan outlook for a criticism of usury. It was only when a new community had been constituted on the basis of Divine commands given in the Qur'ān that 'no usury' could be stated as one of the rules of this community, and even then it was primarily directed against the Jews.[2]

[1] Q. 88. 17. [2] Cf. *Muḥammad at Medina*, 296 f.

This emphasis on the continuity between the Qur'an and the old Arab outlook may seem to contradict the thesis of the celebrated opening chapter of Goldziher's *Muhammedanische Studien* on '*Murūwah* and *Dīn*'; and it is no light matter to go against Goldziher. The contradiction, however, is not complete. That there is some contrast between what Muḥammad preached, on the basis of the Qur'ān, and the old Arab outlook is clear; if it had not been so, there would have been no violent opposition to him. One can, however, distinguish between the religious and the strictly moral aspects of *murūwah*. The religious aspect is what I have usually called humanism; it consists in pride in man and his achievements and in the belief that the significance of life is to be found in human excellence; *that* the Qur'ān clearly and undoubtedly attacks. The purely ethical aspect (which has usually been what I had in mind when I spoke of *murūwah*) is the moral ideal which includes bravery, patience, generosity, fidelity, and the like; this the Qur'ān does not attack; rather it criticizes the Meccans because they do not live up to it.

When one looks closely at Goldziher's chapter one detects various weaknesses. His illustrations of the contrast between *murūwah* and *dīn* are three; against the duty of revenge, Muḥammad preached forgiveness (para. IV); Islam imposed limitations on personal freedom, e.g. in respect of wine and women; Islam prescribed prayer which involves an attitude thoroughly uncongenial to the independence-loving nomads. Over the latter point there is no dispute; it is the religious aspect of *murūwah*. The other illustrations, however, are not so satisfactory. The changes with regard to marriage and wine-drinking are probably not due to anything specifically Islamic but to the difference between nomadic and settled conditions, while the teaching about forgiving enemies which Goldziher mentions is at best a minute facet of the Qur'anic message; one passage (24. 22) traditionally refers to forgiving close relatives, and another (3. 128) is at least within the Islamic community. For a proper parallel to the old Arab attitudes one would have to consider enemies outside the Islamic community, since that had replaced the tribe or clan as social unit. Thus on the strictly ethical side the case for a deep and wide cleavage between Islam and the Jāhilīyah is weak.

Finally, there is the question of the relation of the Qur'ān to Judaeo-Christian conceptions. Let us try to get this question into the true perspective. The Qur'ān is a creative irruption into Meccan life. To discuss 'sources' is somewhat like discussing the 'sources' of Shakespeare's *Hamlet*. At most the 'sources' of *Hamlet* suggest where Shakespeare got certain features of the plot. They neither explain, nor explain away, Shakespeare's creative originality. Even this analogy is not in all respects suitable, since the parallel would be with the relation of the 'sources' to the work of Muḥammad in producing the Qur'ān. This latter conception, however, is contrary to the beliefs of orthodox Muslims, and therefore to be avoided. As in any case, on the assumption of Muḥammad's sincerity, the Qur'ān is not the product of his consciousness, it is preferable to consider it in its relation to the minds of those to whom it was addressed and for whom it was adapted, that is, Muḥammad, the early Muslims and the other Meccans. In this connexion one can ask how far the Qur'anic parallels to Judaeo-Christian ideas were references to ideas present in the minds of these people before the Qur'ān came to them. This topic enables the Western scholar interested in 'sources' to discuss practically all the points he wants to discuss, and yet does not obviously contradict Islamic dogma. It will be convenient to treat separately (1) fundamental ideas and (2) illustrative material and secondary ideas.

In the case of fundamental ideas, such as the conceptions of God and His judgement, both the Qur'ān itself and Western scholarship hold that the Qur'anic conceptions are broadly identical with those of Judaism and Christianity. Does this mean the Qur'ān is not original, is not a creative irruption? Not at all. The identity, in so far as there is identity, is due to the fact that the Qur'ān is addressed to people (including Muḥammad) some of whom were already familiar with these ideas, though perhaps only dimly and vaguely. Here as elsewhere the Qur'ān starts with people as they are. No Arabic-speaking Jew or Christian could have had the success Muḥammad had, if he had stood up in Mecca and repeated his Jewish or Christian ideas; his expression of them would have been too alien. The Qur'ān makes use of these Judaeo-Christian ideas in the 'arabized' form in which they were already present in the minds of the more enlightened Meccans. Its originality consists in that it gave them greater precision and detail, presented them more forcefully, and, by its varying emphasis, made a more or less coherent synthesis of them; above all, it gave them a focus in the person of Muḥammad and his special vocation as messenger of God. Revelation and prophethood are certainly Judaeo-Christian ideas; to say 'God is revealing Himself through Muḥammad', however, is no mere repetition of the past, but part of a creative irruption.

The early passages discussed above deal mainly with fundamental ideas and there is none which might not already have been in the minds of Muḥammad and his more enlightened contemporaries. The difficulty is greater when we come to illustrative material, like the stories of the prophets. There are close parallels between the Qur'ān and Judaeo-Christian documents—usually not the canonical books of the Bible, but rabbinical works and the heretical New-Testament-apocryphal writings. In such cases Western scholars find it difficult to resist the conclusion that the Qur'ān is the work of Muḥammad and that he repeats stories he had heard. From the Muslim standpoint the following would be an alternative view.

'When the early Muslims accepted Muḥammad as a prophet, they (like Muḥammad himself) became interested in previous prophets and found out what they could about them. Thus their store of information gradually increased, and this is reflected in the Qur'ān. Some of the phrases of the Qur'ān itself show that the illustrative material was not unfamiliar: e.g. "Has there come to thee the story of the hosts, of Pharaoh and Thamūd?" (85. 17f.). On the other hand, the words "That is from the stories of the Unseen . . ." (3. 39) suggest that not all details were already familiar even to Muḥammad. Here, however, it must be remembered that the Western distinction between a bare fact and its significance is not so clearly drawn in the East. Muḥammad may have known the bare facts—in the passage referred to the stories are about Mary and Jesus, Zechariah and John, about whom Muḥammad already knew something; but perhaps he had not appreciated the significance of the bare facts, and required to have this shown to him by further statements. The primary function of these statements, in Western terms, would be to convey significance, not to inform about bare fact; but in the Arabic East where men were not interested in this distinction it was sufficient for the Qur'ān to call them *anbā'*, information.'

Thus conceivably might a Muslim argue if he was trying to convince a Westerner who did not believe in miracles that the

Qur'ān is original and not merely repetitive; and this account is perhaps better than the usual Western one. The problem, however, is theológical rather than historical. The historian will merely note that there is something original in the Qurān's use of the stories and in its selection of points for emphasis.

IV

THE FIRST MUSLIMS

1. TRADITIONAL ACCOUNTS OF THE EARLIEST CONVERTS

SINCE nobility in Islam depended theoretically on service to the cause of the Islamic community, later Muslims made the most of their ancestors' claims to merit in this respect, and the traditional accounts of the earliest conversions have therefore to be handled with care. When we find it claimed by the descendants or admirers of X that he was among the first twenty Muslims, it is usually safe to assume that he was about thirty-fifth.

It is universally agreed that Khadījah was the first to believe in her husband and his message, but there was a hot dispute about the first male. Aṭ-Ṭabarī[1] has a large selection of source material, and leaves the reader to decide for himself between the three candidates, ʿAlī, Abū Bakr, and Zayd b. Ḥārithah. The claim of ʿAlī may in a sense be true, but for the Western historian it cannot be significant, since ʿAlī was admittedly only nine or ten at the time and a member of Muḥammad's household. The claim made for Abū Bakr may also be true in the very different sense that, at least from the time of the Abyssinian affair, he was the most important Muslim after Muḥammad; but his later primacy has probably been reflected back into the early records. As a matter of sheer fact Zayd b. Ḥārithah has possibly the best claim to be regarded as the first male Muslim, since he was a freedman of Muḥammad's and there was a strong mutual attachment; but his humble status means that his conversion has not the same significance as that of Abū Bakr.[2]

The statement[3] that after the first three there was an important group of converts introduced by Abū Bakr, is also suspect. The men named are in fact the five who together with ʿAlī were acknowledged as leaders at the death of ʿUmar and nominated by him to settle the succession to the caliphate. It is hardly credible that, more than twenty years earlier, at the very beginning of Islam, the same five should have come to Muḥammad as a group. Their names are: ʿUthmān b. ʿAffān; az-Zubayr b. al-ʿAwwām;

[1] *Ann.* 1159–68.
[2] Cf. Excursus F; Nöldeke, ZDMG, 52. 18–21.
[3] Ṭab. 1168; cf. IH, 162.

ʿAbd ar-Raḥmān b. ʿAwf; Saʿd b. Abī Waqqāṣ; Ṭalḥah b. ʿUbaydallāh. Of these ʿAbd ar-Raḥmān is also reported to have been converted along with a different group whose leader was ʿUthmān b. Maẓʿūn.[1] Aṭ-Ṭabarī further quotes reports from Ibn Saʿd according to which other four persons claimed to be 'fourth or fifth'—Khālid b. Saʿīd, Abū Dharr, ʿAmr b. ʿAbasah, az-Zubayr.

Despite the existence of such grounds of suspicion about claims to early conversion, the 'list of Early Muslims' given by Ibn Isḥāq[2] may be accepted as roughly accurate. It is noteworthy that this list contains the names of a number of people who were *not* prominent in later times, though apparently to the fore in the earliest period. Among these were: Khālid b. Saʿīd b. al-ʿĀṣ, whose father was the leading financier of Mecca at the time; Saʿīd b. Zayd b. ʿAmr, whose father had been a 'seeker of religion' before the time of Muḥammad's preaching; and Nuʿaym an-Naḥḥām, who was possibly the leading man of the clan of ʿAdī, but did not go to Medina until A.H. 6. So far as I have noticed all those whom Ibn Saʿd describes as 'Muslims before Muḥammad entered the house of al-Arqam' are included in this list, and there are also one or two others, usually described by Ibn Saʿd as 'early in conversion' (*qadīm al-Islām*). Since Ibn Isḥāq does not mention the house of al-Arqam, he was presumably using different sources; and thus the list represents the rough agreement of two different lines of tradition.

In surveying the lives of the early Muslims it will be useful to have in mind a passage from az-Zuhrī:[3]

The Messenger of God (God bless and preserve him) summoned to Islam secretly and openly, and there responded to God whom He would of the young men and weak people, so that those who believed in Him (or 'him') were numerous and the unbelieving Quraysh did not criticize what he said. When he passed by them as they sat in groups, they would point to him, 'There is the youth of the clan of ʿAbd al-Muṭṭalib who speaks (things) from heaven'. This lasted until God (in the Qur'ān) spoke shamefully of the idols they worshipped other than Himself and mentioned the perdition of their fathers who died in unbelief. At that they came to hate the Messenger of God (God bless and preserve him) and to be hostile to him.

[1] IS, iii. 1. 286, &c

[2] IH, 162–5; repeated and numbered by Caetani in *Ann.* i. 236 f.

[3] IS, i. 1. 133.

One of the aims of the survey will be to try to discover the precise meaning of the phrases 'young men' (*aḥdāth ar-rijāl*) and 'weak people' (*ḍuʿafāʾ an-nās*), and it will therefore pay special attention to the age and social position of the early Muslims. These are to be taken as two distinct classes. Ibn Saʿd says of several persons that they were among those 'considered weak' (*mustaḍʿafīn*); it is implied that these constituted a small and distinct class.[1] On the other hand, some of the young men who gathered round Muḥammad belonged to the most influential families in Mecca and could not be called 'weak'.

2. SURVEY OF THE EARLIER MUSLIMS

The chief items of information about the early Muslims and their opponents are summarized in Excursus E, and the aim here is to comment on that information and to draw attention to points of importance. Since a man's social standing depended on his position within his clan and on his clan's position within the community as a whole, it is advisable to consider each clan separately. Where statements are based on the information given in Excursus E or derived from the relevant article in the *Ṭabaqāt* of Ibn Saʿd no special reference has been given. The order in which the clans are taken is based on the remarks towards the end of I. 2 a, above.

Hāshim. The place of the clan of Hāshim in Meccan society has already been discussed (II. 1), and it has been suggested that under Abū Ṭālib's leadership it was losing ground. Apart from Muḥammad and his household, including ʿAlī and Zayd b. Ḥārithah, the chief early converts were Jaʿfar b. Abī Ṭālib and Ḥamzah b. ʿAbd al-Muṭṭalib. Ḥamzah, Muḥammad's uncle, though about the same age as Muḥammad, was respected as a warrior but possibly did not carry much weight in the counsels of the clan. The inferior position of Ḥamzah and Jaʿfar in the clan is shown by the fact that they had wives from the nomadic tribe of Khathʿam, whereas Abū Lahab, who probably became chief of the clan on the death of Abū Ṭālib and bitterly opposed Muḥammad, was able to marry[2] a daughter of Ḥarb b. Umayyah, for a time chief of the clan of ʿAbd Shams and one of the strongest men in Mecca.

Al-Muṭṭalib. This clan had apparently become very weak and was much dependent on Hāshim. ʿUbaydah b. al-Ḥārith had ten children but all were by slave-concubines. Misṭaḥ was apparently

[1] Cf. IH, 260; Q. 28. 4; p. 96 below.

[2] IS, iv. 1. 41 f.

poor—his father perhaps dead—for he got help from Abū Bakr, whose mother was a sister of Umm Misṭaḥ's mother. 'Ubaydah, who was some years senior to Muḥammad and one of the oldest among the Muslims, was the primary convert from the clan. The other Muslims at Badr were his brothers and his cousin Misṭaḥ, who was probably also influenced by his mother's connexion with Abū Bakr. Some of the clan fought as pagans at Badr, but none was prominent in any way.

Taym. This clan also counted for little in the affairs of Mecca. In Muḥammad's youth the leading member of it was 'Abdallāh b. Jud'ān, for the meeting to set up the Ḥilf al-Fuḍūl was held in his house, and we also hear of Muḥammad meeting Abū Jahl there.[1] He was probably dead by now, and his son 'Amr who was killed as a pagan at Badr, had not the same importance. Abū Bakr had presumably some influence within the clan at the time of his conversion, but he was not strong enough to carry many of the clan with him. His fortune of 40,000 dirhams when he became a Muslim was that of a merchant in a small way.[2] The other early convert from Taym, Ṭalḥah, was much younger and came from a different branch. An uncle and nephew of his, still pagans, were killed at Badr. He was engaged in trade with Syria and was intimate with Abū Bakr who took him to Muḥammad. The conversion of Ṣuhayb b. Sinān was seemingly independent of these two. A Byzantine by education, if not by birth, his only connexion with Taym was that he had once been slave to 'Abdallāh b. Jud'ān. He was a friend of 'Ammār b. Yāsir, a confederate of B. Makhzūm, who also had Byzantine connexions. His wealth was sufficient to attract the cupidity of the pagans, and Taym was either unwilling or unable to protect him.

Zuhrah. The clan of Zuhrah seems to have been more prosperous than those of Taym and al-Muṭṭalib. Certain branches had business relations, cemented by marriage, with 'Abd Shams; the mother of Sa'd b. Abī Waqqāṣ was a granddaughter of Umayyah b. 'Abd Shams, and 'Abd ar-Raḥmān b. 'Awf before his conversion had married daughters of 'Utbah b. Rabī'ah b. 'Abd Shams and his brother Shaybah. Again Makhramah b. Nawfal of Zuhrah was one of the leaders along with Abū Sufyān of the caravan which was the occasion of the battle of Badr. The clan was in the curious

[1] IH, 85, 451; cf. also p. 32 above.

[2] Lammens, *Mecque*, 226–8 (322–4).

position that at least from Muḥammad's visit to aṭ-Ṭā'if (when Muḥammad asked him for protection) till after Badr the leading man was a confederate (*ḥalīf*), al-Akhnas b. Sharīq. Al-Aswad b. ʿAbd Yaghūth who had been prominent earlier was doubtless now dead.

The principal man to be converted was ʿAbd ar-Raḥmān b. ʿAwf, who was forty-three at the Hijrah and had the reputation of being an astute business man. Another important convert, belonging to a different branch of the clan (B. ʿAbd Manāf b. Zuhrah) was Saʿd b. Abī Waqqāṣ, said to have been only seventeen when converted. According to one account both were brought to Muḥammad by Abū Bakr, but another account makes ʿAbd ar-Raḥmān come along with ʿUthmān b. Maẓʿūn. In the train of Saʿd came his brothers ʿĀmir and ʿUmayr, and probably the obscure confederate, Masʿūd b. Rabīʿah; but it is noteworthy that another brother, ʿUtbah b. Abī Waqqāṣ was one of the four who, before Uḥud, swore to kill Muḥammad or be killed. ʿAbdallāh b. Masʿūd, a confederate of the B. ʿAbd b. al-Ḥārith b. Zuhrah, the branch to which ʿAbd ar-Raḥmān belonged, may have followed the latter into Islam, or may have come independently. He is said to have met Muḥammad and Abū Bakr while pasturing the flocks of ʿUqbah b. Abī Muʿayṭ (of B. Umayyah b. ʿAbd Shams). The occupation may be a sign of youth rather than of poverty, as he was only a little over twenty-eight at the Hijrah, and the connexion with ʿAbd Shams should not be overlooked. He became prominent in Islam, and is to be regarded as the leader of the group comprising his brother ʿUtbah, the latter's grandson, ʿAbdallāh b. Shihāb, and a relative ʿUmayr b. ʿAbd ʿAmr Dhū 'l Yadayn. The confederate Khabbāb b. al-Aratt was not closely connected with any of the above. He was a poor man; his mother was a professional circumciser and he himself a blacksmith; and his complete lack of protection meant that he had to suffer for his faith. Al-Muṭṭalib b. Azhar and his brother Ṭulayb had the same grandfather as ʿAbd ar-Raḥmān b. ʿAwf, and that, and the fact that their mother was of the clan of al-Muṭṭalib, may have weighed with them. Al-Miqdād b. ʿAmr, the confederate and adopted son of the old leader, al-Aswad b. ʿAbd Yaghūth, was in Abyssinia as a Muslim, but did not leave the Meccans till some time after Muḥammad's Hijrah, though before Badr;[1] he was probably rich and is said to have had a horse at Badr. Shuraḥbīl was separate

[1] IH, 416.

from all these and connected rather with Sufyān b. Maʿmar and the clan of Jumaḥ.

ʿAdī. The clan of ʿAdī had formerly belonged to the Aḥlāf, and it will be noticed that the mothers of the Muslims from ʿAdī are mostly from Sahm and Jumaḥ, while the mother of ʿUmar himself was from Makhzūm. ʿAdī changed sides about this time, perhaps because ʿAbd Shams, with whom they had a bitter feud, was coming closer to Makhzūm and the Aḥlāf.[1] The general position of ʿAdī was probably also deteriorating. The fact that Maʿmar b. ʿAbdallāh was the primary authority for a tradition condemning monopolistic practices suggests that ʿAdī was being squeezed out. No members of the clan other than ʿUmar seem to have been of much consequence in Mecca. His father and grandfather, al-Khaṭṭāb and Nufayl, had been prominent men, if we may judge from the number of their confederates and from al-Khaṭṭāb's treatment of Zayd b. ʿAmr;[2] and al-Khaṭṭāb had at least one wife from Makhzūm. The first convert from the clan was probably Saʿīd b. Zayd b. ʿAmr, whose father had been one of the seekers of the true religion and had adopted certain ascetic practices. He may have influenced the six confederates who are named as 'early Muslims'. Another early convert was Nuʿaym b. ʿAbdallāh an-Naḥḥām, who was in the habit of feeding the poor of the clan monthly. He was probably chief of the clan for the first six years of the Islamic era, for, despite his early acceptance of the faith, he did not join Muḥammad in the Hijrah. ʿUmar b. al-Khaṭṭāb was probably the leading man of the clan, certainly one of the leaders, and his conversion, though a little later than that of those on Ibn Isḥāq's list, was a great step forward for the Islamic community. He was doubtless influenced by the examples of Saʿīd b. Zayd, son of his father's cousin, of Saʿīd's wife, ʿUmar's own sister, of ʿUthmān b. Maẓʿūn, his brother-in-law, and of the confederates of the family; and the economic decline may have played a part, even if unconsciously.

Al-Ḥārith b. Fihr. This clan was on the border-line between Quraysh al-Biṭāḥ and Quraysh aẓ-Ẓawāhir. Its position had perhaps been improving, but it was not of first importance. We hear of no influential man from it among the pagans. Its marriage alliances outside the clan were with weaker clans like ʿĀmir and Zuhrah. The chief early converts were Abū ʿUbaydah b. al-

[1] Cf. p. 7 above. [2] IH, 147.

Jarrāḥ and Suhayl b. Bayḍā', the former a friend of 'Uthmān b. Maẓ'ūn, and the latter perhaps a younger friend of Abū Bakr.

'Āmir. This was another clan on the border-line between Quraysh al-Biṭāḥ and Quraysh aẓ-Ẓawāhir. About the time of the Hijrah it seems to have been improving its position, and was able to intermarry with Hāshim, Nawfal, and even Makhzūm. The chief man up to Badr at least was Suhayl b. 'Amr, and it is significant that the only two members of the clan in the list of early Muslims were his brothers Ḥāṭib and Salīṭ. The most notable Muslim from the clan was Ibn Umm Maktūm, whose mother was of Makhzūm.

Asad. The clan of Asad had evidently grown in importance and had left its old associates of the Ḥilf al-Fuḍūl to enter the circles of 'big business'. Zam'ah b. al-Aswad, Abū 'l-Bakhtarī, Nawfal b. Khuwaylid, and Ḥakīm b. Ḥizām were prominent among the pagans of Mecca. Zam'ah had married into Makhzūm, and Nawfal into 'Abd Shams. Az-Zubayr was apparently the only early convert to Islam. He was only about sixteen at the time and can have had no influence in the clan, not even in the sub-clan of Khuwaylid. Perhaps his relationship to Khadījah through his father and to Muḥammad through his mother made conversion easy. The others who went to Abyssinia seem to be junior members of the main families.

Nawfal. The clan of Nawfal does not seem to have been strong in numbers, but its leading men had considerable influence, perhaps because of their close association with 'Abd Shams. They worked in with the Makhzūm group, but were not subservient to them, since at times along with Asad (and 'Āmir) they would go their own way. The only Muslim mentioned by Ibn Sa'd in III and IV—and not one of the earliest—was a confederate of the clan and his freedman.

'Abd Shams. The clan of 'Abd Shams disputed with that of Makhzūm the leading place in Mecca, but both realized the wide sphere of common interest, and the rivalry was not unduly bitter. After Badr Abū Sufyān b. Ḥarb was the first citizen of Mecca, since several of the chief men of Makhzūm had been killed. But in the early days of Muḥammad's mission also Abū Uḥayḥah Sa'īd b. al-'Āṣ had wielded great power,[1] and, until their deaths at Badr, 'Uqbah b. Abī Mu'ayṭ, and the two sons of Rabī'ah,

[1] Cf. Lammens, *Mecque*, index.

'Utbah and Shaybah, were to the fore. The early converts from this clan were 'Uthmān b. 'Affān, Abū Ḥudhayfah b. 'Utbah b. Rabī'ah, Khālid b. Sa'īd (Abī Uḥayḥah), and the family of the confederate Jaḥsh, 'Ubaydallāh, 'Abdallāh, and Abū Aḥmad. Abū Ḥudhayfah and Khālid were sons of leading men, but the fact that their mothers were from Kinānah, a tribe which was, as it were, a poor relation of Quraysh, suggests that they were inferior members of their families. 'Uthmān's immediate forebears were not so prominent, and he, too, probably felt envious of his richer and more powerful relatives. Ten years before the Hijrah Abū Ḥudhayfah and 'Uthmān were men of about 30, an age at which their future prospects would be comparatively clear, but perhaps not attractive. The fact that 'Uthmān's maternal grandmother was a sister of Muḥammad's father may have further smoothed the path. The family of Jaḥsh was not directly connected with any of the above, but were confederates of Ḥarb, the father of Abū Sufyān, and their mother was yet another daughter of 'Abd al-Muṭṭalib. They were early converts and went to Abyssinia where 'Ubaydallāh became a Christian. Most of the other confederates of 'Abd Shams who became Muslims before Badr were probably influenced by this family.

Makhzūm. The Makhzūm were apparently the dominant political group in Mecca in the decade or so before Badr, and a certain Abū Jahl was the leader of the opposition to Muḥammad. The clan was a numerous one and the descendants of al-Mughīrah (the grandfather of Abū Jahl) were specially strong. The two chief early converts Abū Salamah and al-Arqam, were grandsons of brothers of al-Mughīrah. Al-Arqam, though young, was probably head of his family, since he was able to offer his house as headquarters for the Muslims. Abū Salamah had a brother among the pagans killed at Badr, and two cousins who joined him in Abyssinia. Apart from that it is difficult to say how they stood within the clan. A third convert 'Ayyāsh was a cousin and uterine brother of Abū Jahl, but, though he went to Medina at the Hijrah, he was persuaded by Abū Jahl to return to Mecca. Shammās, who also went to Abyssinia and fought at Badr, belonged to a quite separate, and presumably obscure, branch of the clan. To Makhzūm is also reckoned 'Ammār b. Yāsir, the confederate of Abū Ḥudhayfah b. al-Mughīrah. His father had settled in Mecca and they had doubtless lost touch with their tribe. He had contact with Christianity through his mother's second husband, a freedman of Greek origin and therefore presumably a Christian. The family seems to have been a sincerely religious one.

Sahm. Sahm was one of the more powerful clans. It was against them that the Ḥilf al-Fuḍūl was ostensibly directed in the first place, and it was to them that ʿAdī appealed for help when they proved unable to stand up to ʿAbd Shams.[1] Al-ʿĀṣ b. Wā'il and al-Ḥārith b. Qays b. ʿAdī are mentioned among the chief enemies of Muḥammad. At Badr, however, the leaders appear to have been Munabbih b. al-Ḥajjāj and his brother Nubayh. The only early convert named was Khunays b. Ḥudhāfah b. Qays, who had already married a daughter of ʿUmar b. al-Khaṭṭāb; his family was presumably one of the less important branches of the clan, and he himself was in no way prominent. It is worth mentioning also the attitude of the sons of al-Ḥārith b. Qays. Six of them went to Abyssinia as Muslims, but one at least, al-Ḥajjāj,[2] rejoined the pagan party, fought against the Muslims at Badr, was taken prisoner, and later accepted Islam once more. One might conjecture that after the death of al-Ḥārith his family found it difficult to maintain their position.

Jumaḥ. This clan was also powerful, but not quite so powerful as Sahm. The leadership was in the hands of the family of Khalaf b. Wahb, first in that of Umayyah b. Khalaf, and at a later time in that of Wahb b. ʿUmayr b. Wahb b. Khalaf. ʿUthmān b. Maẓʿūn was one of the most important of the early Muslims, and was possibly head of the family of Ḥabīb b. Wahb, brother of Khalaf. The others in the list of early Muslims were his brothers ʿAbdallāh and Qudāmah, his son as-Sā'ib, and his sister's sons, Maʿmar b. al-Ḥārith, Ḥāṭib, and Khaṭṭāb (or Ḥaṭṭāb). ʿUthmān, of whom we shall have to say more later, seems to have been tending to monotheism and asceticism before he met Muhammad.

ʿAbd ad-Dār. 'Abd ad-Dār had once been foremost of the sons of Quṣayy, and his descendants retained certain privileges such as that of carrying the standard, but they now counted for little in Meccan affairs. Muṣʿab (al-Khayr) b. ʿUmayr was not a specially early convert; friendship with ʿĀmir b. Rabīʿah, a confederate of the caliph ʿUmar's father, may have helped. A brother was made prisoner fighting at Badr as a pagan.

[1] Azraqī, 472.
[2] Cf. Excursus H, below.

It remains to summarize some of the points that are to be learned from this survey. The principal 'early Muslims' can be divided into three classes as follows:

1. *Younger sons of the best families.* Khālid b. Sa'īd would be the foremost representative of this class, but there are several others. These were young men from the most influential families of the most influential clans, closely related to the men who actually wielded power in Mecca and who were foremost in opposing Muḥammad. It is noteworthy that at Badr there were instances of brothers, or father and son, or uncle and nephew, being on opposite sides.

2. *Men, mostly young, from other families.* This group is not sharply distinguished from the previous one, but, as we move down the scale to the weaker clans and to the weaker branches of the chief clans, we find among the Muslims men of greater influence within their clan or family. There are one or two comparatively old men like 'Ubaydah b. al-Ḥārith, who was sixty-one at the Hijrah, but the majority were probably under thirty when they became Muslims, and only one or two were over thirty-five.

3. *Men without close ties to any clan.* There was also a comparatively small number of men who were really outside the clan system, though nominally attached to some clan. Either the clan did not recognize the man's claim to be its confederate (as perhaps happened in the case of Khabbāb and B. Zuhrah), or it was too weak to give effective protection. It is not surprising that B. Taym did not protect slaves freed by Abū Bakr since it did not even protect Abū Bakr himself and Ṭalḥah when they were ignominiously tied together. Others said by Ibn Sa'd to be 'considered weak' were Suhayb b. Sinān and 'Ammār b. Yāsir, who were confederates of B. Taym and B. 'Abd Shams respectively.

The confederates (*ḥulafā'*) do not constitute a separate class. The principle of confederacy (*ḥilf, taḥāluf*) does not imply the inferiority of one party, but rather mutual help and protection. In view of the influential position of the Quraysh among the Arabs, however, their confederate, especially when he resided in Mecca, usually received far more than he gave, and in that sense was a dependant. Nevertheless, the position of the individual confederate was very much what he made it by his own abilities. In general the confederates were perhaps about the level of the less important families of a clan, but al-Akhnas b. Sharīq was for a time the leading man in B. Zuhrah, and others were comparatively wealthy. They intermarried freely with the Quraysh. Most of the confederates who became Muslims are in the second class; those in the third class are there for accidental reasons.

There is thus an obvious interpretation of the phrases 'young men' and 'weak people', namely, that the former refers to the first two classes and the latter to the third. Ibn Sa'd defines 'considered weak' (*mustaḍ'afūn*) as 'those who had no clan to protect them',[1] and must have taken az-Zuhrī in this sense. It is just conceivable that 'weak' might be interpreted as applying to those belonging to the less influential clans and families, and in that case it would refer to the second and third classes.

The most important point which emerges from this survey is that the young Islam was essentially a movement of young men (as has been emphasized by an Egyptian writer, 'Abd al-Muta'āl aṣ-Ṣa'īdī).[2] The great majority of those whose ages are recorded were under forty at the time of the Hijrah—some well under it—and many had been converted eight or more years previously. Secondly, it was *not* a movement of 'down-and-outs', of the scum of the population, of 'hangers-on' with no strong tribal affiliations who had drifted into Mecca. It drew its support not from the bottom layers of the social scale, but from those about the middle who, becoming conscious of the disparity between them and those at the top, were beginning to feel that they were underprivileged. It was not so much a struggle between 'haves' and 'have nots' as between 'haves' and 'nearly hads'.

3. THE APPEAL OF MUḤAMMAD'S MESSAGE

Having formed some idea of the sort of men who responded to Muḥammad's call, let us consider more fully their reasons for doing this, so far as we can discern them. In a well-known passage Ibn Isḥāq[3] tells of four men who went in search of the *Ḥanīfīyah*, the 'religion of Abraham', and apart from this previous chapters have given us grounds for holding that a tendency towards a vague monotheism had been widespread.[4] Although the Qur'ān does not mention these matters and ostensibly makes a completely fresh start, the nascent Islam did in fact act as a centre of integration for these vague and nebulous tendencies. One of the four men

[1] iii. 1. 177. 12; cf. IH, 260—Khabbāb, 'Ammār, Abū Fukayhah, Yasār, Ṣuhayb.

[2] *Shabāb al-Quraysh*, Cairo, 1947.

[3] IH, 143 ff.

[4] Cf. also Excursuses B and C.

mentioned by Ibn Isḥāq, ʿUbaydallāh b. Jaḥsh, became a Muslim and took part in the emigration to Abyssinia (even if later he preferred Christianity); and the son of another of the four, Saʿīd b. Zayd b. ʿAmr, was also among the early Muslims. Again, ʿUthmān b. Maẓʿūn, though apparently not connected with the group just mentioned, had engaged in ascetic practices in the Jāhilīyah. The accounts of Muḥammad's difficulties with ʿUthmān suggest that he had no easy time in canalizing the hopes and ideas of such pre-existing monotheists.[1]

The question of how economic facts and religious ideas are related to one another is relevant to this early monotheistic tendency, but it can most conveniently be discussed in connexion with those men who, so far as we know, had taken no definite steps to break with paganism, before they embraced Islam.

Among the first of the classes we distinguished—the younger sons of the best families, there was probably no explicit awareness that economic and political factors were involved in what they were doing. Khālid b. Saʿīd, for example, was presumably conscious only of religious reasons when he became a Muslim. His long residence in Abyssinia[2] probably indicates that he disagreed with Muḥammad's policy, and in particular with the increasingly political orientation of Islam and the insistence on Muḥammad's political leadership in virtue of his prophethood. Had Khālid been interested in the political aspects he would surely have sunk whatever differences he had with Muḥammad and returned to Mecca or Medina long before A.H. 7. But, though Khālid was attracted chiefly by the religious aspects of Islam, the whole social and political situation, especially the growing concentration of wealth in a few hands (not including his own, he might feel), would have an unsettling effect upon him and cause him to be aware of his need for a religious faith.

Khālid's is one of the few cases in which we are given some details about the conversion. He had a dream in which he saw himself standing on the brink of a fire; his father was trying to push him into it, while a man—whom Abū Bakr apparently identified for him as Muḥammad—took him by the middle and kept him from falling.[3] This sounds like authentic material, though probably it has been rewritten in accordance with later ideas. Our ignorance of the date, however, makes it difficult to interpret. It

[1] Cf. further V. 2. [2] Cf. V. 2. [3] IS, iv. 1. 67 f.

may refer to his position after his father discovered that he was attracted by Muḥammad, but before he finally broke with his family; in that case the application is obvious. But certain details suggest that it was prior to an actual meeting with Muḥammad; in that case the dream might signify that—to change the metaphor—his father was forcing him to enter the whirlpool of Meccan finance, which he regarded as soul-destroying, perhaps because it involved practices which he considered mean and ignoble. Whatever be the truth on this matter, his conscious thought appears to have been entirely on the religious plane.

In the case of Ḥamzah and 'Umar there are accounts of the circumstances in which each was converted—for 'Umar two quite different versions.[1] If the traditional accounts may be accepted, then the conversion was immediately occasioned by two factors; both men were impressed by the behaviour of Muḥammad himself or other Muslims, and 'Umar was also mysteriously attracted by the words of the Qur'ān and the religious content of the new faith. In both cases, though in different ways, loyalty to the family or clan was also involved; Ḥamzah was roused to defend Muḥammad from injury and insult at the hands and mouths of another clan; 'Umar felt his clan disgraced when he learned that his sister and her husband were Muslims (in the first version). There is no whisper of economics. Yet 'Umar, though secure in his position within the clan, was probably worried about the position of his clan in Mecca; this anxiety may have intensified his rage against his clansmen in the first place, through the fear that their conversion might lead to a further deterioration of the general position of the clan.

The members of the third class, those 'considered weak', were almost certainly influenced more by their own insecurity outer and inner, than by any prospect of economic or political advantage. If explicit hopes of reform were present among the early Muslims, we should expect to find them in the second class. The earliest passages of the Qur'ān did speak of such matters as well as of the greatness of God, and the whole message, as has been argued above, was relevant to the total situation of the Meccans at that period. It would not be surprising if some men were attracted chiefly by the political and economic implications of the message. Yet it is unlikely that there were many such. Muḥammad, it cannot

[1] IH, 184 f., 225–9, &c.

be too firmly insisted, was in no wise a socialistic reformer but the inaugurator of a new religion.[1] We may describe the position in our own terms by saying that, while Muḥammad was aware of the economic, social, political, and religious ills of his time and country, he regarded the religious aspect as the fundamental one and concentrated on that. This determined the ethos of the young community. The little group took their religious beliefs and practices with deadly seriousness. During the Meccan period a man interested chiefly in politics would have been uncomfortable among them, especially as the struggle with the opponents became more bitter and Muḥammad's prophethood was made the central issue. Their thinking must have been primarily upon the religious plane, and it was on the religious plane that men were summoned to Islam; conscious thoughts about economics or politics can have played hardly any part in conversion. Yet, when this has been said, we may go on to admit that Muḥammad and the wiser among his followers must have been alive to the social and political implications of his message, and that, in directing the affairs of the Muslims, such considerations certainly weighed with them.

[1] Cf. C. Snouck Hurgronje's review of H. Grimme's *Mohammed* in *Verspreide Geschriften*, i. 319–62.

V

THE GROWTH OF OPPOSITION

1. THE BEGINNING OF OPPOSITION; THE 'SATANIC VERSES'

THERE are grounds for thinking that in the early days of Muḥammad's mission he had a certain amount of success. Eventually, however, opposition appeared and soon became formidable. There are two main questions to discuss here: When and how did this opposition manifest itself, and what were the main motives underlying it? The second question is the more important, but before we can tackle it we must try to answer the first.

(a) *The letter of 'Urwah*

Aṭ-Ṭabarī has preserved for us a copy of a written document of early date, which has every appearance of being genuine.[1] It is desirable, therefore, to start with a translation of this.

Hishām b. 'Urwah related to us on the authority of 'Urwah that he wrote to 'Abd al-Malik b. Marwān (*sc.* caliph from 685/65 to 705/86): . . . Now as for him, that is, the Messenger of God (God bless and preserve him), when he summoned his tribe to accept the guidance and the light revealed to him, which were the purpose of God's sending him, they did not hold back from him when he first called them, but almost hearkened to him, until he mentioned their idols (*ṭawāghīt*); from aṭ-Ṭā'if there came some of the Quraysh, owners of property (*sc.* there), and rebutted him with vehemence, not approving what he said, and roused against him those who obeyed them. So the body of the people turned back from him and left him, except those of them whom God kept safe, and they were few in number. Things remained like that such time as God determined they should remain. Then their leaders took counsel how they might seduce (*yaftinū*) from the religion of God those who followed him (*sc.* Muḥammad) of their sons and brothers and fellow-clansmen. Then there was a time of extreme trial (*fitnah*) and upheaval for the people of Islam who followed the Messenger of God (God bless and preserve him). Some were seduced, but God kept safe (*sc.* and faithful) whom He would. When the Muslims were treated in this way, the Messenger of God (God bless and preserve him) told them

[1] Ṭab, *Ann.* 1180 f.; cf. Caetani, *Ann.* i, p. 267 f.

to go away to the land of the Abyssinians. Over the Abyssinians there was a good king called the Najāshī (or Negus); in his land no one suffered wrong; and moreover he himself was praised for his uprightness. Abyssinia was a market where the Quraysh traded, finding in it ample supplies, security and good business. The Messenger of God (God bless and preserve him) gave them this order, then, and the main body of them went there when they were oppressed in Mecca and he feared (the effects of) the trials (*fitnah*) upon them. He himself continued without a break (*sc.* as he was). For years they (*sc.* Quraysh) continued to act harshly to those of them who became Muslims. Afterwards Islam spread in it (*sc.* Mecca), and some of their nobles entered it (? Islam).

If we leave aside for the moment what is said about the emigration to Abyssinia, there are three main points to be noticed. Firstly, the first active opposition is said to be due to the mention of idols (presumably in the Qur'ān); secondly, some Quraysh with property in aṭ-Ṭā'if were the leaders of the movement against Muḥammad; thirdly, all this preceded the migration to Abyssinia. There is not much difficulty about accepting the last two statements, but there is some about the first. Any dating of the Qur'ān of the Nöldeke or Bell type gives many passages prior to the mention of idols in which opposition to Muḥammad is asserted or implied. Indeed there is little about idols through the whole Meccan period. It is possible that 'Urwah who was writing at least seventy years after the events *inferred* merely that the attack on polytheism must have been the cause of the opposition then because it led to much opposition later. It is conceivable, but not likely, that the 'mention of idols' refers to the satanic verses to be discussed below; in that case we should have to suppose that Quraysh were annoyed because the shrine of aṭ-Ṭā'if was being given too much prominence and the inhabitants perhaps being placed on an equal footing with the Meccans. On the whole, the simplest and most likely solution is that in some way more active opposition appeared after the mention of the idols. The reference to the Quraysh of aṭ-Ṭā'if seems to show that 'Urwah had some good source of evidence independent of the Qur'ān. Let us therefore accept the first point provisionally.

(b) *The satanic verses; the facts*

The most notable mention of idols in the Meccan part of the Qur'ān is in Sūrat an-Najm (53), and thereby hangs a tale. The account which aṭ-Ṭabarī places first[1] is as follows. When Muḥammad saw that the Meccans were turning from his message, he had a great desire to make it easier for them to accept it. At this juncture Sūrat an-Najm was revealed; but when Muḥammad came to the verses, 'Have ye considered al-Lāt and al-'Uzzā, And Manāt, the third, the other?' then, the tradition continues, 'as he was saying it to himself, eager to bring it to his people, Satan threw upon his tongue (the verses), "These are the swans exalted, Whose intercession is to be hoped for" '. On hearing this the Meccans were delighted, and at the end when Muḥammad prostrated himself, they all did likewise. The news of this even reached the Muslims in Abyssinia. Then Gabriel came to Muḥammad and showed him his error; for his comfort God revealed 22. 51, and abrogated the satanic verses by revealing the true continuation of the sūrah. Quraysh naturally said that Muḥammad had changed his mind about the position of the goddesses, but meanwhile the satanic verses had been eagerly seized by the idolators.

In his Commentary on 22. 51[2] aṭ-Ṭabarī gives a number of other versions of the tradition on this matter. Two attributed to a certain Abū 'l-'Āliyah are important since they contain details not in the commoner versions and have the appearance of being more primitive. The first runs as follows:

> Quraysh said to the Messenger of God (God bless and preserve him), Those who sit beside you are merely the slave of so-and-so and the client of so-and-so. If you made some mention of our goddesses, we would sit beside you; for the nobles of the Arabs (*sc.* the nomads) come to you, and when they see that those who sit beside you are the nobles of your tribe, they will have more liking for you. So Satan threw (something) into his formulation, and these verses were revealed, 'Have ye considered al-Lāt and al-'Uzzā, And Manāt, the third, the other?' and Satan caused to come upon his tongue, 'These are the swans exalted, Whose intercession is to be hoped for, Such as they do not forget (or "are not forgotten")'. Then, when he had recited them, the Prophet (God bless and preserve him) prostrated himself, and the Muslims and the idolators prostrated themselves along with him. When he knew what Satan had caused to come upon his tongue, that weighed upon him; and God revealed, 'And We have not sent before thee any messenger or prophet but when he formed his desire Satan threw (something) into his formulation . . .' to the words '. . . and God is knowing, wise'.

The second version from Abū 'l-'Āliyah is similar but does not

[1] *Ann.* 1192 ff.; cf. *Tafsīr*, xvii. 119.

[2] xvii. 119–21.

have the third interpolated verse. It records, however, as do some of the other versions, how some of the grandees of Quraysh on account of age did not prostrate themselves but instead raised some earth to their foreheads, but, unlike the other versions, adds that Abū Uḥayḥah Sa'īd b. al-'Āṣ remarked, 'At last Ibn Abī Kabshah has spoken good of our goddesses'. The remark may very well be genuine, since the same, possibly rude, way of referring to Muḥammad is found in another remark attributed to this man.[1]

If we compare the different versions and try to distinguish between the external facts in which they agree and the motives which the various historians ascribe in order to explain the facts, we find at least two facts about which we may be certain. Firstly, at one time Muḥammad must have publicly recited the satanic verses as part of the Qur'ān; it is unthinkable that the story could have been invented later by Muslims or foisted upon them by non-Muslims. Secondly, at some later time Muḥammad announced that these verses were not really part of the Qur'ān and should be replaced by others of a vastly different import. The earliest versions do not specify how long afterwards this happened; the probability is that it was weeks or even months.

There is also a third fact or group of facts about which we can be tolerably certain, namely, that for Muḥammad and his Meccan contemporaries the primary reference of the verses would be to the goddess al-Lāt worshipped at aṭ-Ṭā'if, the goddess al-'Uzzā worshipped at Nakhlah near Mecca, and the goddess Manāt, whose shrine lay between Mecca and Medina, and who was worshipped primarily by the Arabs of Medina. Al-'Uzzā was worshipped in the first place by Quraysh, but the priestly family was from B. Sulaym, and Kinānah, Khuzā'ah, Thaqīf, and some of Hawāzin are also mentioned as participating in her worship. We hear of Medinan nobles having wooden representations of Manāt in their houses,[2] but on the whole the Arabs of that period probably hardly ever thought of the worship of any deity apart from the ceremonies that took place at particular shrines. It was unlike, for example, the Catholic Christian veneration of the Blessed Virgin Mary; the 'Hail Mary' can be said in any place. Manāt, on the other hand, according to the predominant view among the Arabs, could only be worshipped *at her shrine*.[3] Thus the implication of

[1] IS, iv. 1. 69. 3; but cf. i. 2. 145. 27.
[2] IH, 303. 11.
[3] Cf. Ibn al-Kalbī, *K. al-Aṣnām*, 13–19; Wellhausen, *Reste*, 24–45; IH, 55.

the satanic verses is that the ceremonies at three important shrines in the neighbourhood of Mecca is acceptable. Further, the implication of the abrogating verses that the worship at these shrines is unacceptable is *not* a condemnation of the worship of the Ka'bah. Unless there were also some other verses condemning that, which were later abrogated and removed from the Qur'ān—and we have no real grounds for assuming this—then the abrogating verses in Sūrat an-Najm exalt the Ka'bah at the expense of the other shrines. It is worth remembering in this connexion that with the growth of Muhammad's power, these shrines were all destroyed.[1]

(c) *The satanic verses: motives and explanations*

The Muslim scholars, not possessing the modern Western concept of gradual development, considered Muḥammad from the very first to have been explicitly aware of the full range of orthodox dogma. Consequently it was difficult for them to explain how he failed to notice the heterodoxy of the satanic verses. The truth rather is that his monotheism was originally, like that of his more enlightened contemporaries, somewhat vague, and in particular was not so strict that the recognition of inferior divine beings was felt to be incompatible with it. He probably regarded al-Lāt, al-'Uzzā, and Manāt as celestial beings of a lower grade than God, in much the same way as Judaism and Christianity have recognized the existence of angels. The Qur'ān in the (? later) Meccan period speaks of them as jinn,[2] although in the Medinan period they are said to be merely names.[3] This being so, it is perhaps hardly necessary to find any special occasion for the satanic verses. They would not mark any conscious retreat from monotheism, but would simply be an expression of views which Muḥammad had always held.

Even so, the political implications of the verses are interesting. Did Muḥammad accept them as genuine because he was interested in gaining adherents at Medina and aṭ-Ṭā'if and among the surrounding tribes? Was he trying to counterbalance the influence of the leaders of Quraysh, who were opposed to him, by having large numbers of supporters? At the very least the mention of these shrines is a sign that his vision is expanding.

The tradition from Abū 'l-'Āliyah quoted above indicates that

[1] IH, 839 f., al-'Uzzā; 917, al-Lāt; Ṭab. 1649, Manāt, &c.
[2] 6. 100 f.; 18. 48 f.; 37. 158.
[3] 53. 23.

Quraysh made an offer to Muḥammad to admit him into their inner circle, if he would mention their goddesses. There are also other similar traditions. Sometimes he is said to have been offered wealth, a good marriage, and a position of importance; sometimes the offer was in more general terms that the leaders of Quraysh would associate with him in worship and business.[1] Quite apart from the question of details, on which one may justifiably have some hesitation, there is the question whether these stories are not for the most part inventions designed to magnify the importance of Muḥammad at this period. Was he already sufficiently important to be treated almost as an equal by the leading men of Mecca? On the whole the picture of Muhammad's position given by the stories is probably near the truth. We must remember that the original success of Muḥammad tends to be minimized, probably because the descendants of those who followed him for a time and then fell away did not wish to recall such things. In Abū 'l-ʿĀliyah's version, Muḥammad is prominent among visitors to Mecca, even though no leading Meccans joined him; and this contrast would hardly have been expressed so bluntly, if it had been a mere invention. Let us take it, then, that the leading Quraysh made some sort of offer to Muḥammad; he was to receive certain worldly advantages, and in return make some acknowledgement of their deities. The Qur'ān, as we shall see presently, supports this. Of the details we cannot be certain. The promulgation of the satanic verses is doubtless to be linked up with this bargain.

On this view the abrogation of the verses would similarly be linked up with the failure of the compromise. There is no suggestion that Muḥammad was double-crossed by the Meccans. But he came to realize that acknowledgement of the Banāt Allāh, as the three idols (and others) were called, meant reducing God to their level. His worship at the Kaʿbah was outwardly not very different from theirs at Nakhlah, aṭ-Ṭā'if and Qudayd. And that would mean that God's messenger was not greatly different from their priests and not likely to have much more influence; hence the reform on which Muhammad had set his heart would not come about. Thus it was not for any worldly motive that Muḥammad eventually turned down the offer of the Meccans, but for a genuinely religious reason; not, for example, because he could not trust these men nor because any personal ambition would remain

[1] Ṭab. *Ann.* 1191; cf. *Tafsīr*, xv. 82 f., to 17. 75–77.

unsatisfied, but because acknowledgement of the goddesses would lead to the failure of the cause, of the mission he had been given by God. A revelation may first have made this clear to him, but the matter can be thought out on the lines suggested, and he may have felt uneasy even before the revelation came.

If one takes an abstract view of the situation, there would seem to be little objection to the recognition of al-Lāt and the others as inferior celestial beings. The recognition of angels is held to be quite compatible with monotheism not only in Judaism and Christianity, but also in orthodox Islam. Two factors in the Meccan situation, however, made such a recognition impossible at this juncture. Firstly, the worship at the Ka'bah, which had previously been polytheistic, was being purified and for the Muslims at least being made monotheistic. If similar worship was carried on at several shrines, the people of the Ḥijāz would inevitably suppose that several roughly equal deities were being worshipped. Secondly, the phrase *Banāt Allāh*, 'daughters of God' or 'daughters of the god', had serious implications, even though in general it was not taken literally.[1] *Banāt* and similar words are often used metaphorically in Arabic; cf. *bint ash-shafah* (daughter of the lip), a word; *bint al-'ayn* (daughter of the eye), a tear; *banāt ad-dahr* (daughters of fate or time), calamities. Probably, then, the phrase originally meant no more than 'celestial or supernatural beings', *al-Lāh* here being simply 'the god', 'the supernatural', and not the unique or supreme god, that is, God. But as *Allāh* or *al-Lāh* came to be used almost exclusively for God, the phrase could be interpreted to mean that these were beings roughly equal with God; and that could not be reconciled with monotheism.

The view that Muḥammad's break with the leading men of Mecca is linked up with the abrogation of the satanic verses (and his rejection of an offer they made to him) is in accordance with the second of the points noted above in the letter of 'Urwah, namely, that some Quraysh with property in aṭ-Ṭā'if took the lead in actively opposing Muḥammad. Various explanations of this fact are possible, but the most likely is that these were some of the leading members of Quraysh who were specially interested in the commerce of aṭ-Ṭā'if and had brought the mercantile activities connected with that centre within the orbit of Meccan finance. The removal of recognition from the shrine of al-Lāt must some-

[1] Wellhausen, *Reste*, 24.

how or other have threatened their enterprises and stirred their anger against Muḥammad.

The view contained in the letter of 'Urwah, that the 'mention of the goddesses' marked the critical stage in the relation of Muḥammad to the leaders of Quraysh is further confirmed by the Qur'ān. Two passages, traditionally connected with the incidents under consideration, speak of a temptation to which Muḥammad almost succumbed. In one of these (17. 75–77) the nature of the temptation is unspecified; in the other (39. 64–66) it is definitely to acknowledge 'partners' to God. These passages also state that for Muḥammad the consequences of compromise would have been serious, eternally as well as temporally. These passages are possibly 'early Medinan',[1] but, whatever the date of revelation, there seem to be no strong reasons for denying that they are connected with the satanic verses and their abrogation. Another verse (6. 137) may also be connected with these events; it states that though 'they' (*sc.* the idolators) acknowledge God formally, in practice He is not so fully acknowledged as are the idols. That is the sort of fact which may have shown Muḥammad that the compromise would not work.

Sūrat al-Kāfirīn (109) is traditionally what Muḥammad was told to give by way of answer to the suggestion that he should compromise: 'Say: O ye unbelievers, I serve not what ye serve, And ye are not servers of what I serve. . . . Ye have your religion and I have mine.' This is a complete break with polytheism, and makes compromise impossible for the future. Two other passages are somewhat similar, though not so strong (6. 56 and 70), and the latter also speaks of the worship of idols as 'going back upon our steps'. The fact that there are three separate passages suggests that the temptation to compromise was present to Muḥammad for a considerable time.

The precise teaching of the Qur'ān about idols during the Meccan period is also worthy of note. The main purpose is apparently to show that worship of idols is pointless. Idols are powerless to benefit or harm a man,[2] and in particular they do not intercede on his behalf.[3] This will become clear on the Last Day, when their worshippers will appeal to them and they will disown them.[4]

[1] Bell, *Translation of Q.*

[2] 6. 46, 70; 10. 19, 35; 17. 58; 21. 44.

[3] 10. 19; 19. 90; 30. 10–12; 43. 86.

[4] 16. 88 f.; 18. 50; 19. 84–86; 28. 62–63, 74 f.

These verses seem to be addressed to people whose religious views were in process of transition. The idolators are said to regard the objects of their worship as 'intercessors' (10. 19), and this, if taken strictly, would imply that they recognized some higher being, and perhaps also that they accepted the Qur'anic doctrine of the Day of Judgement; but the latter point cannot be taken as certain, since the statements about the attitude of the idols on the Last Day would have some effect even on those who did not fully accept the doctrine. Again, when the idolators are said to make jinn partners to God, this need not imply that the idolators regarded them as jinn; the Qur'ān may express the matter thus because this was the view taken at the time by Muḥammad and others who had abandoned idol-worship. The Qur'anic attack on idols is thus not extreme at this period; it does not assert their non-existence as supernatural beings; but it was probably sufficient to cause serious doubts among those whose views on religion were already in a state of flux.

The phrase *Banāt Allāh* is a prominent object of attack. An *argumentum ad hominem* which occurs several times and is traditionally connected with the abrogation of the satanic verses is that it is impossible that God should have only daughters when the Meccans have both sons and daughters and considered the daughters inferior to the sons.[1] God cannot have any offspring at all since He has no spouse.[2] A careful distinction is made between children or offspring and servants; servants perform commands and do not intercede.[3] Thus it seems to have been felt that the word *banāt* implied or was capable of implying that the idols were roughly comparable with God. This was what chiefly was denied when the satanic verses were abrogated. The other points were presumably added later, along with some miscellaneous arguments not mentioned above.[4]

The Qur'ān thus fits in with what we learnt from the traditional accounts. Muḥammad must have had sufficient success for the heads of Quraysh to take him seriously. Pressure was brought to bear on him to make some acknowledgement of the worship at the neighbouring shrines. He was at first inclined to do so, both in

[1] 16. 59–60; 37. 149; 43. 15 ff.; 53. 21–22.

[2] 6. 100–1; cf. 17. 111.

[3] 21. 26–28; 7. 193–4; 19. 91–95.

[4] 21. 52–71—Abraham's trick; 6. 74, 80–82—Abraham and his father; 18. 48–49—hostility of the jinn to men; 28. 71–73—argument about night and day; 34. 26—challenge to show gods.

view of the material advantages such a course offered and because it looked as if it would speedily result in a successful end to his mission. Eventually, however, through Divine guidance as he believed, he saw that this would be a fatal compromise, and he gave up the prospect of improving his outward circumstances in order to follow the truth as he saw it. The rejection of polytheism was formulated in vigorous terms and closed the door to future compromise.

Westerners tend to think that Muslims confuse religion and politics in an undesirable way (though, of course, this is not confined to Muslims; oriental Christians and others do much the same). Perhaps, however, the truth is that Muslims see the religious bearing of political questions more clearly than do Westerners. Muḥammad was concerned with social, political, and religious conditions in Mecca, but he treated the religious aspect as fundamental. Yet because he was dealing with live issues his religious decisions had political implications. If the stories of offers from the leading Quraysh are correct, then Muḥammad must have been aware of the political aspects of his decisions, and in particular of his promulgation of the satanic verses and of the abrogating verses. Likewise he must have been aware, when he finally rejected compromise by repeating Sūrat al-Kāfirīn, that there could be no peace with Quraysh unless they accepted the validity of his mission. That further implied, according to Arab ideas of the authority of wisdom, accepting him as prophet, and therefore as the leading political figure; but Muḥammad may not have been aware of all this to begin with. He doubtless accepted the Qur'anic view that he was only a warner, and sought for no more than a religious function. Yet in the circumstances, that is, in view of the Arab conception of what constituted fitness or worthiness to bear rule, this divorce between prophethood and political leadership could not be maintained. How could any secular leader carry out a policy if the word of God, or even the word of His prophet merely, was against it? The mention of the goddesses is thus properly the beginning of the active opposition of Quraysh, and Sūrat al-Kāfirīn, which seems so purely religious, made it necessary for Muḥammad to conquer Mecca.

2. THE ABYSSINIAN AFFAIR

If the relative dating of events given in the letter of 'Urwah quoted above is to be trusted, then the *hijrah* or 'emigration' to

Abyssinia took place after the public recitation of Sūrat al-Kāfirīn with the abrogating verses. This order fits quite well the conclusions about the Abyssinian adventure to which we shall come on general grounds.

(a) *The Traditional Account*

The story as given by Ibn Hishām[1] is as follows:

Ibn Isḥāq said: When the Messenger of God (God bless and preserve him) saw the suffering which had come upon his companions, while he himself, through his position with regard to God and to his uncle Abū Ṭālib, was untouched, and when he saw that he was unable to protect them from such suffering, he said to them, Why do you not go away to the land of the Abyssinians, for there is a king there under whom no one is wronged, and it is a land of uprightness; (and remain there) until God gives you relief from this present situation. At that the Muslims, companions of the Messenger of God (God bless and preserve him), set out for the land of the Abyssinians through fear of trial (*fitnah*) and to escape to God with their religion. This was the first *hijrah* which took place in Islam. The first Muslims to set out were . . . (the names of ten adult males and their dependants follow).

These ten were the first of the Muslims to set out for Abyssinia according to my sources. Ibn Hishām said: Over them was ʿUthmān b. Maẓʿūn, according to what a scholar told me. Ibn Isḥāq said: Then Jaʿfar b. Abī Ṭālib set out, and the Muslims followed him one after another and joined together in Abyssinia. Some of them had gone there with their families, others had gone alone without their families. . . . (Then follow the names of 83 adult males, including those in the first list.)

On the basis of this account it is commonly said by later Muslim historians that there were two *hijrahs* to Abyssinia, and that certain persons, namely, those on the first list, took part in both. Some returned to Mecca and later took part in the *hijrah* to Medina; others did not return until the year A.H. 7 when they joined the Messenger of God at Khaybar.

(b) *The interpretation of the two lists*

The view that there were two separate and distinct emigrations to Abyssinia has been questioned by Western historians, notably Caetani[2] to whose treatment the following discussion is greatly

[1] 208 ff.

[2] *Ann.* i, pp. 262–72; cf. Buhl, in *Nöldeke-Festschrift*, Giessen, 1906, i. 13–22.

indebted. The main reason for rejecting the two *hijrahs* is that Ibn Isḥāq, as reported both by Ibn Hishām and by aṭ-Ṭabarī, does not in fact say that there were two *hijrahs*. He says, 'The first Muslims to set out were . . .' and gives a short list; then he continues, 'Then Ja'far b. Abī Ṭālib set out, and the Muslims followed him one after another. . . .' There is no mention of the first list returning in order to go back a second time; and the lists are not in order of priority in travelling to Abyssinia, but follow the order of precedence in which names, we may presume, were arranged in the public registers of the caliphate. Abū Sabrah is said to have been first to arrive in Abyssinia;[1] and 'Amr b. Sa'īd b. al-'Āṣ is said to have gone two years after his brother Khālid;[2] such facts and the word *tatāba'a* (followed one after another, or consecutively) suggest that there were not two large parties but a number of smaller groups. The impression one gets from Ibn Isḥāq is that there were two lists extant in his time of people who had gone to Abyssinia, but that he was uncertain about the exact relation of the two lists. If on the assumption that there was a single stream of emigrants, spread out possibly over years, and not two main parties, we are able to give a simple explanation of how there came to be two lists and what they were lists of, then that will go a long way to confirm the hypothesis of the single successive *hijrah*.

In the year A.H. 15 the caliph 'Umar revised the system whereby the Muslims received an annual grant from the public treasury in return for their services in war and administration. These annuities varied according to the date of a man's adhesion to Islam, those who became Muslims earliest receiving most. In the new system of the year 15 the highest class after the wives and kinsmen of the Prophet was that of those who had fought at Badr. But it seems probable that at some previous time the highest class had been rather that of the Muhājirūn, those who had performed the *hijrah*. From references to disputes about the matter it is certain that to have one *hijrah* or two to one's credit was a special honour and raised one to a higher rank in the new nobility of Islam. These disputes can hardly have been an invention of later times, since they lost most of their point after the reform made by 'Umar. What actually happened may be reconstructed somewhat as follows.

In the year 7 Muhammad specially wanted to strengthen his

[1] Tab. 1184. [2] IS, iv. 1. 73. 14.

position by gaining the support of the little group still in Abyssinia. He sent a messenger to assure them of a warm welcome and to escort them back, and they—or at least some of them—came. They were given a cordial welcome and a share in the spoils of Khaybar which Muḥammad had just captured. It was probably at this time that the name *hijrah* was given to the Abyssinian adventure, and that doubtless by Muḥammad himself as a justification for his more than generous treatment of Ja'far and his party; in virtue of their *hijrah* to Abyssinia these were presumably to be treated as *muhājirūn* and the equals of those to whom this title of distinction had hitherto been applied. Unfortunately this made it possible for some people, namely, those who had been in Abyssinia for a short time and had then made the *hijrah* from Mecca to Medina with Muḥammad, to retort that they had two *hijrahs* to their credit. Muḥammad managed to parry this to some extent: 'Well, so have the others; one to Abyssinia, and one from Abyssinia to me.'[1] When the first of the two lists mentioned above is closely scrutinized, it will be found that it is probably a somewhat incomplete list of those who made two *hijrahs*, only they were not both to Abyssinia, but one to Abyssinia and one to Medina. Most of those who were in Abyssinia and are also reckoned as having made the *hijrah* to Medina with Muḥammad are in the longer forms of this first list.[2]

'Umar, the later caliph, appears to have been one of the chief opponents of this favourable treatment of those who had remained so long in Abyssinia. At least an account has been preserved of an altercation between him and the wife of Ja'far b. Abī Ṭālib, in which Muḥammad intervened.[3] This throws light on what is involved in the classifications selected by 'Umar for his revised scheme of annuities. There is no mention of either *hijrah*, and the result is that those who had returned from Abyssinia only at the time of the Khaybar expedition were two classes below those who had fought at Badr.

(c) *The reasons for the emigration*

The above considerations, even if sound, do not greatly advance our understanding of the Abyssinian affair, for it is not so simple

[1] IS, iv. 1. 79. 8; cf. viii. 205, foot.
[2] Cf. Excursus G.
[3] Bukhārī, 64. 38 (iii. 128 f.); tr. iii. 165.

as the standard Muslim accounts suggest. This will become evident as we try to answer the question, For what reason did so many Muslims emigrate to Abyssinia?

The first possible answer is that they went to Abyssinia to avoid the hardships and persecution they faced in Mecca. This is implied in the letter of ʿUrwah and in the account of Ibn Isḥāq, although Muḥammad is there made to take the initiative; one could hardly suggest that these early worthies of Islam were moved chiefly by fear of suffering. In support of this answer it may be urged that those from Ibn Isḥāq's list of 'early Muslims' who did *not* go to Abyssinia belonged with two exceptions to the clans of Hāshim, al-Muṭṭalib, Zuhrah, Taym, and ʿAdī, either as full members or as confederates. These are the clans of the Ḥilf al-Fuḍūl with ʿAdī substituted for Asad, and it was apparently they who constituted the opposition to the groups round Makhzūm and ʿAbd Shams in which the chief financial power lay.[1] The leading opponents of Muḥammad belonged to the Makhzūm and ʿAbd Shams groups, and their persecution of his followers consisted in bringing pressure to bear on them from within the clan and even within the family. In the rival group, however, of Zuhrah, Taym, and the others, there would not be—it may be argued—the same eagerness to persecute the followers of Muḥammad, since he was primarily attacking the high finance which they also disliked, and therefore there would not be the same need for Muslim members of these clans to flee to Abyssinia. Of the two exceptions, al-Arqam (Makhzūm), though a young man, was apparently in a strong position—possibly head of his branch of the clan—since he was able to offer his house to the Muslims for a meeting-place, and therefore not so exposed to persecution as others. The other, Abū Aḥmad b. Jaḥsh (confederate of ʿAbd Shams), was a blind poet, and so in a special position; moreover Ibn Saʿd says he went to Abyssinia, though Ibn Isḥāq does not mention him.

There seems to be something in this argument and in the answer in support of which it is given. But there is also a telling objection to that answer. If the Muslims went to Abyssinia merely to avoid persecution, why did some of them remain there until A.H. 7, when they could safely have rejoined Muḥammad in Medina? There is no record of Muḥammad having told them to remain in Abyssinia after his own *hijrah* until he could provide for them adequately in

[1] Cf. I. 2 (a) above.

Medina; yet, had he done this, it would surely have been recorded. Any answer to this counter-question implies that the emigrants had some reason for what they did other than avoiding persecution, and probably more important than that.

A second possible reason for the emigration has been suggested by Western scholars. Noting that the earliest accounts speak of Muḥammad's initiative, they have inferred that he was concerned not so much to alleviate the physical hardships of his followers as to remove them from the danger of apostasy; if they remained in Mecca exposed to family pressure, they might easily deny their new faith. Yet this second reason is no more satisfactory than the first. To what could it lead? What grounds were there for expecting a reversal of fortune so that these people could safely return to Mecca? Meanwhile, some of them were staunch Muslims and would probably not have been seduced from their religion; would it not have been better to keep them in Mecca where their example would have inspired others?

A third possible reason is that they went in order to engage in trade. Now, since some of them lived there for perhaps a dozen years, they must have had some source of livelihood, and that would almost certainly be some form of mercantile operations. 'Urwah speaks of Abyssinia as within the sphere of Meccan commerce. Yet again this reason by itself is not sufficient to account for the actions of Muḥammad and the Muslims, unless we suppose that in sheer despair they were abandoning all hopes of religious reform in Mecca. But, even if that was the attitude of the emigrants, it was not the attitude of Muḥammad. We must therefore look for further reasons.

Fourthly, could it be that this was part of some subtle plan of Muḥammad's? Was he hoping to get military help from the Abyssinians, as his grandfather had possibly tried to get military support from Abrahah? They would probably not have been averse to an excuse for invading South Arabia in an attempt to recapture their lost dominion; and the Byzantine emperor—it was a year or two after the capture of Jerusalem by the Persians—would have approved of a diversion on the Persian flank. Or was Muḥammad hoping to make Abyssinia a base for attacking Meccan trade, as he did later from Medina? Or was he attempting to develop an alternative trade route from the south to the Byzantine empire, out of reach of Meccan diplomacy, and so to break the monopoly of the Meccan capitalists? It has been suggested above[1] that Meccan policy was essentially one of neutrality, but Abyssinia doubtless disapproved of Meccan readiness to trade with the Persians and was ready to do what it could to weaken Mecca economically. The story of how the Meccans sent two men as envoys to the Negus is to be accepted, and would support the view that the emigration had economic and political implications. But the precise nature of the mission and its result must remain matter for conjecture. It may have been successful in restraining the Negus from giving active help to the Muslims by informing him of their weakness in Mecca, even if it failed in its primary object (according to the standard account) of gaining their repatriation. Once again, however, this fourth reason, attractive as it is in some respects, does not explain why some of the Muslims remained so long in Abyssinia.

It is difficult to resist the conclusion that most weight must be attached to a fifth reason, namely, that there was a sharp division of opinion within the embryonic Islamic community. After giving the first list of emigrants from Ibn Isḥāq, Ibn Hishām adds a note to the effect that the leader was ʿUthmān b. Maẓʿūn; and Ibn Saʿd[2] records how even in the Jāhilīyah he avoided wine, and how, later, he wanted to introduce into Islam an ascetic note of which Muḥammad disapproved. ʿUthmān originally came to Muḥammad with four friends, quite important men, and was doubtless the foremost of them. He is thus almost certainly to be regarded as the leader of a group within the Muslims which was in some sense a rival to the group led by Abū Bakr. The remark of ʿUmar's, mentioned by Ibn Saʿd, that, until after the deaths of Muḥammad and Abū Bakr, he thought little of ʿUthmān because he died in his bed, is a relic of the rivalry between ʿUthmān b. Maẓʿūn and the group of Abū Bakr and ʿUmar.

There are also other hints of differences among the Muslims. Khālid b. Saʿīd (of ʿAbd Shams) was a very early Muslim who is said to have been the first to go to Abyssinia,[3] but he did not return till Khaybar; after Muḥammad's death he appears to have shown some hostility to Abū Bakr—probably another indication that there was a faction opposed to the latter. Interesting also is the case of al-Ḥajjāj b. al-Ḥārith b. Qays (Sahm); he is perhaps to be identified with al-Ḥārith b. al-Ḥārith b. Qays. He was taken a

[1] I. 2 (d). [2] iii. 1. 286–91. [3] ISaʿd, iv. 1. 67–72.

prisoner fighting against the Muslims at Badr;[1] but he also seems to have been one of the Muslims who emigrated to Abyssinia;[2] the latter point is admittedly doubted by some of the Muslim authorities, but, in view of his later record, their doubts are understandable and are not a reason for denying that he was an emigrant. If one emigrant to Abyssinia adopted such an attitude, may not others have done so also? There are a number for whose arrival in Medina no date is given in the sources.[3] Finally there is Nu'aym b. 'Abdallāh an-Naḥḥām ('Adī); he seems to have been the leading man in the tribe of 'Adī, and he and Abū Bakr were the most prominent men among the 'early Muslims' who did not go to Abyssinia. But a coolness seems to have sprung up between him and the main body, which was primarily Abū Bakr's party; at least he did not go to Medina until A.H. 6. Perhaps it was in part facts like this that 'Urwah had in mind when he said 'some were seduced'; of course 'Urwah is not an unbiassed witness, since his father, az-Zubayr b. al-'Awwām, had followed in the footsteps of 'Uthmān b. Maẓ'ūn, and he may not be accurate about motives and relative dating.

The conclusion of this discussion of reasons for the emigration is that, in so far as all the emigrants had the same reason—which is not a necessary assumption—it was the fifth. We need not suppose, however, that the difference of opinion had reached extreme lengths nor that the other reasons were entirely inoperative. Probably what happened was something like this.

The emigrants to Abyssinia were apparently men with genuine religious convictions. These convictions had in some cases been firmly held even before Muḥammad came forward as a prophet, as by 'Uthmān b. Maẓ'ūn and by 'Ubaydallāh b. Jaḥsh (who became a Christian in Abyssinia). Such men would be disinclined to accept the policy of Abū Bakr, with the probable implication that Abū Bakr was to be second in command to Muḥammad. What that policy was we can only conjecture. It may have been the insistence that Muḥammad must be accepted as political as well as religious leader because of the socio-political implications of the message he proclaimed. Those who remained in Mecca belonged to clans which (with the possible exception of 'Adī) would be most ready to follow a leader from the clan of Hāshim

[1] IH, 514; IḤajar, *Iṣābah*, i, no. 1608.
[2] IS, iv. 1. 144.
[3] Cf. Excursus H.

in view of the old Ḥilf al-Fuḍūl. Whatever Abū Bakr's policy, Muḥammad no doubt came to approve of it.

The statement that Muḥammad took the initiative may be an attempt to conceal base motives among those who abandoned him in Mecca; but it is not necessary to interpret the data in this way. It is in accordance with Muḥammad's character that he should quickly have become aware of the incipient schism and taken steps to heal it by suggesting the journey to Abyssinia in furtherance of some plan to promote the interests of Islam, of whose precise nature we remain unaware since in its ostensible aim it met with little success. The comparatively speedy reconciliation with 'Uthmān and the others who returned to Mecca before the *hijrah* to Medina at least suggests that there was never a complete break between them and Muḥammad. Certainly they came in the end to accept Muḥammad's leadership and the special position of Abū Bakr, and fought bravely as Muslims at Badr.

3. THE MANŒUVRES OF THE OPPOSITION

While the details given by Ibn Hishām and aṭ-Ṭabarī for the rest of the Meccan period are meagre, they do give a tolerably consistent picture of the outward manifestations of the opposition to Muḥammad. This is in keeping with that derived from the Qur'ān but not identical with it. Allowance must be made for exaggerations in certain directions, but there is probably less of this than has often been supposed by Western writers.

(a) *Persecution of Muslims*

The following description of Abū Jahl by Ibn Isḥāq[1] seems to be free from exaggeration.

> It was the wicked Abū Jahl who used to incite the men of Quraysh against them (*sc.* the Muslims). When he heard of the conversion of a man of high birth with powerful friends, he criticized him vigorously and put him to shame. 'You have left your father's religion,' he said, 'although he is a better man than you; we shall make your prudence appear folly and your judgement unsound, and we shall bring your honour low.' If he was a merchant, he said, 'By God, we shall see that your goods are not sold and that your capital is lost'. If he was an uninfluential person, he beat him and incited people against him.

Thus it is not asserted that Abū Jahl's persecution of the

[1] IH, 206 f.

Muslims was more severe than verbal attacks on influential persons, economic pressure on lesser men, and bodily violence towards those without any influential backing. As most of the clans of Quraysh were sufficiently strong to cause serious inconvenience, if not worse, to anyone who maltreated a clansman or confederate, those exposed to physical violence were very few and comprised slaves and persons without any clear clan connexion (like Khabbāb b. al-Aratt). Clansmen and confederates could be formally disowned by the clan, though this tended to lower the clan's honour. This seems to have happened to Abū Bakr, since we find him accepting the protection of Ibn ad-Dughunnah,[1] and we also hear of Ṭalḥah and him being bound together. In any case his clan, Taym, was not powerful. Muḥammad may also have been deprived of clan protection at the time of his visit to aṭ-Ṭā'if, for he was badly handled there, and before he re-entered Mecca he appealed to members of other clans for protection.

It is doubtless actions like those of Abū Jahl which the sources have in mind when they speak of the seduction or trial (*fitnah*, *yaftinū*) to which the Muslims were subjected. This is not, however, severe persecution. The point is confirmed by a study of the details in Ibn Hishām, aṭ-Ṭabarī, and Ibn Sa'd's biographies, for what are mentioned there are presumably the worst cases and not average ones. All goes to suggest that the persecution was slight. The accusations made by Western scholars that the extent of persecution has been exaggerated thus hardly apply to the earliest sources. Perhaps the chief instances of exaggeration would be those cases where it serves to clear a man from a possible charge of apostasy.

The materials at our disposal illustrate the different manifestations of opposition mentioned in the passage from Ibn Isḥāq. Muḥammad was attacked verbally and subjected to minor insults, such as having his neighbours' rubbish and waste dumped at his door; the unpleasantness possibly increased after the death of Abū Ṭālib.[2] The reduction of Abū Bakr's capital from 40,000 to 5,000 dirhams between his conversion and the Hijrah[3] was probably mostly due to economic pressure such as Abū Jahl threatened and not to the purchase of slaves as is stated in Ibn Sa'd, since a slave cost only about 400 dirhams.[4] The most

[1] IH, 245 f.
[2] IH, 183–5; Ṭab. 1198 f.
[3] IS, iii. 1. 122.
[4] Cf. IS, iii. 1. 27. 21.

notable examples of bodily violence were the sufferings of the slaves like Bilāl and 'Āmir b. Fuhayrah.[1] Closely akin to this was the refusal of al-'Āṣ b. Wā'il to pay a legitimate debt to Khabbāb b. al-Aratt.[2] Yet a fourth type of persecution might be named —the application of pressure (including physical measures) to members even of influential clans and families by fathers, uncles, and elder brothers. The treatment of al-Walīd b. al-Walīd, Salamah b. Hishām, and 'Ayyāsh b. Abī Rabī'ah by Abū Jahl and other kinsmen is perhaps the best-known instance,[3] but several others are to be found in the pages of Ibn Sa'd. The man-handling of the confederate 'Ammār b. Yāsir and his family by B. Makhzūm[4] is probably to be regarded as falling under this head.

The persecution of the Muslims was thus mostly of a mild nature. The system of security in force in Mecca—the protection by each clan of its members—meant that a Muslim could not be seriously molested by a member of another clan, even though his own clan had no liking for Islam; failure to defend a clansman attacked by an outsider was a stain on the honour of the clan. Thus persecution was limited to (*a*) cases where clan-relationships were not affected, as when the persecutors were fellow clansmen or the victim had not effective protection from any clan, and (*b*) actions not considered in the traditional code of honour, such as the economic measures and perhaps also verbal and other minor insults that affected only the individual and not his clan. This very limited persecution was perhaps sufficient to give a fillip to the nascent Islam, but not sufficient to deter any serious believer. It may even have strengthened Islam by causing converts of poor quality to apostatize.

(b) *Pressure on B. Hāshim*

What made it possible for Muḥammad to continue preaching in Mecca until 622 despite opposition from powerful members of the community was the system of security just described. The chief of the clan of Hāshim at this time was Muḥammad's uncle Abū Ṭālib who, though he was not a Muslim, was ready to accord to Muḥammad the full protection due to a member of the clan. The leaders of Quraysh, headed by Abū Jahl, appealed more than once, it would seem, to Abū Ṭālib either to stop Muḥammad proclaiming his new religion or else to withdraw his protection from

[1] IH, 205, &c. [2] IS, iii. 1. 116. [3] IH, 206, &c. [4] IH, 206.

him. Abū Ṭālib, however, refused to do either of these things, and managed to secure the approval of the clan for the course he adopted.[1] (The clan of al-Muṭṭalib, though formally separate, joined with Hāshim for many purposes and acted as if they were one clan.)

To uphold the honour of the clan would in itself be a sufficient reason for Abū Ṭālib's acting in this way; but there was probably more in the matter than that. It has been noticed above that the clan of Hāshim seems to have been going down in the world during the previous decades. To abandon one of their best younger men at this stage would have been a serious loss of strength, and the implied confession of weakness would have still further impaired their position. Moreover, underlying the question of Muḥammad and the honour of the clan there was probably also a question of economic policy. The movement led by Muḥammad, though primarily religious, impinged upon economic matters, and in this respect it could perhaps be regarded as continuing the attitude of the Ḥilf al-Fuḍūl of opposition to unscrupulous monopolists. To this extent Muḥammad might be regarded as continuing the traditional policy of Hāshim, and it would therefore not be surprising if he also received a certain measure of general support from his clan. It is noteworthy that Abū Ṭālib also gave protection to another Muslim, Abū Salamah b. ʿAbd al-Asad, his sister's son, who belonged to the clan of Makhzūm,[2] and that Abū Lahab supported him in this.

The case of Abū Lahab is interesting since he yielded to the pressure that was being exerted upon the clan of Hāshim. He was a younger brother of Abū Ṭālib, but he had managed to marry a sister of Abū Sufyān, one of the principal men of ʿAbd Shams and after A.H. 2 the principal leader of Mecca as a whole. When the opposition against Muḥammad hardened, he took his stand with his wife's clan against his nephew. It was doubtless about this time that the engagement of Muḥammad's daughters to his two sons was broken off. We may suppose that Abū Lahab's line of conduct was influenced by his business relations with ʿAbd Shams.

Eventually Muḥammad's opponents, foiled in their attempt to detach him from his clan, managed to bring together a grand alliance of nearly all the clans of Quraysh against Hāshim (with

[1] IH, 168–70; Ṭab. 1178–80. [2] IH, 244.

al-Muṭṭalib). On the one hand, this was a stage in the campaign against Muḥammad; but on the other hand, it was also a stage in the aggrandizement of Makhzūm and their associated clans at the expense of the Ḥilf al-Fuḍūl, for it involved the disruption of the latter. The poem of Abū Ṭālib with Ibn Isḥāq's notes[1] is important confirmatory evidence. Even if some of it is a later forgery, much must have been written by someone familiar with the state of affairs in Mecca at this time, and may very well be a genuine work of Abū Ṭālib himself. Some of the names mentioned are not usually included in the lists of opponents of Muḥammad. What is most important is that the men who are reproached for turning against Hāshim are *all* members of clans in the Ḥilf al-Fuḍūl. Their names, if we accept Ibn Isḥāq's identifications, are: from 'Abd Shams, Asīd and his son, Abū Sufyān, Abu 'l-Walīd 'Utbah; from Taym, 'Uthmān b. 'Ubaydallāh and Qunfudh b. 'Umayr b. Jud'ān; from Zuhrah, Ubayy or al-Akhnas b. Sharīq and al-Aswad b. 'Abd Yaghūth; from al-Ḥārith b. Fihr, Subay'; from Asad, Nawfal b. Khuwaylid; from Nawfal, Abū 'Amr and Muṭ'im. Moreover these men are reproached for allying themselves with the old enemy: al-Ghayāṭil or B. Sahm, B. Khalaf or B. Jumaḥ, and Makhzūm.

With the formation of the grand alliance a boycott of the clans of Hāshim and al-Muṭṭalib was instituted. None of the other clans was to have any business dealings with them, and there was to be no intermarriage. This boycott was apparently maintained for over two years, though perhaps not always with absolute strictness, since various members of the boycotting clans were closely related to Hāshim by marriage. If Hāshim was able to maintain its own caravans to Syria, it would possibly be not too badly off; at any rate there is no record of any complaint, and that tends to confirm the point that the giving of protection to Muḥammad was not the sole reason for the dispute.

According to Ibn Isḥāq's account of the end of the boycott,[2] the initiative was taken by Hishām b. 'Amr (of 'Āmir), and he was supported by Zuhayr b. Abī Umayyah (Makhzūm), al-Muṭ'im b. 'Adī (Nawfal), and Abū 'l-Bakhtarī and Zam'ah b. al-Aswad (both of Asad). In the assembly of Quraysh, however, it was Zuhayr who rose first. His mother was 'Ātikah bint 'Abd al-Muṭṭalib, and Abū Ṭālib was his maternal uncle, so that he had reasons of affinity for

[1] IH, 172–8.

[2] IH, 247–9.

helping Hāshim. It is noteworthy that in the poem of Abū Ṭālib's mentioned above[1] the highest praise is given to Zuhayr for coming to the assistance of Hāshim; and that may well refer to this incident.

Once again it is important to notice the clans to which these five belonged, for this gives us some clue to the nature of the opposition within the grand alliance. Zuhayr was presumably moved primarily by the tie of blood; but as a member of Makhzūm he was a most suitable person to lead the attack on a policy inaugurated mainly by members of that clan. The others, however, were probably moved chiefly by other factors. They belonged to the clans of Nawfal, Asad, and 'Āmir, which had joined the grand alliance, but had not been members of the old Aḥlāf, which probably constituted the inner circle. The absence of the other members of the Ḥilf al-Fuḍūl is probably not significant except that of 'Abd Shams; but the latter suggests that this clan was now coming to have very close business relations with Makhzūm and in consequence common interests, and that these rather than traditional alliances were now moulding its policy. If we may hazard a guess about the motives of the boycott-breakers, it would be that with the passage of time they had realized that the grand alliance and the boycott were strengthening the position of the strong clans which aimed at establishing monopolistic controls over Meccan trade, and were consequently weakening the position of the other clans.

With the death of Abū Ṭālib after the end of the boycott Muḥammad's relations with his clan passed into a new phase; but this topic belongs to the next chapter.

(c) *Offers of compromise to Muḥammad*

There is an interesting reference, placed by both Ibn Isḥāq and aṭ-Ṭabarī after the beginning of the boycott, but probably earlier, to an attempt by some of the leading men of Mecca to get Muḥammad to agree to a compromise. Aṭ-Ṭabarī has two forms of the story, and Ibn Isḥāq a third;[2] aṭ-Ṭabarī's second version is said to come from Ibn Isḥāq, but does not occur in Ibn Hishām's recension. Apparently what happened was that four men met Muḥammad and offered him wealth and influence if he would cease reviling their idols; they would worship God, and he was to

[1] From IH, 172–8.
[2] Ṭab. 1191; IH, 239.

acknowledge the idols. Such a compromise, as was said above, would have been fatal to Muḥammad's claims, and he wisely rejected it. The identity of the four men is interesting. They were: al-Walīd b. al-Mughīrah (Makhzūm), al-'Āṣ b. Wā'il (Sahm), al-Aswad b. al-Muṭṭalib (Asad), Umayyah b. Khalaf (Jumaḥ). Three of these were leaders of clans belonging to the Aḥlāf, the old rivals of Hāshim and the Ḥilf al-Fuḍūl; and this tends to confirm the authenticity of this report. The mention of al-Walīd suggests that this event may have taken place before Abū Jahl assumed the leadership of Makhzūm, and therefore before the beginning of the boycott; the motive would then be a realization that Muḥammad's prophethood, if accepted, would inevitably lead to his political leadership. It is also possible, however, that the event occurred after the beginning of the boycott, as the sources place it, and that the four men were not in entire agreement with the policy of the boycott. Al-Walīd, as an older man, could not have regarded Muḥammad as a serious personal rival, as Abū Jahl may have done; and he might also have been more genuinely concerned about the worship of idols. The offer, if genuine, would imply that these men realized something of Muḥammad's gifts as a statesman.

4. THE WITNESS OF THE QUR'ĀN

The Qur'ān, as Caetani noticed,[1] tends to confirm the impression received from a critical study of the early historians that the persecution of the Muslims was mild and did not include any acts strictly forbidden by custom. The frequent references in the Qur'ān to Muḥammad's opponents are largely concerned with their verbal criticisms of his message and of himself. There is, as we shall see, mention of plots and schemes against Muḥammad and the Muslims, but hardly of anything that really merits the name of persecution. The verbal criticisms may have started long before the affair of the satanic verses; they certainly seem to belong to strata of the Qur'ān earlier than those where idols are mentioned and where it is asserted that God has no children.

(a) *Verbal criticisms of the message*

The form of criticism referred to most frequently in the Meccan passages is criticism of the resurrection. The Meccans, regarding the body as an essential part of the man, could not conceive how

[1] *Ann.* i, p. 244.

a human body could possibly be restored to life after it had mouldered in the grave. This seemed to them to be a crushing retort to Muḥammad's assertions.

> And when they are reminded, they do not keep it in mind,
> And when they see a sign, they seek to make fun,
> And say: 'This is nothing but magic manifest;
> When we die and become dust and bones, are we to be raised up,
> And our fathers of olden time as well?'[1]

While this question may have been asked chiefly for polemical reasons, it was in fact in line with the real beliefs of the Meccans.

> They say: 'There is nothing but this present life of ours; we die and we live, and it is only Time (or Fate) which destroys us.' (45. 23 DE.)

Again and again in the Qur'an they are reproached for disregarding the future life and thinking only of prosperity in this life.

The passage from Sūrah 37 quoted above also illustrates a further point sometimes connected with the one just mentioned. The Meccans described this restoring to life of mouldering bodies as magic; and the word 'magic' seems to have had the connotation that the thing was a trick and not genuine.[2] This thought probably lies at the back of most of the references to magic in the Qur'ān, though it is also possible that some of them, and especially those to Muḥammad as a magician, refer rather to the process of revelation.

The Qur'ān is not concerned with resurrection in abstraction, but only with resurrection as implicit in the judgement of the Last Day and the resulting eternal reward and punishment. The question about mouldering bodies was doubtless popular with the opponents of Muḥammad because it seemed to them to be a telling objection to the whole eschatological doctrine. The Qur'ān makes it clear that they rejected that doctrine in its entirety, though the references are mostly brief.[3] This brevity suggests that the mouldering bodies may have bulked more largely in popular discussion, but the rejection of judgement would have more serious practical consequences, since it would mean that the sanction that was being introduced for the code of individual behaviour would remain ineffective.

[1] 37. 13–17 C; cf. 79. 10 D; 75. 3 f. C; 56. 46–48 ED; 44. 34 f. C; 50. 2 f. D; 19. 67 C; 23. 37–39 E; 23. 84 f. EF; 17. 52–54 CE; 17. 100 E?; 27. 69 C?; 32. 9 C.

[2] 52. 15 C; 43. 29 E.

[3] Cf. 74. 47 E?; 83. 10 f. E?; 52. 11–14 C; 37. 20 f. C; 37. 50 f. E; 25. 12 D; 107. 1 E?.

Disbelief in the Last Day probably also was behind the question addressed to Muḥammad, 'When is the Hour?'[1] The Qur'ān has answers to this question, or at least responses which parry it, but it may have caused embarrassment to Muḥammad, which was perhaps the chief aim of the questioners.

The many passages in the Qur'ān which speak about God's 'signs' appear to be the response or reaction to the difficulty about the resurrection of the body. The Qur'ān regards God's creation of man through the process of conception and the slow development of the embryo in the womb and His subsequent provision for sustaining man's life as a 'sign' that He is also able to restore him to life after he has lain in the grave. While some of the 'sign passages' are chiefly concerned with showing God's existence and His power in general, there are others that make it clear that the primary importance of many of the signs was as evidence of God's abilities to restore men's bodies.

> Does man think that he will be left roaming at will?
> Was he not a drop of semen emitted in desire?
> Then he was a blood-clot; and He created and formed him;
> And made of him the two sexes, the male and the female.
> Is not That One able to restore the dead to life?[2]

Needless to say, the stubborn opponents of Muḥammad and of the religion he preached were not convinced by the signs, and disbelief in the signs is added to the other forms of disbelief.[3] Sometimes apparently the unbelievers retorted to the mention of signs by saying, 'Produce our fathers, then'.[4] Sometimes they dismissed the signs as 'old-world tales' (*asāṭīr al-awwalīn*).[5] The phrase occurs a number of times in the Qur'ān, and many of the instances may have behind them this criticism of the signs and the theodicy implied in them.

All the criticisms of the content of the Qur'ān that have been mentioned so far are various aspects of the attack upon its eschatological teaching. This emphasis on eschatology in the discussions between Muḥammad and his opponents tends to confirm the view maintained in chapter III that some teaching about the Last Day was part of the primary message of the Qur'ān. This whole line of thought is summed up in the word *takdhīb*, 'unbelief' in the

[1] 79. 42–44 C; 51. 12 D?; 36. 48 C; 67. 25 f.?; 21. 39–41 C; 17. 53 C?.

[2] 75. 36–40 C. Cf. 79. 27–33 C; 56. 57–73 C; 50. 6–11 B; 19. 68 C; 36. 77–83 CE; 17. 52–54 C?.

[3] 90. 19 C; 78. 28 C; &c.

[4] 45. 24 DE.

[5] 83. 13 E?.

sense of 'counting false' (as distinct from *kufr* which is 'unbelief' as contrasted with *īmān* or 'faith'). One can 'disbelieve' or 'count false' the resurrection, the Last Day, the future life, the signs and, more generally, the warning and the message. Sometimes the object of attack is unbelief and unbelievers without qualification, *takdhīb* and *mukadhdhibūn*; and the latter term comes to be a synonym for Muḥammad's opponents.

The other main focus of discussion in respect of the content of the revelation was the question of idols and the unity of God. Here it was rather the Qur'ān that took the initiative in attack, while the pagans of Mecca were on the defensive. Something has been said in the first section of this chapter about this point, so that it need not be treated again here. Mention may be made, however, of the appeal to the customs of the fathers. The Meccans (and others) are represented as saying that they found their fathers following a certain religion and that the wisest course for themselves is to follow in their fathers' footsteps.[1] This is not explicitly an accusation against Muḥammad of deviating from the way of the fathers, but that was perhaps implied. It has the outward appearance of being rather a defensive position; they are not prepared to follow Muḥammad even though he brings them better guidance, and they refer to the customs of the fathers as a justification in general terms of their conservative attitude.

Part of the point of the stories of the prophets which occupy so much of the Meccan passages of the Qur'ān is that they are a counterblast to this claim to follow in the steps of the forefathers. The Muslims must have felt they were deserting their ancestors, especially when asked difficult questions about the present or future state of deceased pagans. The stories of the prophets doubtless helped them to realize that, as followers of a prophet, they had a distinguished spiritual lineage. Thus these stories served not merely to encourage the Muslims; they also corresponded roughly to the *mafākhir* where the poet boasted of the excellence of his tribe—a common feature of pre-Islamic poetry—and so helped the Muslims to realize that they were members of a community with roots deep in the past.[2]

[1] 43. 21–23 C?; cf. 21. 54 DE.

[2] Cf. G. von Grünebaum, *Von Muḥammads Wirkung und Originalität*, in *Wiener Zeitschrift für die Kunde des Morgenlandes*, xliv, 1937, pp. 29–50, esp. 44 f.; Rudi Paret, *Das Geschichtsbild Mohammeds*, in *Die Welt als Geschichte*, 1951, pp. 214–24, esp. 217 f.

It is noteworthy that there is no overt criticism of the insistence on generosity in the primary message of the Qur'ān. This is possibly due to the fact that, though the practice of the pagans did not exemplify the virtues commended in the Qur'ān but rather the vices castigated, they did not feel inclined in public to make a theoretical defence of their practice. To be selfish is one thing; to uphold selfishness as an ideal is another. We need not suppose that the pagans had a bad conscience on the matter, though a few of the more sensitive may have felt some twinges. They need only have been aware of the fact that their conduct, while not formally breaking any accepted rules, was contrary to the spirit of the traditional Arab code of honour. If this is correct, then it tends to show that the Qur'ān does not set out a completely new morality, but extends the traditional Arab ethical conceptions to circumstances and conditions outside the range of the nomad's experience.

(b) *Verbal criticisms of Muḥammad's prophethood*

Besides criticisms of the message there are criticisms of the messenger—criticisms of Muḥammad's claim to have received revelations from God and of the process of revelation. The belief that the words which came to him were a revelation from God must have been present to Muḥammad from a very early period, whatever the precise form of the original experience of receiving a revelation; and the claim that this was so must have been involved in his public preaching from the first. Some of the early passages of the Qur'ān record attempts of the opposition to discomfit Muḥammad by suggesting other explanations of his experiences than that they 'came down' from God.

The commonest allegation against Muḥammad was apparently that he was *majnūn*, mad, or, more precisely, possessed by jinn.[1] But they also suggested that he was a *kāhin* or soothsayer,[2] a *sāḥir* or magician-sorcerer,[3] and a *shā'ir* or poet.[4] It is difficult to think ourselves back into the mentality of the pagan Meccans when they used these words; but from the Qur'anic handling of the matter and from many facts recorded elsewhere[5] the main points are clear. Those who made allegations of this kind did not deny that Muḥammad's experiences had in some sense a supernatural cause;

[1] Cf. 81. 22 B; 68. 2 C; &c.
[2] 69. 42 B; 52. 29 B?.
[3] 38. 3 C.
[4] 69. 41 B; 52. 30 B?; &c.
[5] Cf. A. Guillaume, *Prophecy and Divination*, lecture 6; D. B. Macdonald, *The Religious Attitude and Life in Islam*, Chicago, 1909, esp. pp. 24–36.

but they implied that this was either a demonic being or a supernatural power of low grade, quite other than the Power that controls the universe. Even the assertion that Muḥammad was a poet had this reference to the supernatural, since the view of his contemporaries was that the poet has a familiar spirit or jinn; we actually find the phrase *shā'ir majnūn*, poet possessed, in the Qur'ān.[1] These assertions about the origin of the revelations had the consequence that the warnings and other matter contained in the revelations need not be taken seriously; they were not necessarily true. The underlying thought is probably that the supernatural beings who produce or bring the revelations may be either malevolent or lacking in knowledge. These allegations may have been made solely in order to discredit Muḥammad and not because the people who made them believed in them; but on the whole it is most likely that they thought they were true. To these charges the Qur'ān usually gives the lie direct; indeed, in some cases the charges are inferred from the denial. There are two interesting passages, however, where the reality of Muḥammad's visions is put forward as a refutation of the suggestion of demonic origin.[2] These have been discussed in another context, and mere reference to them will suffice here.

A second attempt by opponents to account for the revelations was the assertion that they were a completely human production, the work either of Muḥammad himself or of a human assistant.[3] If these passages are from the Medinan period,[4] one can easily imagine such charges being made by the Jews of Medina. But the traditional accounts regard this accusation as having been made during the Meccan period, and name several persons who were supposed to have helped Muḥammad.[5] The historian will acknowledge Muḥammad's complete sincerity in his belief that the revelations came to him from outside himself, and will also admit as a possibility that prior to the revelation Muḥammad heard some of the stories recounted or alluded to in the Qur'ān from the alleged informants; and he will then leave it to the theologian to effect some sort of reconciliation. In any event, whether there was any justification for the charge, it is a fact that the charge was made, and made with a view to discrediting Muḥammad and his mission.

1 37. 35 c.
2 81. 15–27 B; 53. 1–18 B.
3 25. 5 f. E; 32. 2 E; 16. 103–5 ED.
4 Bell, *Translation of Q.*
5 Cf. Sale and Wherry on 16. 105.

These allegations that Muḥammad invented the message with human help are, of course, distinct from the charge, which occurs in several passages where magic is mentioned,[1] that the revelations are human speech. In these latter cases the thought is perhaps that the rhythmic and assonanced prose is a spell produced by the sorcerer from his esoteric knowledge, and in this sense human; but he was doubtless supposed to have received the knowledge from the jinns.

A third line of attack was to say that Muḥammad was not the sort of person to whom revelations would come. He was not sufficiently important,[2] and so when he appeared and made his claims men simply ridiculed him.[3] Once again such remarks are not to be taken as impartial statements of fact. The narratives about the prophets are commonly taken to reflect Muḥammad's circumstances; and we find Thamūd saying to Ṣāliḥ that he was one of whom they had good hopes,[4] and Midian address Shu'ayb as 'the clement, the right-minded one',[5] even although a little later they say, 'we see thee to be weak amongst us, and were it not for thy company we should stone thee; to us thou art not of much account'.[6] These assertions of Muḥammad's unimportance must, one would think, have been made originally at Mecca, since by the time he had settled in Medina he had acquired a certain importance. The references to the followers of other prophets as vile or slaves[7] perhaps indicate a taunt against Muḥammad; but the point cannot be pressed.

It was presumably another type of opponent who expected revelation to have supernatural accompaniments observable by all. When they saw that Muḥammad was no more than a human being, they argued that he could not be a messenger from God.

They say: 'We shall not give thee credence till thou causest for us to bubble up from the earth a spring;
Or until thou hast a garden of palm and vine, and thou cause in the midst of it rivers to gush forth;
Or until thou cause the heaven to fall upon us in fragments as thou hast said, or thou producest God and the angels assenting;
Or until thou hast a house of ornamental work, or thou ascendest into the heaven; nor shall we give credence to thy ascent until thou bringest down to us a writing which we may read.' Say: 'Glory be to my Lord! am I anything but a human being (sent) as a messenger?'

[1] 74. 24 B?; 21. 3 E; 38. 3 C; &c. [2] 43. 30 E. [3] 25. 43 DE. [4] 11. 65 C. [5] 11. 89 C?. [6] 11. 93 C–E+. [7] 26. 111 C–E; 23. 49 E; &c.

Nothing prevents the people from believing when the guidance has come to them, but that they say: 'Hath God sent a human being as a messenger?'[1]

There is some variation in the precise nature of what is expected or demanded, but the underlying assumption is always the same, namely, that the Divine can only be manifested in time through a disturbance of the natural order. The old Semitic idea that the righteous prosper in this world may also have been present. Another criticism—the question why the revelation did not come to Muḥammad all at once[2]—may belong to the same train of thought.

Coupled with some of the above assertions there appears to have been a criticism of Muḥammad's motives, if we may judge from what is said about Noah.[3]

But the nobility, those of his people who disbelieved, said: 'This is only a man like yourselves who wishes to gain pre-eminence over you; if God had willed, He would have sent angels; we never heard of this among our fathers of old.
He is only a man possessed; wait and see (what befalls him) for a time.'

Most of the phrases used here fit in best with the situation in Mecca and the mentality of its people; and the Meccan leaders' offer to Muḥammad of wealth and position, if authentic, shows that it had occurred to them to credit him with ambition. His rejection of this offer, however, and the general tenour of his conduct at Mecca make it improbable that political ambition was among his dominant motives. The Qur'ān, too, insists again and again that he is only a warner. His function is simply to warn people that there is a Judgement followed by eternal reward or punishment. How they respond to the warning is their own responsibility; they have been warned! In one passage it is expressly stated that Muḥammad is not a *muṣayṭir*, that is, a person who has some sort of control over other people.[4] The further insistence that Muḥammad, like other prophets, does not seek any reward from men but only from God, doubtless is a reaction to this accusation of self-seeking.[5] Finally, a passage, apparently from the

[1] 17. 92–96 E?; cf. 21. 7 f. D; 25. 8 f. DE; 25. 22 f. DE; 26. 154 C–E; 41. 13 C.
[2] 25. 34 D?. [3] 23. 24 f. C–E. [4] 88. 22 C.
[5] 38. 86 C; cf. 36. 20 C; 26, vv. 109, 127, 145, &c., C–E; 11. 31 and 53 C–E; 12. 104 C?.

early Medinan period, indicates the acceptance of the political leadership which had come to Muḥammad as conferred by God.

But We wished to bestow favour upon those who had been held weak in the land, and to make them leaders, and to make them the inheritors;

To give them position in the land, and to let Pharaoh, Hāmān, and their hosts see from them the very thing they were on their guard against.[1]

There is nothing inconsistent in such an attitude. In accordance with the Qur'ān Muḥammad conceived his function as primarily religious, that of being a warner; but in the circumstances of Mecca such a function had political implications, and when events developed these implications to the point at which political action was necessary, Muḥammad did not shrink back, since he regarded the leadership thrust upon him as from God.

(c) *The actions of Muḥammad's opponents*

The verbal criticisms and discussions occupy far the larger part of the picture of the opposition in the Qur'ān; but there is also sufficient material to show that they acted as well as argued. There are no detailed descriptions of their activity, but for the most part only general references to their scheming and plotting; for that two words are used, *kayd*[2] and *makr*[3]; the former word seems to have come into use at an earlier period than the latter. There seems to be no objection to supposing that by these words the Qur'ān in its Meccan passages refers to the manœuvres of the opposition which were considered in the previous section, and especially to the political and economic pressure which culminated in the boycott of the clans of Hāshim and al-Muṭṭalib. The response or reaction of the Qur'ān is to exhort Muḥammad to be patient[4] and to wait for God to act; God will frustrate their knavish tricks as He did those of the Men of the Elephant.[5] Muḥammad had previously been told to bear the verbal criticisms patiently;[6] and such patient endurance was clearly the wisest course at Mecca. The prophetic stories are used to encourage the Muslims to endure by showing how those who rejected the prophets sent to them were punished and how God delivered the prophets and those who

[1] 28. 4 f. E, from the story of Moses.

[2] 86. 15 f. D; 52. 42 C?; 37. 96 C; 20, vv. 62, 67, 72 C–E, &c.

[3] 34. 32 DE; 13. 42 DE, &c.

[4] 76. 24 C?; 86. 17 D; 73. 11 C; &c.

[5] 105 C.

[6] 73. 10 B; 50. 38 BC; 20. 130 C–.

believed in them. It may be that it was in reaction to the hostile activities of the opposition that emphasis came to be laid on temporal punishment as distinct from eternal. Certainly the idea would spring naturally out of such a context. The schemer is hoist with his own petard, or rather is out-schemed by God; and the failure of the scheme and consequent reversal of fortune is essentially temporal.

A more particular instance of hostile activity is the preventing of an *'abd* from praying.[1] Since *'abd* can mean 'servant' with the connotation 'servant of God' this passage is sometimes said traditionally to refer to Muḥammad himself; *'abd*, however, can also mean 'slave', and it seems more likely that the reference is to an actual slave, since the less influential members of the new community suffered most in ways of this sort. The story of the men of the Trench (*ukhdūd*)[2] is traditionally referred to the persecution of the Christians of Najrān, and, if that were sound, might reflect persecution at Mecca; but Western scholars are now inclined to regard the passage as a description of Hell. Certainly by itself the passage cannot be taken as evidence of the persecution of the Muslims. The Medinan passage[3] which speaks of the Muslims as having emigrated after they were tried or tested (*futinū*) need not imply anything more than the *kayd*, together with family pressure. The opening of Sūrat al-Qalam, however, seems to be a reference to the attempts to bring Muḥammad to some sort of compromise, especially when it is said that those who disbelieve 'would like if thou wouldst dissimulate',[4] while he is frequently urged[5] not to obey his opponents, or, as we may interpret it, accede to their requests, or yield to their threats. A passage that tradition refers to the affair of the satanic verses—though it might easily have some other occasion, even a Medinan one, in view—shows that the danger of compromise was a real one.

Verily they nearly tempted (*yaftinūna*) thee from that which We suggested to thee that thou mightest invent about Us something else; and in that case they had taken thee as a friend.
Had it not been that We made thee stand firm, thou hadst almost leaned towards them a little.
In that case We should have made thee taste the double of life and the double of death, and then thou wouldst not find against Us a helper.[6]

[1] 96. 9 ff. BC. [2] 85. 1–7 E. [3] 16. 111 E+.
[4] 68. 9 C?. [5] 96. 19 BC; 76. 24 C?; &c. [6] 17. 75–77 E?.

It is difficult, but not altogether impossible, to see how the refusal to prostrate oneself at the reciting of the Qur'ān could be a valid charge against Muḥammad's opponents;[1] one is therefore tempted to imagine that the verse might refer to some opposition from among the believers or to apostasy. If the passages which speak of people not giving the Zakāt are Meccan, they also might refer to this.[2] The evidence of the Qur'ān on this point is thus somewhat precarious.

In general, then, the Qur'ān tends to confirm the picture derived from the traditional historical material. The verbal criticisms and disputations seem to have been the chief feature of the opposition. The principal hostile activity is described as *kayd* and *makr*, words which suggest subtlety and perhaps danger, yet always within the letter of the law. The criticisms may have included false assertions, the plots may have led potentially to disaster, but there is no evidence for any severe persecution or anything that could be called oppression.

5. THE LEADERS OF THE OPPOSITION AND THEIR MOTIVES

It remains to ask about the character of the group or groups of Meccans who opposed Muḥammad and about their reasons for doing so.

The first part of this investigation is the easier. Even if we admit that the opposition to Muḥammad was milder than is commonly supposed, it is clear that it was led by the most influential men of the chief families of Quraysh. The names of the persons mentioned as opponents during the Meccan period have been regarded with some suspicion by Western scholars, since they are mostly found in the lists of those killed or taken prisoner at Badr, and might therefore reflect the state of affairs about two years after the Hijrah. This suspicion is increased by the fact that the poem of Abū Ṭālib mentioned above, which deals with the political situation about the time of the boycott and is probably genuine, contains several names not usually given as those of Muḥammad's opponents. On the other hand, the lists of opponents include several persons who died before Badr, like al-Muṭʿim b. ʿAdī, and

[1] 84. 21 D?.
[2] 36. 47 E+; 41. 6 E+?; they are Medinan according to Bell, *Translation*.

these appear to fade out of the story about the correct time. It is therefore almost certain that the compilers whose works are still extant possessed genuine historical materials and used these intelligently; and that the lists of opponents are in general sound.

The most prominent opponent for some years before his death at Badr was Abū Jahl of the clan of Makhzūm. Previously the chief man in Mecca had probably been al-Walīd b. al-Mughīrah,[1] head of Makhzūm, but he was possibly not quite so bitterly opposed to Muḥammad. It was Abū Jahl who organized the league of the various clans against Hāshim and al-Muṭṭalib. The break-up of that league shows that there was a strong party of pagans which was not ready to follow Abū Jahl all the way, but it is hardly possible to say anything about their distinctive reasons for opposing Muḥammad.

It is sometimes suggested that the strongest motive underlying the opposition was the fear that, if Mecca adopted Islam and abandoned idolatry, the nomads would cease to come to the sanctuary and Meccan trade would be ruined. This is not very satisfactory, however. There is no record of any attack on the worship at the Ka'bah in the Qur'ān or elsewhere; it was only subsidiary features that were altered and purified at the conquest of Mecca. The original attack on idols, as has been maintained above, was an attack on the worship at specific shrines in the neighbourhood. These shrines would hardly be sufficiently important for their desertion to lead to a general ruin of Meccan trade. Indeed, it seems probable that a great deal of Meccan trade was now independent of the visits of nomads to the Ka'bah or other sanctuaries. Consequently this theory of economic fears because of the attack on idolatry is best forgotten.

What is almost certainly true, however, is that those particular individuals who had trade connexions with the particular shrines involved in the attack were extremely annoyed. The shrine of al-Lāt at aṭ-Ṭā'if was one of the three, and in the letter of 'Urwah we read that it was some Quraysh who had property in aṭ-Ṭā'if who began the active opposition to Muḥammad. It is likewise possible that there were other groups whose special interests were adversely affected by some point of Muḥammad's preaching.

The chief reason for opposition, however, was almost certainly that the leaders of Quraysh saw that Muḥammad's claim to be a

[1] IH, 238.

prophet, if taken seriously, had political implications. The old Arab tradition was that rule in the tribe or clan should go to him who had most wisdom, prudence, and judgement. If the Meccans believed Muḥammad's warning, and then wanted to know how to order their affairs in the light of it, who would be the best person to counsel them if not Muḥammad? Doubtless they remembered the connexion between the Christianity of 'Uthmān b. al-Ḥuwayrith and his attempt to become prince of Mecca. Even if Muḥammad is sincere in professing to be merely a warner, they may have thought, will he be able to resist the opportunity of attaining supreme power when circumstances offer it to him?

The leaders of Quraysh were probably also sufficiently far-sighted to recognize the opposition between the ethics of the Qur'ān and the mercantile activities which were their life. There was no whisper of the forbidding of usury till long after the Hijrah. But from the very first there was criticism of their individualistic attitude to wealth. This must have been little to the liking of the financiers of Mecca, even if they avoided discussing it publicly. Perhaps they felt that these ethical ideas would gain Muḥammad much political support if he became politically minded. Some may even have felt that this was a reopening of the old dispute about policy between Makhzūm with its friends and the Ḥilf al-Fuḍūl.

In placing these grounds of opposition in the forefront we do not imply that the Qur'anic attack on idolatry met no resistance. The Arabs were by nature or nurture conservatives, and the Qur'ān frequently describes pagans adhering to their paganism merely because it was the way of their fathers and they did not choose to leave it. Even in later Islam this conservative tendency continued, and 'innovation' (*bid'ah*) is the regular word for heresy. It has been suggested above that certain strands among the opposition—notably elder statesmen like al-Walīd for whom Muḥammad could not be a serious personal rival—were moved mainly by this point. They had no theoretical defence of paganism to offer; it was change as such that they detested, perhaps felt to be immoral, although the gods meant little to them. It is significant that another early historical passage (that from az-Zuhrī quoted in IV. 1) gives as a reason for opposition, in addition to the attack on idols, the assertion that their pagan ancestors would be in Hell. This piety towards ancestors is closely related to reverence for tradition.

While some of the opponents were thorough-going individualists, the more conservative probably retained a certain group-loyalty. They would therefore see in the tendency of Islam to cause sharp divisions within a family a further proof that this departure from the beaten track of the ancestors led to unpleasant results. It might seem to be undermining the whole social structure. Indeed, in a sense, it was doing so.

The grounds of opposition to Islam were thus, besides self-interest, fear of its political and economic implications, and sheer conservatism. The situation which confronted Muḥammad was a malaise which had social, economic, political, and intellectual symptoms. His message was essentially religious in that it attempted to remedy the underlying religious causes of the malaise, but it affected the other aspects, and consequently the opposition also had many facets.

VI

EXPANDING HORIZONS

1. THE DETERIORATION IN MUḤAMMAD'S POSITION

NOT long after the end of the boycott, and within a short time of one another, Muḥammad lost by death his uncle and protector Abū Ṭālib, and his faithful wife and helpmate, Khadījah. The year was probably A.D. 619. We have no evidence of what Khadījah meant to Muḥammad at this period; earlier, we are told, she had confirmed his resolution when it wavered, and we may conjecture that, at the very least, her support still meant something to him. If so, it was doubtless good for him to be compelled to be more self-reliant. He did indeed marry again at no great interval—the woman was Sawdah bint Zamʿah, one of the earliest Muslims and now a widow—and this may indicate a need for spiritual companionship. But we hear little further about Sawdah, and may suppose that her relations with Muḥammad were chiefly in the domestic sphere. The experience of Muḥammad at Nakhlah on his return from aṭ-Ṭā'if, when he received comfort in his mood of depression, might be taken as marking a stage in his weaning from reliance on human companionship.

The repercussions of the death of Abū Ṭālib were in the political sphere. His successor as chief of the Banū Hāshim appears to have been his brother, Abū Lahab. Although Abū Lahab had joined the 'grand alliance' against Hāshim during the boycott, he is said at first to have promised to protect Muḥammad in the same way as Abū Ṭālib had done.[1] This account may well be accepted, for the self-respect of an Arab *sayyid* would dictate such a course. If this conduct seems to contradict his previous hostility, the contradiction may be softened by supposing that his hostility to Muḥammad prior to Abū Ṭālib's death has been exaggerated because of his hostile conduct later.

After a time, however, Abū Lahab formally refused protection to Muḥammad on the grounds that Muḥammad alleged ʿAbd al-Muṭṭalib to be in Hell. The traditional account is that ʿUqbah b. Abī Muʿayṭ and Abū Jahl suggested that he should question Muḥammad on this point. The form in which the story has come

[1] IS, i. 1. 141.

to us is naïve, but there is no reason to doubt its essential truth. Muḥammad's enemies would point out to Abū Lahab that, because Muḥammad made such remarks about their common ancestor, Abū Lahab could abandon him without any loss of self-respect.

The loss of security was on the surface a great disaster for Muḥammad and for the cause of Islam. There had been no important conversions to Islam since that of 'Umar, probably three or four years before this time, but the failure of the boycott might have been regarded as the beginning of a movement which would lead to an improvement in the prospects of the new religion. The abandonment of Muḥammad by Abū Lahab, however, nipped all such hopes in the bud. Even if the Muslims could still maintain themselves in Mecca—which was by no means certain—there was little likelihood of the adherence of others to Islam. In such circumstances, if Islam was not to fade away, some fresh line of activity was urgently required. All that could be done in Mecca had been done; therefore the chief hope lay in advances elsewhere. Muḥammad had originally regarded himself as a prophet sent solely or primarily to Quraysh, and there is no way of telling whether prior to the death of Abū Ṭālib he had thought of an expansion of his mission to the Arabs in general. The deterioration in his position, however, now forced him to look farther afield, and during his last three years in Mecca we hear only of dealings with nomadic tribes and with the citizens of aṭ-Ṭā'if and Yathrib.

2. THE VISIT TO AṬ-ṬĀ'IF

In some ways aṭ-Ṭā'if was a smaller replica of Mecca, though there were also important differences. Aṭ-Ṭā'if was a mercantile centre which had specially close connexions with the Yemen. The tribe of Thaqīf, the inhabitants of aṭ-Ṭā'if, engaged in long-distance trading, often in collaboration with Quraysh. At the same time aṭ-Ṭā'if had a much better climate than Mecca, and parts of the surrounding country were very fertile. The district was noted for raisins, and one of the distinctive features of the Thaqīf was that they lived on cereals whereas other Arabs were content with dates and milk. Many of the wealthier Meccans had land in aṭ-Ṭā'if, and used it as a summer resort. In particular the clans of Hāshim and 'Abd Shams had close relations with aṭ-Ṭā'if, and Makhzūm had at least financial dealings with Thaqīf. On the whole Thaqīf were less powerful than Quraysh and—possibly as a result of the war of the Fijār[1]—had to acknowledge their supremacy in finance, with all that that entailed. Yet the relationship was not entirely one-sided since a confederate from aṭ-Ṭā'if, al-Akhnas b. Sharīq, was for a time the leading man of the clan of Zuhrah at Mecca.[2]

There were two main political groups in aṭ-Ṭā'if, the Banū Mālik and the Aḥlāf. The latter were probably those longest settled in the district since they were custodians of the sanctuary of the goddess; it is misleading to speak of them as plebeians. The Banū Mālik were intimately connected with the great tribe of Hawāzin which dominated the surrounding country, while the Aḥlāf, to counterbalance this advantage, sought support from Quraysh. That the inferiority of Thaqīf to Quraysh was due to their greater internal disunity is possible but by no means certain.

It was to aṭ-Ṭā'if that Muḥammad apparently first turned in his quest for fresh adherents to Islam. The traditional account[3] is that, in view of the increasingly humiliating treatment to which he was subjected after the death of Abū Ṭālib, he went to seek a protector. But this cannot have been his sole reason. The sources speak of him hoping for converts, and such a hope perhaps already implies the idea of inaugurating an Islamic community, such as later came into existence at Medina. At the same time the possibility should not be entirely overlooked that he expected some calamity to befall Mecca after its rejection of him, and wanted to remove his followers. There must almost certainly have been some point of dissension in local politics of which Muḥammad wanted to take advantage, but we have not sufficient evidence to say what it was. The particular men approached by Muḥammad, 'Abd Yalīl and his brothers, belonged to the clan of 'Amr b. 'Umayr which was included in the Aḥlāf, and so were presumably favourable to Quraysh. Perhaps Muḥammad hoped to attract them by the bait of financial deliverance from the clutches of Makhzūm.[4]

Whatever the precise nature of Muḥammad's proposals and the reasons of the B. 'Amr b. 'Umayr for rejecting them, they sent Muḥammad away with nothing accomplished and even encouraged the town rabble to fling stones at him. It is said that in this sorry plight he found shelter in the garden of two brothers of the Meccan

[1] Cf. I. 2 d.
[2] Cf. Lammens, *Ṭā'if*.
[3] IH, 279–81; Ṭab. 1199–1202.
[4] Cf. Lammens, *Ṭā'if*, 100/212.

clan of 'Abd Shams, who are often mentioned among his leading opponents.

He eventually set out on his way back to Mecca, doubtless in great dejection of spirits. Tradition tells how at Nakhlah during the night, while he was engaged in worship, a company of jinn came and listened, and went off believing;[1] and even if this story owes much to later editing, we may well believe that at this critical period of his life Muḥammad 'took refuge with God'.

Muḥammad did not immediately re-enter Mecca but proceeded to Ḥirā' on the outskirts, and from there began to negotiate for the protection (*jiwār*) of the head of one of the clans. This must indicate that his own clan under Abū Lahab had refused to protect him further. Moreover, as soon as his visit to aṭ-Ṭā'if and its political implications became generally known to his opponents in Mecca, their hostility would be more active. The first men whom he approached, al-Akhnas b. Sharīq of B. Zuhrah and Suhayl b. 'Amr of B 'Āmir, refused his request. Eventually al-Muṭ'im b. 'Adī, head of B. Nawfal, agreed to take Muḥammad under his protection. We may suppose that he laid down certain conditions, though there is no mention of these in the sources. This is not surprising, however, since the story is repeated in honour of the clan of Nawfal. Later it was passed over lightly, since it was discreditable to Hāshim; it is seemingly omitted by Ibn Isḥāq.[2] It is noteworthy that none of the Muslims, not even 'Umar, was sufficiently powerful to give Muḥammad protection.

3. APPROACHES TO THE NOMADIC TRIBES

The traditional accounts mention at this point that Muḥammad took the opportunities provided by various fairs to preach to some of the nomadic tribes. In particular the earliest sources[3] mention the B. Kindah (and a chief Mulayḥ), the B. Kalb, the B. Ḥanīfah, and an individual of B. 'Āmir b. Ṣa'ṣa'ah. The first three rejected Muḥammad outright, the last after Muḥammad had refused to promise them the political succession to his own position.

It is difficult to know why these tribes and no others are mentioned. It may be largely a matter of accident, but it is also possible that Muḥammad had some special reasons for expecting that they

[1] Cf. Sūrah 72.
[2] IH, 281; inserted on p. 251 by Ibn Hishām himself.
[3] IH, 282 f.; Ṭab. 1204–6.

might listen to what he had to say. A section of B.ʿĀmir b. Ṣaʿṣaʿah was apparently attracted to Muḥammad, as is learnt from the events surrounding the affair of Bi'r Maʿūnah in A.H. 4. The other three tribes all had territories at a considerable distance from Mecca, and were either wholly or partly Christian. But it is impossible to be certain that these facts are the reason for their mention in this connexion. What we are justified in believing is that at this period Muḥammad began to summon members of nomadic tribes to accept Islam, and that behind this activity there was at least a vague idea of the unity of all Arabs.

4. NEGOTIATIONS WITH MEDINA

(a) *The existing state of affairs in Medina*

Medina is the usual English form of *al-Madīnah*, the city (or perhaps 'place of justice'); it is said to be a shortening of *Madīnat an-Nabī*, the city of the Prophet. Prior to Muḥammad's connexion with it it was known as Yathrib. It was not so much a city as a collection of hamlets, farms, and strongholds scattered over an oasis, or tract of fertile country, of perhaps some twenty square miles, which was in turn surrounded by hills, rocks, and stony ground—all uncultivable.

The dominant section of the population was the Banū Qaylah, later known as the Anṣār (or Helpers, *sc.* of Muḥammad). This tribe or tribal group consisted of the related stems of the Aws and the Khazraj, each of which was divided into a number of clans and sub-clans. According to tradition the Aws and the Khazraj had migrated to Yathrib from South Arabia and settled in apparently unoccupied lands as clients of the existing inhabitants. Eventually they were sufficiently numerous, with some assistance from outside, to gain political supremacy in the oasis. This took place about the middle of the sixth century A.D. or a little later.[1]

Of these earlier inhabitants two strong and wealthy groups occupying fertile lands remained largely independent of the Aws and the Khazraj, namely, the Banū Qurayẓah and the Banū 'n-Naḍīr. While similar to their neighbours in many ways, these two groups adhered to the Jewish faith and vigorously maintained their credal and ritual distinction. It is not clear whether they were of

[1] Cf. Wellhausen, *Medina vor dem Islam*, in *Skizzen u. Vorarbeiten*, iv, 1889, p. 7.

Hebrew stock or were judaized Arabs; possibly isolated Arabs had attached themselves to small groups of Hebrews.[1] In Muḥammad's time there was also a third, less influential, Jewish tribe, Banū Qaynuqāʿ, and some small bodies of Arabs, quite distinct from the Aws and the Khazraj, which were perhaps the remains of the Arabs who had inhabited the oasis prior to the arrival of Jewish settlers.

The Aws and the Khazraj had frequent feuds with one another. Mostly these involved only one or two clans on each side. But the so-called war of Ḥāṭib involved almost the whole of the Aws and the Khazraj (and the Jewish tribes as well), and culminated in the battle of Buʿāth a few years before the Hijrah—perhaps in A.D. 617. This restored an uneasy balance, chiefly owing to the exhaustion of all concerned.

Medina was thus suffering from a malaise as serious as that of Mecca, but completely different in its symptoms, though the underlying disease is similar, namely, the incompatibility of nomadic standards and customs—in fine, nomadic ideology—with life in a settled community.

The economic aspect of the troubles was doubtless the pressure of increasing population on limited food-supplies. The result of the petty warfare in which the people of Yathrib engaged was frequently that the victors occupied the lands of the vanquished.[2] When, as after the battle of Buʿāth, there was no formal peace but only a cessation of hostilities, men had to be constantly on guard against sudden murderous assaults and to refrain from entering the territory of the other side. Even though the date-palm can produce fruit with less attention than other crops require, this state of affairs must have led to some deterioration in the quantity and quality of the yield. The trees themselves were not usually harmed, but the insecurity of tenure must have kept men from thinking of long-term schemes of improvement. What in fact was happening was that the desert principle of 'keep what you have armed strength to keep' was being applied to cultivated land. When one is dealing with flocks and herds spread over vast areas this principle is satisfactory, but within the narrow bounds of an oasis it leads to an unpleasant situation.

[1] Cf. Caetani, *Ann.* i, p. 383; Torrey, *Jewish Foundation*, ch. 1; D. G. Margoliouth, *Relations between Arabs and Israelites, &c.*, London 1924, lecture 3.

[2] Cf. Wellhausen, op. cit., *passim*.

The principles of social organization found in the desert were retained in Yathrib. Each clan was responsible for the life of its members; that is to say, it exacted a life for a life or else compounded for blood-money.[1] Since a man would defend his property with his life (to some extent, at least), tribal solidarity would virtually guarantee security of property. But where the factor of distance found in the desert is absent, this basing of security on force—the armed strength of the group—is disastrous. A settled community requires a single supreme authority to keep the peace between rival individuals and groups, and that is something which lies outside the purview of nomadic thought and, aeroplanes and armoured cars apart, outside the physical possibilities of desert life.

In Mecca commercial interests tended to draw different groups together and fostered a sense of the unity of Quraysh (though the grievances of the underprivileged had a contrary divisive effect). There was no comparable factor at Medina, where the population was less homogeneous. A small family group is an adequate unit for agriculture. On the other hand, there was probably less individualism than in the mercantile atmosphere of Mecca, doubtless because in Arabian conditions agriculture did not give opportunity for such wide divergences in wealth as did commerce.

In Ibn Saʿd's biographies of those who fought at Badr on the Muslim side he arranges Quraysh in fifteen 'clans' whereas thirty-three are mentioned for the Aws and the Khazraj, and this can probably be used as evidence to show that agricultural conditions foster fragmentation. The larger number of the subdivisions of the tribes at Medina might be due to the convenience of genealogists, since there were far more Medinans than Quraysh. Or, again, it may somehow be connected with the persistence of vestiges of matriarchy at Medina, or with the greater number of generations between the Anṣār of Badr and their common ancestor.

Quite apart from the relevance of this evidence, however, Medina was much divided; and the lack of unity, with the suicidal warfare to which it led, meant that the point which had been at the root of the opposition in Mecca—Muḥammad's position as prophet and its political implications—was the very thing which offered the Medinans some hope of peace. The idea may be present in the verse:

Each community has a messenger, and when their messenger comes,

[1] Cf. the Constitution of Medina, IH, 341–4.

judgement is given between them with justice, and they are not wronged.[1]

A prophet, with authority resting not on blood but on religion, could stand above the warring blood-groups and arbitrate between them. The sources speak of the Anṣār imagining that Muḥammad was the Messiah expected by the Jews and hastening to get on good terms with him.[2] But, if there is any truth in this story, it is that the conception of a Messiah helped to familiarize the Anṣār with the idea of a community whose centre of integration was a person with special qualifications of a religious character.

The Anṣār thus had a solid material reason for accepting Muḥammad as prophet, and this reason was doubtless not without influence. But the malaise of Yathrib had also a religious root. In the nomadic outlook shared by the men of the Aws and the Khazraj the meaning of life is found in the honour and prowess of the tribe or clan. Such a conception is best realized in comparatively small closely knit units. It does not apply to a large unit like the Anṣār as a whole, where perhaps most of the members had no contact with outsiders. The nomadic life fosters solidarity only within the smaller groups. In Yathrib, moreover, there was little that was glorious in the petty murdering that went on. ʿAbdallāh b. Ubayy seems to have attempted to be neutral at Buʿāth—at least he took no part in the fighting;[3] this is perhaps a mark of hearty sickness with the endless feuds. To this religious problem, if it may be so called, Islam had a solution. Its doctrine of the Last Day implied that the meaning of life is in the quality of the conduct of the individual. This conception is capable of becoming the basis of a large community, since, where it is accepted, one man's gain no longer entails another's loss. Doubtless the Anṣār had some realization of these implications when they accepted the doctrines of Islam, but the majority of them presumably became Muslims primarily because they believed the doctrines to be true, and in particular because they believed that God had sent Muḥammad with a message to the Arabs.

(b) *The Pledges of al-ʿAqabah*

Tradition records claims made on behalf of two members of the Aws killed prior to the battle of Buʿāth that they died as Muslims. The first definite converts, however, were six men of the Khazraj

[1] Q. 10. 48 c?.
[2] IH, 286; Ṭab. 1210.
[3] Wellhausen, op. cit., 34, 55 f., 59–62.

who came to Muhammad probably in 620. At the pilgrimage of 621 five of these six returned bringing with them seven others, including two of the Aws. These twelve are said to have made a promise to avoid various sins and to obey Muḥammad. This is known as the Pledge of the Women,[1] *bayʿat an-nisāʾ*. Muḥammad sent back to Medina with them Muṣʿab b. ʿUmayr, a trusty follower and one well-versed in the Qurʾān. Within the next year converts were made from all the families of Medina with the exception of that section of the Aws known as Aws Manāt or Aws Allāh. For the pilgrimage of 622 a party of Muslims, seventy-three men and two women, went to Mecca, met Muḥammad secretly by night at al-ʿAqabah and took an oath not merely to obey Muḥammad but to fight for him—the Pledge of War, *bayʿat al-ḥarb*. Muḥammad's uncle ʿAbbās was present to see that the responsibilities of Hāshim to Muḥammad were genuinely shouldered by the Aws and the Khazraj. Muḥammad asked for twelve representatives (*nuqabāʾ*) to be appointed, and that was done. Quraysh got word of the negotiations, which appeared to them hostile, and questioned some of the pagan Medinans, who answered in good faith that there was no truth in the report. Muḥammad now began encouraging his followers to go to Medina—Abū Salamah is even said to have gone *before* the Pledge of al-ʿAqabah —and eventually there were about seventy of them there, including Muḥammad himself. This is the Hijrah or migration of the Prophet; 'hegira' is an old transliteration, and 'flight' an inaccurate translation. The first day of the Arabian year in which the Hijrah took place, 16 July, A.D. 622, was later selected as the beginning of the Islamic era.[2]

With this standard traditional account may be compared an early version of the events by ʿUrwah b. az-Zubayr, preserved by aṭ-Ṭabarī:[3]

On the return from Abyssinia of certain of those who had migrated there, before the migration of the Prophet (God bless and preserve him) to Medina, the adherents of Islam began to increase and be numerous. Many of the Anṣār in Medina were converted, and Islam spread in Medina, and the people of Medina began to visit the Messenger of God (God bless and preserve him) in Mecca. When Quraysh observed that, they were moved to bring pressure to bear on (the Muslims) and

[1] Cf. Buhl, *Muhammed*, 186, n. 147.
[2] Ṭab. 1207–32; IH, 286–325.
[3] 1224–5.

to try to get them to apostatize. They seized them and were eager to make them apostatize. Great distress did (the Muslims) suffer. This was the latter trial (*fitnah*). There were (in all) two trials, one which caused some of them to go away to Abyssinia, when (Muḥammad) gave them this command and permitted them to go away, and one when they returned and saw those of the people of Medina who visited them. Later there came to the Messenger of God (God bless and preserve him) from Medina seventy representatives, the chief of those who had been converted. They met him during the pilgrimage and pledged themselves to him at ʿAqabah, giving him their oaths (in the words), 'We are of you (sing.), and you are of us', and 'If you or any of your companions come to us, we will defend you from whatever we defend ourselves from'. Upon that Quraysh increased their pressure on them and the Messenger of God (God bless and preserve him) gave his companions the word to go away to Medina. This was the latter trial during which the Messenger of God (God bless and preserve him) made his companions go away to Medina, and himself went there. It was in respect of this that God most high revealed the verse (2.189), 'Fight them until there is no *fitnah*, and until the religion is all God's'.

In connexion with this version of ʿUrwah we must remember that he belonged to the family of az-Zubayr which was hostile to that of Umayyah, and that his family tradition would therefore be inclined to exaggerate the persecution and its influence on the course of events seeing that the clan of Umayyah were deeply involved in the opposition to Muḥammad. Hence the motivation suggested by ʿUrwah need not be taken as a balanced account of the matter. The verse of the Qur'ān is to be dated late in the Medinan period,[1] and therefore did not originally have the application here suggested.

The absence of mention of two distinct meetings at ʿAqabah in ʿUrwah's version might seem to confirm the view held by some Western scholars that there was only one such meeting. The main ground for this view is that the oath sworn at the first Meeting, the Pledge of the Women, is based on a Qur'anic passage which is admittedly later.[2] But, even if this is the source of the precise wording of the pledge in the standard account, it does not follow that there was no meeting. On the contrary, it is clear that there must have been long and careful negotiations between Muḥammad and the Medinans. When he sent Muṣʿab to Medina, it was not merely to instruct the new converts, but also to report on the

[1] Bell, *Translation of Q.*

[2] Cf. Buhl, *Muhammed*, 186; Q. 60. 12.

situation there. We may therefore accept the broad lines of the traditional account. The first effective contacts were with the Khazraj, but Muḥammad insisted on meeting a more representative group, since he could not trust himself to one of the rival clans without the other. At this meeting, whatever the exact details may have been, there must have been a provisional agreement between Muḥammad and the Medinans which included some acknowledgement of Muḥammad as prophet (though such an acknowledgement doubtless meant less now than it did after al-Ḥudaybiyah).

Again, in connexion with the second or main Meeting at al-'Aqabah, there are details which may be questioned, but the general outline must be accepted. The whole incident of 'Abbās is probably to be rejected as a later invention to conceal the dishonourable treatment of Muḥammad by the Banū Hāshim at this juncture; on his return from aṭ-Ṭā'if Muḥammad was under the protection of the head of the clan of Nawfal, and in view of the absence of references to any change of status in the sources it is practically certain that Muḥammad was under the protection of B. Nawfal and not of his own clan. The argument that the incident is genuine because 'Abbās is represented speaking as a pagan is unsound; paganism gave less of a handle to opponents (at the end of the first Muslim century) than dishonour. The account attributed to Wahb b. Munabbih and preserved in a papyrus[1] tends to confirm the above view. In this version 'Abbās praises Muḥammad highly; then Muḥammad permits one of the Medinans to reply, refuting 'Abbās and showing that they thought more highly of Muḥammad than he did. The impression given is that this is an anti-'Abbasid reply to 'Abbasid propaganda. Quite apart from this version of Wahb (which by itself raises some difficult questions) the most satisfactory supposition is that the visit of 'Abbās to al-'Aqabah was a sheer invention of 'Abbasid propagandists.

There is also some difficulty about the appointment of the twelve *nuqabā'* or representatives since they do not appear to have fulfilled any function. Some Western writers have suspected that they were introduced into the story in order to make Muḥammad similar to Moses and Jesus. In the version of Wahb one of the Medinans pledged himself to Muḥammad 'on the same terms as the *nuqabā'* from the tribe of Israel pledged themselves to Moses', and another

[1] G. Mélamède, 'The Meetings at al-'Akaba', in *Le Monde Orientale*, xxviii, 1934, pp. 17–58.

'on the same terms as the *ḥawārīyūn* did to 'Īsā b. Maryam'.[1] The story of how Muḥammad became *naqīb* for the Banu 'n-Najjār when their original representative died, however, shows that that suspicion is unfounded, and also that there was no deliberate imitation of these great exemplars. The probability is that the *nuqabā'* are a part of the primitive organization of the new community or *ummah* in Medina, which soon fell into disuse.

On the other hand, the main point about the Meeting, namely, that some Pledge of War was involved, is to be accepted, though we cannot be certain just how far this pledge went. The Medinans must also have agreed to receive the Muhājirūn or emigrants from Mecca on favourable terms. What is not clear is how far the Medinans committed themselves to hostility to Quraysh. Doubtless they were suspicious of the growing power of Mecca, and the fact that Muḥammad was *persona non grata* in Mecca would be a guarantee that he would not be used for the extension of Meccan influence. But in welcoming him and giving him a position of influence in Medina were they not throwing down the gauntlet to the Meccans?

The answer to this question is bound up with the answer to others. What plans had Muḥammad for his companions after they went to Medina? How did he propose that they were to exist? He cannot have intended them to remain permanently the idle guests of the Medinans, and he can hardly have expected them to settle down as farmers. In Medina they could gain a livelihood only as merchants sending out caravans or else as organized raiders of Meccan caravans. But even the former alternative, if it was the original plan—and there are few signs of that—would soon have led to active hostility with Quraysh, and Muḥammad would have foreseen that. In short, Muḥammad must have realized that his migration to Medina would lead sooner or later to fighting with the Meccans. How much of this did he communicate to the Medinans and in what form? And how much did they realize of themselves? Much more, we may suspect, than our sources indicate.[2]

Caetani has expressed the view[3] that the Medinans accepted Muḥammad as a superior soothsayer merely because they were interested in the internal peace of Medina and not because they accepted the full teaching of the Qur'ān, at least in the sense

[1] Text, *ap.* Mélamède, op. cit., p. 4. Cf. Q. 5. 15.

[2] But cf. IH, 313 f., &c.

[3] *Studi*, iii. 27–36.

intended; only a handful, he thinks, were genuine converts. This view rightly emphasizes the material factors (as indeed does Ibn Isḥāq), but it unnecessarily minimizes the religious or ideological, and the two are not opposed but complementary. We may agree that the essential division in Medina was between those who wanted to bring in Muḥammad and those who did not, and also that the 'conversions' would not have proved lasting but for Muḥammad's political successes. It is also possible that to some extent the Medinans interpreted the Judaeo-Christian ideas of the Qur'ān in pagan-Arabian terms, and so misunderstood them, as Caetani suggests. Yet we must hold that the bulk of the Medinans who supported Muḥammad understood in essence and accepted the main principles of Islam: God as creator and ruler of the world and as judge on the Last Day, and Muḥammad as the mediator of God's message to the Arabs. The Muslims were creating a community of a fresh type in Medina, and this new creation required a clear and definite ideological basis. Few of the Medinan Muslims may have been religious enthusiasts, but all of them must have been sufficiently convinced of the reality of religious relationships to join in the experiment of a community based on bonds of religion instead of those of kinship.

5. THE HIJRAH

Once the Medinans had pledged themselves to support Muḥammad he lost no time in carrying out his plans. The Pledge had been kept secret and he had to achieve as much as possible before his overt actions gave his opponents some indication of his plans. He therefore gave the word to his followers in Mecca to leave Mecca and betake themselves to Medina. Ibn Isḥāq's version[1] makes it clear that what moved him and them was the brighter prospects of the movement in Medina. 'Urwah's suggestion that they went to escape persecution gives a wrong emphasis; there is no trace of a fresh wave of persecution prior to the Hijrah or emigration to Medina with the possible exception of the case of Abū Salamah[2] and of the insults addressed to Muḥammad himself and Abū Bakr; there was probably some persecution or at least vigorous opposition *after* the leaders realized what Muḥammad was doing. Under these circumstances we may suppose that Muḥammad's word to his companions was exhortation and per-

[1] IH, 314. 6 ff. [2] IH, 314 ff.

suasion, not command; some, such as Nuʿaym an-Naḥḥām, who had once been a prominent Muslim, remained in Mecca, but these men were never charged with apostasy.[1] In this first wave about seventy persons in all are said to have migrated to Medina; they travelled in small groups and all arrived safely. The Muslims in Medina provided the *Muhājirūn* or Emigrants with lodging.

At length, according to the standard account, only ʿAlī and Abū Bakr were left in Mecca along with Muḥammad. Muḥammad's reasons for thus waiting until the majority had reached Medina were probably to ensure that waverers did not abandon the enterprise and to make it certain that he would be in a strong and independent position when he reached Medina and would not have to rely solely on the support of the Medinan Muslims.[2] Meanwhile the leaders of Quraysh had become aware that something was afoot and held a council in which after some discussion they agreed to Abū Jahl's plan that a band of young men, one from each tribe, should strike Muḥammad simultaneously with their swords so that the blood-guilt was spread over them all and therefore could not be exacted.[3] It is worth noting that at this council the clan of Nawfal was represented by Ṭuʿaymah b. ʿAdī and Jubayr b. Muṭʿim, the brother and son of the man who had given protection to Muḥammad; but whether he himself was dead or was merely staying away we do not know. The other tribes whose representatives are named are ʿAbd Shams, ʿAbd ad-Dār, Asad, Makhzūm, Sahm and Jumah; these are in fact groups B and C of the table on p. 6. There seems to be no reason for denying that some such meeting took place and that those who were present, as Ibn Isḥāq suggests, realized that Muḥammad was planning hostile activities against them. On the other hand, subsequent events make it clear that there was no resolute attempt to kill Muḥammad; and it may therefore be that there was less agreement at the meeting than the sources assert. The imminence of danger, however, perhaps precipitated Muḥammad's departure.

It is difficult to be certain about the exact extent and nature of the danger. The whole story of the Hijrah has been much embellished and even the earliest sources are probably not free from additions. After the meeting of the council it is possible that Muḥammad might have been molested in Mecca itself, but, to

[1] Cf. Caetani, *Ann.*, p. 364; Q. 8. 73.

[2] Ibid., p. 365.

[3] IH, 323 f.

judge from Muḥammad's actions, the greatest danger was while he was on the road. There was doubtless a point at which he might be presumed to have left the sphere in which his Meccan protectors were responsible for him and yet not to have become the responsibility of the Medinans; in this middle region he could be killed without involving his murderer in a blood-feud. Abū Bakr who accompanied him was probably in a similar position since his clan appears to have renounced him.[1]

Ibn Isḥāq's account is that when Muḥammad realized that he must leave he got ʿAlī to take his place in bed to make the Meccans think he was safely asleep, then he himself slipped out unobserved and along with Abū Bakr secretly made his way to a cave not far from Mecca to the south and there he lay in concealment for a day or two until Abū Bakr's son reported that the search for him had slackened off. Then the two set out on two camels, accompanied by Abū Bakr's freedman, ʿĀmir b. Fuhayrah, and by a guide from the tribe of ad-Du'il b. Bakr called ʿAbdallāh b. Arqaṭ. For the first part of the journey they followed devious paths and only joined the beaten track when they were well away from Mecca. They arrived safely in Qubā' on the edge of the Medinan oasis on the 12th of Rabīʿ I (= 24 September 622).[2]

An early Medinan verse of the Qur'ān (9. 40) confirms the story of the cave:

> If ye (*sc.* the Medinans) do not aid him, God hath already aided him, when the unbelievers (*sc.* the Meccans) expelled him with only one companion; the two of them were in the cave, and he was saying to his companion: 'Grieve not, verily God is with us.' . . .

Another verse (8. 30) may refer to the meeting of Quraysh, but that is not altogether certain:

> (Recall) when the unbelievers were plotting against thee, to bring thee to a stand (or 'to detain thee prisoner'), or kill thee, or expel thee; they were plotting and God was plotting, but God is the best of plotters.

With Muḥammad's arrival in Qubā' the second or Medinan phase of his career begins.

6. THE MECCAN ACHIEVEMENT

The great achievement of the Meccan period of Muḥammad's career was the founding of a new religion, the religion which eventually came to be known as Islam. In its broad outlines

[1] Cf. IH, 245 f.

[2] IH, 325–33.

Islam may be said to be complete by the time of the Hijrah, but most of its institutions were still in a very rudimentary state. The formal Prayers or Worship cannot have been fully organized, though something of this kind had doubtless been started. On the other hand, night prayers seem to have been much in vogue.[1] Still less were the other 'pillars of Islam'—fasting, alms-giving, confession of faith and going on pilgrimage—fully developed. Yet the basic conceptions—God, the Last Day, Paradise and Hell, the sending of prophets—were all prominent.

Some scholars have questioned the genuineness of the majority of the 'conversions' to Islam and have tended to assert that in most cases men were acting mainly from material motives. This is a point on which it is best not to be dogmatic since Islamic ideas are so different from Western. It is probably true that there were few conversions and little genuine piety as these matters are conceived in the West; but that is because Western conceptions are not strictly applicable to the manifestations of religion in the Near East. By Near Eastern standards the conversions and the piety probably were genuine; to make a public declaration of faith presumably meant far more to an Arab of that time than it does to a Westerner of today. The material motives would not exclude religious, but the two would be complementary. Indeed, the religious ideas would be necessary to make men aware of the total situation in which they were and of the aims of their activity. In religious thinking a movement with political, social, and economic aspects came to consciousness of itself. This has often, perhaps always, been true in the Near East, yet it is a phenomenon which the modern West finds strange. This strangeness to our ideas, however, should not blind us to the fact that the religious aspect of the movement focused in Muḥammad was always quite genuine and always closely knit with the other aspects.

Because this new religion or ideology corresponded very exactly to the needs of the non-nomadic communities of Western Arabia, it was capable of being the vehicle of a profound social change. In both Mecca and Medina the nomadic ethics and outlook, however well suited to desert conditions, were proving unsatisfactory for settled communities. In Mecca the chief trouble was probably selfish individualism; in Medina the need for a supreme judicial authority was most prominent. In a sense the great work of Islam

[1] Cf. Q. 73 and commentaries.

was to modify the nomadic ethics for use in settled conditions; and the key to this was a new principle of organization for society. Hitherto the bond of society had been blood-relationship; but this was very weak in the case of larger groups—the common ancestry of the Aws and the Khazraj did not prevent their bitter feud; and group loyalty was proving an insufficient sanction for conduct as individualism grew.

It is difficult to formulate the new principle succinctly. Its kernel was the conception of the prophet as a focus of integration for society. The new social unit may contain several kinship groups (which may or may not be related to one another), and these are held together by the fact that a prophet has been sent to them jointly. The members of the community therefore have in common the duty of obeying the commands of God to them as revealed through the prophet. There is thus a principle of cohesion, and a supreme authority above the rival groups, namely, the prophet—or perhaps one should say, the Word of God. The advance of the new conception seems to be reflected in the Qur'ān by the increasing use of the word *ummah*, community, in the later passages. Specially frequent are references to the Last Day, when each *ummah* will come before the Judge as a separate unit, though, of course, each individual will be rewarded or punished according to his deserts; members of an *ummah* may disbelieve their own prophet (cf. 27. 85). In contrast the word *qawm*, tribe or people, represents a group held together solely by ties of kinship. The use of *ummah* as an official description in the 'Constitution of Medina'[1] is noteworthy: 'they (*sc.* the believers of Quraysh and Yathrib and those associated with them) are one *ummah*.'

These thoughts and conceptions doubtless only received their full development some time after the Hijrah, but they must have been present in embryo when Muḥammad began his negotiations with the men of Medina. That Muḥammad should have had in mind—albeit in rudimentary form—an ideology capable of being elaborated to form the basis of the great movement of Arab expansion, is a measure of the width of his perception of the needs of his time and the vastness of his achievement during the Meccan period.

[1] IH, 341.

EXCURSUS A

The Aḥābīsh

THE cynical view of H. Lammens in his article, *Les 'Ahabiš' et l'organisation militaire de la Mecque, au siècle de l'hégire*,[1] is not supported by the sources. Lammens held that the Meccans who opposed Muḥammad had ceased to be warlike and in military affairs relied chiefly on a force of 'Aḥābīsh', consisting of Abyssinian and other negro slaves with a backbone of free-lance Bedouin who were little better than brigands.

There is much that is sound in what Lammens says. In particular he is right in contending that the Aḥābīsh were not simply 'die politischen Verbündeten' or 'confederates' as Wellhausen had held. Unfortunately, however, he goes far beyond the evidence in another direction. His high-handed treatment of the sources is unscientific. He rejects this and accepts that statement according to his own ideas and preconceptions and not according to any objective principle. Thus, in the phrase 'Aḥābīsh and slaves of the people of Mecca' the *and* is explicative and indicates that the Aḥābīsh are identical with the slaves, whereas in the phrase 'Aḥābīsh and those who obeyed them (*sc.* Quraysh) of the tribes of Kinānah and the people of Tihāmah' the *and* marks a sharp disjunction. But why? The reason appears to be that Lammens is assuming the truth of the theory he is trying to prove.

In order to form a more balanced view it will be helpful to consider first the main references to the Aḥābīsh in Ibn Hishām, al-Wāqidī and aṭ-Ṭabarī.

A. In connexion with Abū Bakr's withdrawal from Mecca and appeal for protection to Ibn ad-Dughunnah (or ad-Dughaynah), it is said that Ibn ad-Dughunnah, who was of B. al-Ḥārith b. ʿAbd Manāt b. Kinānah, 'was then *sayyid al-Aḥābīsh* . . . the Aḥābīsh are B. al-Ḥārith b. ʿAbd Manāt b. Kinānah and al-Hūn b. Khuzaymah b. Mudrikah and B. al-Musṭaliq of Khuzāʿah'.[2] The reason for the name was that they formed a confederacy (*taḥālafū*) in a wādī called Aḥbash.[3]

B. 'When Abū Sufyān and the partners in the caravan did that (*sc.* gave money), Quraysh agreed to war against the Messenger of God with their Aḥābīsh and those who obeyed them (*sc.* Quraysh) of the tribes of

[1] *Arabie*, pp. 237–94; originally in *Journal Asiatique*, 1916, pp. 425–82.

[2] IH, 245.

[3] IH, 246; also variant readings.

Kinānah and the people of Tihāmah.'[1] WK. 199 has 'those who followed us of the Aḥābīsh'; ibid. 201 foot records that one of the three standards was 'among the Aḥābīsh, carried by one of them'. All this refers to the campaign of Uḥud.

C. At Uḥud, 'when battle was joined, the first to meet the enemy was Abū 'Āmir with the Aḥābīsh and the slaves of the people of Mecca.'[2]

D. At the close of the battle of Uḥud, al-Ḥulays b. Zabbān, who 'was then *sayyid al-Aḥābīsh*', reproached Abū Sufyān for disfiguring the corpse of Ḥamzah, and Abū Sufyān acknowledged his fault.[3]

E. From a poem on Uḥud by Ḥassān b. Thābit: 'You collected them (as) Aḥābīsh, of no honour (or "without number"), models of unbelief, whose presumptuous ones led them astray'; Lammens prefers a different text, which I should translate: 'You collected Aḥābīsh without ancestry . . .', though there are other possibilities. In view of the uncertainty of the text and the interpretation, little weight can be laid on this use of the word.[4]

F. From a poem by Ka'b b. Mālik: 'We came to a wave of the sea, in whose midst were Aḥābīsh, some without mail, some helmeted, three thousands, while we. . . .'[5]

G. At the Khandaq or siege of Medina, 'Quraysh advanced . . . with ten thousand men of their Aḥābīsh and those who followed them (*sc.* Quraysh) of B. Kinānah and the people of Tihāmah.'[6]

H. At al-Ḥudaybiyah, 'al-Ḥulays b. 'Alqamah (or b. Zabbān) was then *sayyid al-Aḥābīsh*'. He was of B. al-Ḥārith b. 'Abd Manāt b. Kinānah. On being sent as an envoy to Muḥammad, he was so impressed by the serious purpose of the Muslims that he threatened to go over to Muḥammad with the Aḥābīsh unless the Meccans allowed them to perform the pilgrimage.[7]

I. In a poem by al-Akhzar b. Lu'ṭ ad-Du'alī taunting B. Ka'b (part of B. Khuzā'ah), it is suggested that they are now useless in war because the Aḥābīsh are far away.[8]

J. Aḥābīsh, who were in Mecca when it fell, were among the few who offered resistance to the Muslims.[9]

To these may be added the following references to events prior to the Hijrah.

K. After the incident which led to the war of the Fijār, 'Quraysh and others from Kinānah and Asad b. Khuzaymah and those who joined with them of the Aḥābīsh—they are (the tribe of) al-Ḥārith b. 'Abd Manāt b. Kinānah and 'Aḍal, al-Qārah, Dīsh and al-Musṭaliq of

[1] IH, 556 = Ṭab. 1384. [2] IH, 561. [3] IH, 582.
[4] IH, 613. [5] IH, 614. [6] IH, 673.
[7] IH, 743 = Ṭab. 1538 f., WW, 252 f. [8] IH, 804. [9] Ṭab. 1635.

Khuzāʿah, because of their league with Banū 'l-Ḥārith b. 'Abd Manāt—remained quiet preparing for this conflict. . . .'[1]

L. Before the two wars of the Fijār, Ḥarb b. Umayyah was leader of Quraysh in the war with B. Bakr b. ʿAbd Manāt b. Kinānah. 'The Aḥābīsh on that occasion were with the B. Bakr; they made a league on a mountain called al-Ḥubshī against Quraysh, and are called Aḥābīsh because of that.'[2]

From the general stand-point towards the sources which I adopt—which is rather different from that of Lammens—the following conclusions seem to be tolerably certain.

1. There is nothing to suggest that Aḥābīsh are not Arabs, and much to suggest that they are, esp. passage J. The chief weight of Lammens's case falls on the etymology of the word. But while it may be a derivative of *Ḥabash*, 'Abyssinians', that is not the only possibility. Besides the derivation given by Ibn Hishām, it may be a plural of *uḥbūsh* or *uḥbūshah*, meaning 'a company or body of men, not of one tribe' (Lane). Even if derived from *Ḥabash*, it would not necessarily imply that these people were negroes; they might be pure Arabs in the male line, with considerable negro admixture in the female, and consequent dusky hue. Thus there are no compelling reasons for holding that the Aḥābīsh were Abyssinian slaves, and many grounds for regarding such a view as improbable.

2. The Aḥābīsh were apparently tribally organized; *sayyid* is the usual title for the chief of a tribe.[3] Some of the expressions used, however, suggest that they were not an ordinary tribe or group of tribes; e.g. the phrase '*their* Aḥābīsh'.[4] This would fit in with the meaning given by Lane for *uḥbūsh*. If this is so, the Aḥābīsh may have consisted largely of tribeless people, who had become confederates of the tribes named in passage A. They can hardly have been the ordinary *ḥalīfs* or confederates of Quraysh, who probably fought along with the families to which they were attached. Some of the *ḥalīfs* were persons of importance in Mecca; e.g. al-Akhnas b. Sharīq, to whom Muḥammad appealed for protection at one point. The phrase *bi-lā nasab*,[5] if genuine, might simply mean 'of poor ancestry'. The fact that their first appearance

[1] IS, i. 1. 81. 8–11.

[2] Azraqī, *ap.* Wüst., *Mekka*, i. 71. 14.

[3] Cf. Lammens, *Berceau*, 208.

[4] Cf. WW. 225, where there is apparently a reference to the Aḥābīsh of Sufyān al-Hudhalī.

[5] Cf. E.

is in opposition to Quraysh (L) tends to confirm that they were a weak quasi-tribal group from the neighbourhood of Mecca.

3. The actions of Ibn ad-Dughunnah might show that he had a special position at Mecca, but his importance could easily be overemphasized, as he was not in fact prepared to go against 'Quraysh'. In passages D and H al-Ḥulays acts as an independent chief who deals with Quraysh as an equal. Such conduct would be sufficiently explained if the relation of the Aḥābīsh to Quraysh was analogous to that, say, of B. Bakr b. ʿAbd Manāt.

4. The Meccans had black slaves, probably numerous, and these took part in the battles. Some seem to have fought along with their masters, but passage C suggests that at Uḥud there was a separate corps of them, though distinct from the Aḥābīsh. The slaves presumably lived in Mecca, whereas the Aḥābīsh seem to have lived about two days' journey from Mecca (passage A).

5. We must keep in mind the possibility of confusion in some passages between the senses of 'Abyssinians', 'men not of one tribe', and 'men of Aḥbash'. The alleged derivations of 'Aḥābīsh' are presumably conjectures of later chroniclers.

6. Whatever and whoever the Aḥābīsh may have been—and there is something mysterious about them—they were not of primary importance in the campaigns mentioned, though their numbers may have added to the difficulties of the Muslims. Lammens's wicked suggestion that the power of Mecca was founded on an army of black slaves is unfounded. The merchant princes were not enamoured of fighting and tried to avoid it, but they could give a good account of themselves if necessary.

EXCURSUS B

Arabian Monotheism and Judaeo-Christian Influences

THE question commonly asked by writers of a generation or two ago was about the extent of Jewish and Christian influences upon Muḥammad himself, and the underlying assumption was that, with some trifling exceptions, there was no monotheism among the Arabs to whom Muḥammad preached. It is becoming increasingly clear, however, that this assumption is unsound. The earliest passages of the Qur'ān presuppose in those to whom they were first addressed familiarity with the conception of one supreme Being and acceptance of it; and other lines of argument tend to confirm that the intellectual atmosphere of Arabia in general and Mecca in particular had been permeated by monotheism.[1] Thus in his article on *The Origins of Arabic Poetry*,[2] D. S. Margoliouth gives a number of instances of the occurrence of monotheistic ideas, later adopted by Islam, in pre-Islamic poetry. He tries to make this a reason for denying the authenticity of the poetry, but the simpler explanation of the fact would be the monotheistic permeation also presupposed by the Qur'ān. Again C. C. Torrey in *The Jewish Foundation of Islam*, while straining the evidence to make his point, almost against himself seems to admit:

> His 'Arabic Koran', a work of genius, the great creation of a great man, is indeed built throughout from Arabian materials. All the properties of the Koranic diction, including the foreign words and proper names, had been familiar in Mekka before he appeared on the scene.[3]

Torrey is to some extent thinking of the religious terms used by Arabic-speaking Jews; but it is certain that many of them were also used by pure Arabs. Now the presence of the words must indicate the presence of the ideas, at least in the form of what I have called 'vague monotheism', that is, a monotheism not expressing itself in definite acts of worship and not fully conscious of its distinction from paganism.

Thus sound scholarship as well as the theological impartiality of the historian suggests that the chief question to be asked in this

[1] Cf. Nicholson, *Lit. Hist.* 139 f.

[2] JRAS, 1925, pp. 417–49, esp. 434 ff.

[3] P. 54; cf. 33 f., 48, 50, 52, 71, 76, &c.; cf. also Jeffery, *Vocabulary*, 10.

field is the extent of Jewish and Christian (and perhaps other) influences upon the Mecca of A.D. 600, *not* upon Muḥammad himself, or rather, upon the Qur'ān; and to this question the answer can be neither simple nor absolutely certain.

The existence of this indirect or environmental influence does not mean that direct influence must be entirely denied. Since, however, ideas that were 'in the air' could easily have been communicated to Muḥammad by Arabs, it would seem best to assume in general that we have to do with monotheistic influences on the Meccan environment, and only to suppose the direct influence of a monotheist informant where there is good evidence for it. The chief piece of evidence is the reference to a teacher of foreign speech in Sūrat an-Naḥl (16. 105 ED). Torrey, who makes much of this point (43 f., &c.), notes that Muḥammad does not deny having a 'human teacher but only insists that the teaching came down from heaven'. Now on the supposition that Muḥammad had such a teacher, he would most naturally be connected with something which appears to be a fact, namely, the growth in accuracy of the acquaintance with Old Testament stories observable in the Qur'ān. For example, in 37. 135 C and 26. 171 E(D) the member of Lot's party not delivered is an old woman; elsewhere it is Lot's wife (27. 58 E(D); 7. 81 D–E; 15. 60 DE; 11. 83 E+; 29. 32 E+). Again, in the first four of the passages just quoted nothing suggests any awareness of the connexion between Abraham and Lot, and indeed some matters suggest ignorance of it; on the other hand, in the last three passages there is explicit mention of the connexion with Abraham. If there were only one or two instances of this sort of thing they could easily be explained away; but there are a great many; and the Western critic therefore finds it difficult to resist the conclusion that Muḥammad's knowledge of these stories was growing and that therefore he was getting information from a person or persons familiar with them.

An orthodox Muslim, if he accepted the observation, could perhaps claim that God suited the wording of the Qur'ān to the understandings of Muḥammad and his followers, and might then admit that they were acquiring familiarity with the stories from human sources, whereas God was revealing to them the point of the stories and the 'teaching' implicit in them. Such a view finds some difficulty in verses like 11. 51 C–E+:

That is one of the stories of the unseen, which We give thee by inspiration; thou didst not know it, neither thou nor thy people before this; so endure. . . .

If we are both to maintain Muḥammad's sincerity and to admit the increase in his information from human sources, three possibilities seem to be open to us; (1) we may suppose that Muḥammad did not distinguish between the story and the 'teaching' implicit in it, and, because the latter came by revelation, regarded the whole as revealed; (2) the stories may have come to him by some supernormal method of a telepathic character; (3) the translation may not be accurate, and in particular the word *nūḥī*, 'give by inspiration', may mean something slightly different such as 'cause to understand the teaching implicit in or the significance of'. The truth probably lies somewhere between the first and third views. Stories in the Qur'ān are always told with a point and told in rather allusive and elliptic fashion so as to make that point. They show, for instance, how the opponents of a prophet who reject his message get the worst of it in the end, and how the faithful are saved. The stories as a whole, too, probably have the further significance that they make clear to the genealogically minded Arab world that the new movement has an honourable spiritual ancestry. There is no great difficulty in claiming that the precise form, the point and the ulterior significance of the stories came to Muḥammad by revelation and not from the communications of his alleged informant.

The embarrassment caused by such a verse to those who want to uphold the sincerity of Muḥammad should not distract attention from the relatively slight importance of what is likely to have been communicated to him by the supposed monotheist. Muḥammad and the Muslims were interested in the accounts of earlier prophets (and presumably tried to get more information about them) partly because they received encouragement and consolation from these accounts, but mainly, as has just been suggested, because this was a form of *fakhr* or boasting of the merits of one's forefathers. But before this interest in the prophets arose, the essential message of the Qur'ān had been proclaimed; and the ideas it presupposed did not require to be specially communicated, for they had permeated the Meccan environment; while their precise form in the Qur'ān, integrated so as to be relevant to the contemporary situation, could have been given them only by the prophetic intuition.

No Jew or Christian told Muḥammad that he was a prophet. Hence for the understanding of Islam the chief question about sources is by what means and to what extent Judaeo-Christian ideas had become acclimatized in the Ḥijāz.

EXCURSUS C

The Ḥanīfs

IBN ISḤĀQ[1] mentions four men of the generation before Muḥammad who agreed together to abandon pagan practices and to seek the *ḥanīfīyah*, the religion of Abraham; and Ibn Qutaybah[2] mentions half a dozen other persons to whom the term *ḥanīf* was applied, including Umayyah b. Abī 'ṣ-Ṣalt and Abū Qays b. al-Aslat.[3] What are we to make of these references? Do they imply the existence of a sect of monotheists in Arabia who were neither Jews nor Christians?

So much ink has been lavished on this controversy from Sprenger onwards that it is impossible here even to summarize the various views and we must content ourselves with noting the points most relevant to the biography of Muḥammad.[4]

The use of the word *ḥanīf* in the Qur'ān affords a fairly firm starting-point. There 'the *ḥanīfs* were the followers of the ideal original of Arab religion; they were no sect or party of historical people'.[5] This aspect of Qur'ānic teaching makes its appearance early in the Medinan period when Muḥammad's relations with the Jews had become strained; it was claimed that the Muslims retained the religion of Abraham in its purity whereas the Jews and Christians had corrupted it.[6] It seems further to be clear that all the references to the *ḥanīfs* in the early sources are attempts to find facts which would illustrate the statements in the Qur'ān, and that none of the persons named would have called himself a *ḥanīf* or said he was in search of the *ḥanīfīyah*.

There are a number of genuine instances of the use of *ḥanīf* in Arabic prior to Muḥammad (though it is not always easy to say which instances are genuine and which are not), but there it has a somewhat different sense, and the latest students of the question hold that it is ultimately derived 'from the dialect of the Nabateans

[1] IH. 143–9. [2] *Ma'ārif*, 28–30. [3] Cf. also IH. 40. 178. 293.

[4] Chief references: F. Buhl, art. *Ḥanīf* in EI; Caetani, *Ann.* i, pp. 181–92; R. Bell, 'Who were the Ḥanīfs?' in *Moslem World*, xx, 1930, pp. 120–4; N. A. Faris and H. W. Glidden, 'The Development of the meaning of the Koranic Ḥanīf', in *Journal of the Palestine Oriental Society*, xix, 1939, pp. 1–13.

[5] Bell, op. cit., 124.

[6] Cf. C. Snouck Hurgronje, *Het Mekkaansche Fest*, 29 ff. = *Verspreide Geschriften*, i. 22 ff.

in whose language it meant a follower of some branch of their partially Hellenized Syro-Arabian religion'.[1] This question of derivation is a secondary matter, however, and, even if the above view is sound, it does not necessarily follow—indeed it is unlikely—that this adaptation of Hellenism made an important contribution to the permeation of Arabia by monotheistic ideas.

Although the four persons in Ibn Isḥāq's story did not call themselves *ḥanīfs*, they may nevertheless have been feeling their way towards monotheism. Of the four two belonged to the clan of Asad of Quraysh, Waraqah b. Nawfal (the cousin of Khadījah) and 'Uthmān b. al-Ḥuwayrith; both of these became Christians, though the Christianity of the latter at least had political implications. Another, 'Ubaydallāh b. Jaḥsh, was a confederate of the clan of 'Abd Shams and son of a daughter of 'Abd al-Muṭṭalib; he became a Muslim and took part in the migration to Abyssinia, but there went over to Christianity. The fourth, Zayd b. 'Amr of the clan of 'Adī, remained a monotheist without definite allegiance. We have further information about these men in the *Aghānī* and elsewhere.[2] Thus when all that may fairly be ascribed to later invention or misunderstanding is removed, a certain amount of presumed fact remains, but it is not of such a character as to warrant a hypothetical reconstruction of the events. We cannot be certain that there was a compact between the four men. If there were, it would almost certainly have had a political aspect as well as a religious, and in that case would probably not be unconnected with the attempt of 'Uthmān to seize power in Mecca. But they may simply have been following parallel lines. Presumably none was completely without awareness of the non-religious factors leading to the contemporary malaise, though they were possibly more interested in the religious factor.

While mystery thus continues to surround those men to whom the label *ḥanīf* has been attached, what we know about them is sufficient to make them an additional illustration of the way in which monotheism was permeating the environment in which Muḥammad grew up and attracting some of the most enlightened among the Arabs. Those who are called *ḥanīfs* were not the only ones who responded to this attraction; there were several others among his early followers, such as 'Uthmān b. Maẓ'ūn, and at

[1] Faris and Glidden, op. cit. 12.
[2] For refs. see Caetani, loc. cit.

least one, Abū ʿĀmir ʿAbd ʿAmr b. Ṣayfī of Medina, who became a bitter opponent. For the student of the life of Muḥammad the so-called *ḥanīfs* are of importance mainly as affording evidence of the monotheism present in the environment.

EXCURSUS D

Tazakkā, &c.

THE translation of *tazakkā* and other derivatives of *zakā* (apart from *zakāt*) in the Qur'ān presents something of a problem. One scholar translates by 'purify oneself' but adds in brackets or in a footnote 'by almsgiving';[1] another simply says 'be charitable'.[2] Apart from the noun *zakāt* the root occurs about 26 times in the Qur'ān, and it is instructive to consider the most important of these instances. They fall into four groups.

In the first group (2. 169 E+; 3. 71 F; 4. 52 E?; 53. 33 E+) the meaning is clear. These are all instances of the second stem *zakkā* used in the sense of 'justify' or 'count just' in much the same way as 'justify' is used in the New Testament. In each case the thought is expressed or implied: Do not justify yourselves, God justifies whom He pleases. All have an eschatological reference, and all, with the possible exception of the last, refer to the Jews. The criticism of Jewish ideas with which this usage is bound up is similar to that in the New Testament.

In the second group (2. 123 F; 2. 146 F—; 3. 158 G; 62. 2 E) it is said that a messenger is sent to 'purify' (*yuzakkī*) a people. These passages are early- to mid-Medinan; the first is in an address to the Jews, though descriptive of Abraham; the others refer to Muḥammad. Since a prophet cannot justify in the sense in which God justifies, we must, if we translate by 'justify', mean that justification (by God) is the result of the prophet's mission. The same holds of 'purify'. Perhaps, however, the word could be extended in meaning and taken as 'to direct to justification or purification'. On the other hand, it might mean 'to appoint *zakāt* for'; this would be specially appropriate if *zakāt* had not yet become a technical term but retained something of the associations of 'means of purification'. Thus where *yuzakkī* is used of a messenger it seems probable that it means 'purifies by instituting almsgiving'.

The Meccan (and perhaps early Medinan) usage of *tazakkā* and *at-tazakkī* which constitutes the third group (20. 78 C–E;

[1] Bell, *Translation of Q.*

[2] J. Obermann in *The Arab Heritage*, ed. by N. A. Faris, Princeton, 1946, p. 108.

35. 19 C?; 79. 18 C; 80. 3, 7 B; 87. 14 C; 92. 18 E?) is slightly different. In 80. 3 and 7 the aim of Muḥammad's preaching is apparently to bring a man to *tazakkī*, which is thus almost equal to conversion. 20. 78 states that Gardens of Eden are the reward of *tazakkī*; and something similar is implied in 35. 19, 79. 18, and 87. 14. Thus *tazakkī* seems to indicate that moral excellence which is part of the supreme aim of life.

This would be in accordance with what Western scholars have written about the analogous uses of similar words in Hebrew, Aramaic, and Syriac.[1] The Arabic root *zakā* properly means to grow or thrive or flourish, but the usages of it just considered have been influenced by these other languages, in which a similar root (corresponding to the Arabic *dhakā*) indicates especially moral purity. The strangeness of this idea to the Arabs—though it was probably not introduced to them by the Qur'ān—would help to account for their use of a term like *tazakkā* to describe it. It was distinct from the ritual purity (cf. *ṭahhir* in 74. 4 B), with which the old religion had doubtless familiarized them. Thus the meaning of *tazakkī* would possibly be better conveyed by 'righteousness' than by 'purity', and would link up with *zakkā* in the first group. Any difficulty in suggesting that people are already righteous could be avoided by taking the word to mean 'aim at righteousness, take it as a principle'; but the distinction implied here was probably not present to the Arab.

We may also include in this group two instances of the second stem of the root, 24. 21 E and 91. 9 C: 'Had it not been for the bounty and mercy of God towards you, not one of you would ever be pure (*zakā*), but God purifieth (*yuzakkī*) whom He willeth'; 'Prospered has he who purifies it (*sc.* his soul or self)'. *Yatazakkā* in 92. 18 E? is possibly to be taken in this sense—'who gives of his wealth to purify himself (*yu'ṭī māla-hu yatazakkā*)'—but in view of the probable Medinan date and the mention of wealth it is perhaps rather 'who gives of his wealth as (purifying) *zakāt*'; that is to say, it perhaps refers to the more technical use of *zakāt* but with the associated meaning of 'purifying' also present. None of the clearly Meccan passages connects *tazakkā* with money; on the contrary, a special reference is sometimes inappropriate, as in the case of Pharaoh (79. 18), while, though there is a rich man in Sūrat 'Abasa (80), yet the blind man is also a possible instance of *tazakkī*.

[1] Cf. Jeffery, *Vocabulary*, *s.v.*

There is also a fourth group where the original Arabic meaning of the root is dominant (2. 232 H; 18. 18 E+; 18. 73 C?; 19. 19 E+; 24. 28 H; 24. 30 G?). These add no fresh elements to our special problem, and need not be discussed, interesting as they are.

The word *zakāt* is frequently used in a technical sense, usually coupled with *ṣalāt*; but there appear to be also some instances of its use in a non-technical sense, that is, in the sense of general moral excellence or righteousness, as in the third group above. The best examples are 18. 80 C? and 23. 4 E; verses 14, 34, and 55 (all E+) of Sūrat Maryam (19) are perhaps further examples, but in view of the connexion with prophets they are probably to be connected with the second group.

Finally, there is 9. 104 I which appears to connect the moral sense of the root *zakā* with the ritual purity of *ṭahara*. Muḥammad is commanded, with regard to some Bedouin, 'Take of their goods a *ṣadaqah* to cleanse and purify them thereby' (*tuṭahhiru-hum wa-tuzakkī-him bi-hā*); another possible interpretation favoured by some Muslim exegetes[1] is, 'Take of their goods a *ṣadaqah* which will cleanse them, and you will justify (or purify) them thereby.' On either interpretation the two ideas have become connected. The commentaries may be mistaken in the occasions named for the revelation of this passage, but they are doubtless sound in suggesting that it has been assimilated to current Arab ideas. These men had done something from which they thought they required purification; it was they who wanted the purification. So far as the word *tuzakkī* itself is concerned, it is close to the second group.

This examination appears to show that in the Meccan period—the third group—the root *zakā* in special religious usages connoted righteousness or moral excellence. The commentator Ibn Zayd quoted by aṭ-Ṭabarī[2] goes so far as to identify *tazakkī* with *islām*. There may have been—though it is not necessarily so—a suggestion of moral purity about *tazakkī*, but there was no suggestion of religious or ritual purity, and no obvious connexion with almsgiving. In the Medinan period, however, notably in the second group and in 9. 104, *zakkā* seems to refer specially to purification by almsgiving and to be connected (to some extent) with ritual purity. Why did such a change come about? With this problem may be linked up that of the use of *zakāt* for almsgiving. This is

[1] Cf. aṭ-Ṭabarī, *Tafsīr, ad loc.* [2] *Tafsīr*, on 79. 18.

probably derived from the Aramaic *zakōt* meaning purity and *not* almsgiving; and, whether the transition from the one meaning to the other was the work of Jews settled in Arabia or was first made by Muḥammad himself, the problem of the reason for the transition is much the same.[1] What is the connexion between righteousness, ritual purity, and almsgiving?

Although *tazakkā* apparently had no connexion with almsgiving originally, the virtue of generosity was prominent in the earlier passages of the Qur'ān, and that of course includes almsgiving. But, as C. Snouck Hurgronje argues,[2] almsgiving was and is not practised in the East for a socialistic or utilitarian reason but because it is the chief of the virtues. The negative aspect of his statement is beyond dispute, but in speaking of beneficence as a virtue sought for its own sake he is perhaps idealizing somewhat. Deep in Semitic thought was the idea of sacrificing something very precious, even a first-born son, doubtless on the assumption that such an act tended to propitiate a jealous deity and so to ensure one's enjoyment of the rest of one's possessions. For people with this thought in their bones it would be natural to regard almsgiving, the giving away of a part of one's money or possessions, as a form of propitiatory sacrifice.[3]

It may be that nothing of this thought was present in the earliest passages with *tazakkā*, and not even in the insistence on generosity. But later passages of the Qur'ān appear to bear witness to the resurgence of old ideas; and these were certainly present in the development of the practice of *zakāt* in later Islam, as evidenced by Tradition.

Thus in Sūrat al-Baqarah (2. 273), alms (*ṣadaqāt*) given in secret are said to cover or atone for (*yukaffiru*) evil deeds, according to the standard interpretation; and earlier in the same sūrah alms is spoken of as a *fidyah* in those cases where the head is not shaved during the pilgrimage, where, according to Lane, *fidyah* means 'property by the giving of which one preserves himself from evil in the case of a religious act in which he has fallen short of what was incumbent, like the expiation for the breaking of an oath. . .'.

Again, in the legal *zakāt* according to later theory, what was

[1] Cf. Jeffery, *Vocabulary*, *s.v.* and refs. there.

[2] 'Une nouvelle Biographie de Mohammed', in *Revue de l'Histoire des Religions*, xxx. 167 f. = *Verspreide Geschriften*, i. 353 f.

[3] Cf. M. Gaudefroy-Demombynes, *Muslim Institutions*, 105.

paid had always to be part of the property of which it was the *zakāt*, and not an equivalent in money.[1] The payment must actually be made too; several traditions about voluntary alms speak of the great misfortune of those who are unable to find someone who will accept their alms.[2] Moreover the object given as *zakāt* may not be bought back by the former owner.[3] It may further be noticed that when al-Ghazālī is listing the possessions on which *zakāt* is to be paid he places first cattle, then crops, and after these money, merchandise, and mines; that is to say, those which are mentioned first correspond to those which are subjects for sacrifices in the Old Testament.

If it was correct to hold that in the Meccan period *tazakkā* meant aiming at moral purity or righteousness, then the disappearance later may be due to the fact that this method of expressing an idea novel to the Arabs became confused with older ideas of ritual purity. The Qur'ān had linked the moral ideal with the Divine command and consequently with the Divine judgement; but the reassertion of the notion of ritual purity would impair this linking. Hence *tazakkā* tended to fade out before *ḥanīfīyah* and *islām*.[4]

[1] Ghazālī, *Iḥyā'*, v, faṣl 2; cf. Bukhārī, 24. 58, tr. i. 485.

[2] Bukhārī, 24. 9. 10.

[3] Ibid. 59.

[4] Cf. p. 76, above.

EXCURSUS E

List of Meccan Muslims and Pagans

MANY of the main points on which the survey of the earlier Muslims is founded can be readily set out in the form of a table. The names of the Muslims in the following table are those contained in vols. iii. 1 and iv. 1 of Ibn Sa'd; the pagans are those in the lists of the killed and the prisoners at Badr (Caetani, *Ann.* i, pp. 512–17), together with a few mentioned in the primary sources as prominent opponents of Muḥammad. The table contains the following particulars:

M's Tribe—Mother's Tribe; this is usually taken from Ibn Sa'd's notice; in the case of confederates and freedmen it is normally not given even where known.

Age—that is, age at the Hijrah; it mostly has to be calculated from other particulars given by Ibn Sa'd, and is not always given exactly.

E—number in the list of first Muslims as given by Caetani, Ann. i, § 229, from IH. 162–5; the entry 'E' in the column indicates that the man's conversion was earlier than that of those in the list.

AA.—number in Caetani's first list of Emigrants to Abyssinia (ibid. § 275, from IH, 208 f., &c.).

AB—number in Caetani's second list of Emigrants (ibid. § 277, from IH, 209–15, &c., omitting names in first list).

R—number in Caetani's list of returned Emigrants (ibid. § 283, from IH, 241–3, &c.); 'Sh' indicates one of those who returned in the two ships (IH, 781–6), and 'X' one of whose return nothing is stated and who was not at Badr as a Muslim.

H—number in Caetani's list of those who made the Hijrah (1 A.H., § 15, from IH, 316–23, &c.).

B—performance at the battle of Badr; for the Muslims the number in Caetani's list (2 A.H., § 85A, from IH, 485–91, &c.); 'PK' and 'PP' indicate that these names are present in Caetani's lists of pagans killed and made prisoner respectively at Badr (ibid., §§ 88, 89, from IH, 507–15, &c.); 'P' means present as a pagan.

'IS' indicates that Ibn Sa'd mentions the man's presence in Abyssinia, as a *Muslim* at Badr, &c.

* indicates that the person so marked should appear in this list, though for reasons that are usually obvious he does not receive a number in Caetani; e.g. Caetani's second list of Emigrants to Abyssinia does not contain the names in his first list although they are included in the list in Ibn Hishām on which his second list is based.

m = *mawlā*, client or freedman.
h = *ḥalīf*, confederate.
h/Tamīm = a confederate coming from the tribe of Tamīm.

	M's tribe	*Age*	*E*	*AA*	*AB*	*R*	*H*	*B*
HASHIM								
Muslims								
Muḥammad . . .	Zuhrah	52	..	..	..	..	*	1
Ḥamzah	Zuhrah	56	..	..	..	..	49	2
'Alī b. Abī Ṭālib . . .	Hāshim	..	E	..	..	..	*	3
Zayd b. al-Ḥārithah . .	(Tayyi')	42–7	E	..	..	..	50	4
— Abū Marthad al-Ghanawī *h*	..	54	..	..	..	..	51	7
— Marthad b. Abī Marthad *h*	..	..	..	..	..	..	52	8
— Anasah m. of Muḥammad	..	..	..	..	..	..	53	5
— Abū Kabshah *m* . .	..	..	..	..	..	..	54	6
— Ṣāliḥ Suqrān (Ḥabashī) *m*	..	..	..	..	..	..	..	IS
'Abbās b. 'Abd al-Muṭṭalib .	Namir	55?	..	..	..	..	..	? P
Ja'far b. Abī Ṭālib . .	Hāshim	..	24	..	1	Sh	..	..
'Aqil b. Abī Ṭālib . .	Hāshim	..	..	..	..	..	..	..
Nawfal b. al-Ḥārith b. 'Abd al-Muṭṭalib	Ḥārith b. F.	..	..	..	..	..	..	PP
Rabī'ah b. al-Ḥārith b. 'Abd al-Muṭṭalib	Ḥārith b. F.	57?	..	..	..	..	..	..
'Abdallāh b. al-Ḥārith b. 'Abd al-Muṭṭalib	Ḥārith b. F.	..	..	..	..	..	..	? P
Abū Sufyān b. al-Ḥārith b. 'Abd al-Muṭṭalib . .	Ḥārith b. F.	..	..	..	..	..	..	? P
Faḍl b. al-'Abbās . . .	'Āmir b. Ṣa'ṣa'ah	..	..	..	..	..	..	..
Ja'far b. Abī Sufyān b. al-Ḥ. .	Hāshim	..	..	..	..	..	..	..
al-Ḥārith b. Nawfal b. al-Ḥ. .	Azd	..	..	..	..	..	..	..
'Abd al-Muṭṭalib b. Rabī'ah .	Hāshim	..	..	..	..	..	..	..
'Utbah b. Abī Lahab . .	'Abd Shams	..	..	..	..	..	..	? P
Mu'attib b. Abī Lahab . .	'Abd Shams	..	..	..	..	..	..	? P
Usāmah b. Zayd b. al-Ḥārithah *m/Hāshim* . . .	..	9	..	..	..	..	..	..
— Abū Rāfi' . . .	..	..	..	..	..	..	..	..
— Salmān al-Fārisī . .	..	..	..	..	..	..	..	..
Pagans								
'Uqayl b. Abī Ṭālib (or 'Aqīl) .	..	..	..	..	..	..	..	PP
Ṭālib b. Abī Ṭālib . .	..	..	..	..	..	..	..	..
Abū Lahab b. 'Abd al-Muṭṭalib	..	..	..	..	..	..	..	..
AL-MUṬṬALIB								
Muslims								
'Ubaydah b. al-Ḥārith b. al-M.	Thaqif	61	7	..	..	..	55	9 k.
aṭ-Ṭufayl b. al-Ḥārith b. al-M.	Thaqif	38	..	..	..	..	56	10
al-Ḥusayn b. al-Ḥārith b. al-M.	Thaqif	..	..	..	..	..	57	11
Misṭaḥ b. Uthāthah b. 'Abbād	Muṭṭalib (her m. Taym)	22	..	..	..	..	58	12

	M's tribe	Age	E	AA	AB	R	H	B
AL-MUTTALIB (*contd.*)								
Pagans								
as-Sā'ib b. 'Ubayd b. 'Abd Yazīd	..	..	..	..	..	..	..	PP
Nu'mān b. 'Amr b. 'Alqamah	..	..	..	..	..	..	..	PP
'Ubayd b. 'Amr b. 'Alqamah	..	..	..	..	..	..	..	PP
— 'Āqil b. 'Amr *h*	..	..	..	..	..	..	..	PP
— Tamīm b. 'Amr *h*	..	..	..	..	..	..	..	PP
— Ibn Tamīm b. 'Amr *h*	..	..	..	..	..	..	..	PP
TAYM								
Muslims								
Abū Bakr b. Abī Quḥāfah b. 'Āmir	Taym	50	E	..	..	..	•	45
Ṭalḥah b. 'Ubaydallāh b. 'Uthmān	Ḥaḍramīyah	26–8	E	..	..	..	47	49
— Ṣuhayb b. Sinān *m*	..	32	45	..	..	..	48	48
— 'Āmir b. Fuhayrah *m*	..	..	35	..	..	..	..	47
— Bilāl b. Rabāḥ *m*	..	..	..	..	..	..	..	46
al-Ḥārith b. Khālid b. Ṣakhr	Taym	..	..	..	32	Sh	..	..
'Amr b. 'Uthmān b. 'Amr	..	..	..	..	34	X	..	..
Pagans								
'Umayr b. 'Uthmān b. 'Amr	..	..	..	..	..	..	..	PK
'Uthmān b. Mālik b. 'Ubaydallāh	..	..	..	..	..	..	..	PK
Mālik b. 'Abdallāh b. 'Uthmān	..	..	..	..	..	..	..	PK
'Amr b. 'Abdallāh b. Jud'ān	..	..	..	..	..	..	..	PK
Musāfi' b. 'Iyāḍ b. Ṣakhr b. 'Āmir	..	..	..	..	..	..	..	PP
— Jābir b. az-Zubayr	..	..	..	..	..	..	..	PP
'Abdallāh b. Jud'ān b. 'Amr	..	dead	..	..	..	..	..	d.
ZUHRAH								
Muslims								
'Abd ar-Raḥmān b. 'Awf b. 'Abd 'Awf	Zuhrah	43	E	7		11	62	37
Sa'd b. Abī Waqqāṣ b. Wuhayb	'Abd Shams	16–29	E	..	..	..	..	38
'Umayr b. Abī Waqqāṣ	'Abd Shams	14	13	13	..	..	..	39 k.
— 'Abdallāh b. Mas'ūd *h*	Zuhrah *h*	29–37	14	17?	29	13	..	41
— al-Miqdād b. 'Amr *h*	..	c. 37	..	..	31	12	..	40
— Khabbāb b. al-Aratt *h*	Khuzā'ah	36	12	..	..	..	..	44
— Dhu 'l-Yadayn 'Umayr b. 'Abd 'Amr	Zuhrah	28+	..	..	..	..	..	43 k.
— Mas'ūd b. ar-Rabī' *h*	..	30+	15	..	..	..	..	42
'Āmir b. Abī Waqqāṣ	'Abd Shams	..	..	..	26	Sh	..	..
al-Muṭṭalib b. Azhar b. 'Abd 'Awf	Muṭṭalib	..	32	..	27	X	..	..
Ṭulayb b. Azhar	Muṭṭalib	..	..	..	IS	..	..	..
'Abdallāh b. Shihāb al-Aṣghar	Khuzā'ah *h/Zuhrah*	dead	..	..	IS	..	..	..
'Abdallāh b. Shihāb	Khuzā'ah; *h*	dead	..	..	..	..	..	..
— 'Utbah b. Mas'ūd *h*	Zuhrah *h*	..	..	..	30	Sh	..	..
— Shuraḥbīl b. Ḥasanah *h*	Jumaḥ (by marriage)	49	..	..	55	X	..	..
Pagan								
'Abdallāh al-Akhnas b. Sharīq *h/Thaqīf*	..	..	..	..	..	..	..	..
'ADĪ								
Muslims								
'Umar b. al-Khaṭṭāb b. Nufayl	Makhzūm	31–39	..	..	..	..	33	55
Zayd b. al-Khaṭṭāb	Asad	..	..	..	..	..	34	56
Sa'īd b. Zayd b. 'Amr b. Nufayl	Khuzā'ah	20–29	8	..	..	..	39	68
'Amr b. Surāqah b. Mu'tamir	Jumaḥ	..	..	..	..	..	35	58
— 'Āmir b. Rabī'ah *h*	..	..	21	11	•	27	2	63

	M's tribe	Age	E	AA	AB	R	H	B
'ADĪ: *Muslims* (*contd.*)								
'Amr 'Āqil b. (Abī) Bukayr *h/Kinānah* . . .	..	32	42	..	..	..	44	65 k.
— Khālid b. (Abī) Bukayr *h/Kinānah* . . .	..	30	40	..	..	..	45	66
— Iyās b. (Abī) Bukayr *h/Kinānah*	..	..	43	..	..	..	43	67
— 'Āmir b. (Abī) Bukayr *h/Kinānah* . . .	..	..	41	..	..	..	46	64
— Wāqid b. 'Abdallāh *h/Tamīm*	..	..	39	..	..	..	40	60
— Khawlā b. Abī Khawlā *h/Madhḥij* . . .	..	..	..	..	..	..	41	61
— Mihja' b. Ṣāliḥ *m* (of 'Umar)	..	..	..	..	..	..	..	57 k.
Nu'aym b. 'Abdallāh b. Asīd .	'Adī	..	34	..	..	..	..	..
Ma'mar b. 'Abdallāh b. Naḍlah	Ash'arī	..	..	..	71	Sh	..	..
'Adī b. Naḍlah b. 'Abd al-'Uzzā	Sahm	dead	..	..	73	d.	..	..
'Urwah b. (Abī Uthāthah) b. 'Abd al-'Uzzā . . .	'Anazah (her m. Sahm)	..	..	..	72	d.	..	..
Mas'ūd b. Suwayd . .	'Adī	..	..	..	..	..	..	..
'Abdallāh b. Surāqah . .	Jumaḥ	..	..	..	..	..	36	59?
'Abdallāh b. 'Umar b. al-Khaṭṭāb	Jumaḥ	10–11	..	..	..	..	..	..
Khārijah b. Ḥudhāfah b. Ghānim	'Adī	..	..	..	..	..	..	..
an-Nu'mān b. 'Adī b. Naḍlah	..	..	..	..	74	X	..	..
Mālik b. Khawlah . .	..	..	..	..	..	..	42	62
AL-ḤĀRITH B. FIHR								
Muslims								
Abū 'Ubaydah b. al-Jarrāḥ .	al-Ḥārith	39–40	1	..	83	36	..	80
Suhayl b. Bayḍā' . .	al-Ḥārith	31–32	..	15	•	38	..	82
Ṣafwān b. Bayḍā' . .	al-Ḥārith	..	..	..	..	..	..	83 k.
Ma'mar b. Abī Sarḥ (or 'Amr)	'Āmir	..	..	..	84	39	..	84/90
Ḥāṭib b. 'Amr b. Abī Sarḥ .	..	..	..	..	..	..	..	86
'Iyāḍ b. (Abī) Zuhayr . .	al-Ḥārith	..	..	..	86	X	..	87?
'Amr b. Abī 'Amr (of B. Muḥārib b. Fihr)	..	30	..	..	..	..	..	..
Sahl b. Bayḍā'	al-Ḥārith	..	..	..	..	..	..	? PP
'Amr b. al-Ḥārith . .	'Āmir	..	..	..	85	37	..	81
'Uthmān b. 'Abd al-Ghanm .	Zuhrah	..	..	..	87	X	..	..
Sa'id (or Sa'd) b. 'Abd Qays .	..	..	..	..	88	X	..	..
al-Ḥārith b. 'Abd Qays. .	..	..	..	..	89	Sh	..	..
'Āmir b. 'Abd Ghanm (as-Sahmī?)	..	..	..	..	91	X	..	..
Pagans								
aṭ-Ṭufayl b. Abī Qunay' .	..	..	..	..	..	..	..	PP
'Utbah b. 'Amr b. Jaḥdam .	..	..	..	..	..	..	..	PP
— Shāfi' *h* . . .	..	..	..	..	..	..	..	PP
'ĀMIR								
Muslims								
Abū Sabrah b. Abī Ruhm b. 'Abd al-'Uzzā . . .	Hāshim	..	..	13	•	31	64	75
'Abdallāh b. Makhramah b. 'Abd al-'Uzzā . . .	Kinānah	28–9	..	15	75	29	..	76
Ḥāṭib b. 'Amr b. 'Abd Shams	Ashja'	..	17	16	•	Sh	..	89?
'Abdallāh b. Suhayl b. 'Amr .	Nawfal	25–6	..	..	76	30	..	77
— 'Umayr b. 'Awf *m* (of Suhayl)	..	..	..	..	..	..	..	78
Wahb b. Sa'd b. Abī Sarḥ .	Ash'ar	32	..	..	..	..	..	85
— Sa'd b. Khawlah *m* .	..	23	..	..	82	35	..	79
Salīṭ b. 'Amr . . .	Yaman	..	16	..	77	X	..	..
as-Sakrān b. 'Amr . .	Khuzā'ah	dead	..	..	78	33	d.	..

	M's tribe	Age	E	AA	AB	R	H	B
'AMIR: *Muslims (contd.)*								
Mālik b. Zam'ah . . .	..	..	..	..	80	Sh	..	..
'Abdallāh b. Qays (Ibn Umm Maktūm)	Makhzūm	..	..	..	..	.	..	..
Pagans								
Suhayl b. 'Amr b. 'Abd Shams	..	..	..	..	..	..	..	PP
'Abd b. Zam'ah b. Qays b. 'Abd Shams . . .	..	..	..	..	..	..	..	PP
'Abd ar-Raḥmān b. Manshū'.	..	..	..	..	..	..	..	PP
Ḥabīb b. Jābir . . .	..	..	..	..	..	..	..	PP
as-Sā'ib b. Mālik . . .	..	..	..	..	..	..	..	PP
+2 confederates								
ASAD								
Muslims								
az-Zubayr b. al-'Awwām b. Khuwaylid . . .	Hāshim	27–8	E	5	*	7	63	32
— Ḥāṭib b. Abī Balta'ah *h* .	..	35	..	..	..	..	..	33
— Sa'd *m* (of Ḥāṭib) . .	..	..	..	..	..	..	..	34
Sā'ib b. al-'Awwām b. Khuwaylid	Hāshim	..	..	..	..	..	..	..
Khālid b. Ḥizām b. Khuwaylid	Asad	dead	..	..	IS	d.	..	..
al-Aswad b. Nawfal b. Khuwaylid	'Abd Shams	..	..	..	15	Sh	..	..
'Amr b. Umayyah b. al-Ḥārith	Taym	..	..	..	17	d.	..	..
Yazīd b. Zam'ah b. al-Aswad	Makhzūm	..	..	..	16	X	..	..
Pagans								
Zam'ah b. al-Aswad b. al-Muṭṭalib	..	..	..	..	..	..	..	PK
al-Ḥārith b. Zam'ah . .	..	..	..	..	..	..	..	PK
'Uqayl b. al-Aswad (or 'Aqīl) .	..	..	..	..	..	..	..	PK
Abu 'l-Bakhtarī (al-'Āṣ) b. Hishām b. al-Ḥārith . .	..	..	..	..	..	..	..	PK
Nawfal b. Khuwaylid . .	..	..	..	..	..	..	..	PK
as-Sā'ib b. Abī Ḥubaysh .	..	..	..	..	..	..	..	PP
al-Ḥuwayrith b. 'Abbād .	..	..	..	..	..	..	..	PP
'Abdallah b. Ḥumayd . .	..	..	..	..	..	..	..	PP
Ḥakīm b. Ḥizām b. Khuwaylid	..	..	..	..	..	..	..	
+2 confederates + 1 client								
NAWFAL								
Muslims								
'Utbah b. Ghazwān *h* . .	..	40	..	..	14	6	68	30
— Khabbāb *m* (of 'Utbah) .	..	31	..	..	..	..	61	31
Pagans								
al-Ḥārith b. 'Āmir b. Nawfal	..	..	..	..	..	..	..	PK
Ṭu'aymah b. 'Adī b. Nawfal .	..	..	..	..	..	..	..	PK
'Adī b. al-Khiyār b. 'Adī b. N.	..	..	..	..	..	..	..	PP
al-Muṭ'im b. 'Adī b. Nawfal .	..	..	..	..	..	..	..	? d.
+2 confederates +1 client								
'ABD SHAMS								
Muslims								
'Uthmān b. 'Affān b. Abi 'l-'Āṣ	'Abd Shams	39/46	E	1	*	1	69	13
Abū Hudhayfah b. 'Utbah b. Rabī'ah .	Kinānah	41–2	38	3	*	3	66	14
— Sālim *m.* (of Abū Hudhayfah)	..	..	..	..	..	..	67	15
— 'Abdallāh b. Jaḥsh *h/Khuzaymah*	Hāshim	38–46	22	..	7	5	4	17

	M's tribe	*Age*	*E*	*AA*	*AB*	*R*	*H*	*B*
ABD SHAMS: *Muslims (contd.)*								
Abū Yazīd b. Ruqaysh *h/Khuzaymah*	..	..	..	..	..	..	14	21
— 'Ukkāshah b. Miḥṣan *h/-Khuzaymah*	..	33	..	..	..	..	7	18
— Abū Sinān b. Miḥṣan *h/-Khuzaymah*	..	35	..	..	..	..	..	22
— Sinān b. Abī Sinān *h/-Khuzaymah*	..	15	..	..	..	..	..	23
— Shujā' b. Wahb *h/Khuzaymah*	..	29–37	..	..	IS	..	8	19
— 'Uqbah b. Wahb *h/Khuzaymah*	..	..	..	..	..	..	9	20
— Rabī'ah b. Aktham *h/-Khuzaymah*	..	31	..	..	..	..	20	25
— Muḥriz b. Naḍlah *h/Khuzaymah*	..	29–32	..	..	..	..	13	24
— Arbad b. Ḥumayrah *h/-Khuzaymah*	..	..	..	..	..	..	10	29
— Malik b. 'Amr *h/Sulaym*	..	..	..	..	..	..	17	26
— Midlāj b. 'Amr *h/Sulaym*	..	..	..	..	..	..	..	27
— Thaqf b. 'Amr *h/Sulaym*	..	..	..	..	..	..	19	28
Khālid b. Sa'id b. al-'Āṣ	Kinānah	..	36	..	5	Sh	..	..
'Amr b. Sa'id	Makhzūm	..	..	..	3	Sh	..	..
— Abū Aḥmad b. Jaḥsh *h/-Khuzaymah*	Hāshim	..	23	..	IS	..	5	..
— 'Abd ar-Raḥmān b. Ruqaysh *h/Khuzaymah*	..	..	..	..	..	..	..	..
— 'Amr b. Miḥṣan *h/Khuzaymah*	..	..	..	..	..	..	16	..
— Qays b. 'Abdallāh *h/Khuzaymah*	..	..	..	..	10	X	15?	..
— Ṣafwān b. 'Amr *h/Sulaym*	..	..	..	..	..	..	18	..
— Abū Mūsā al-Ash'arī *h*	..	..	..	..	13	? Sh	..	..
— Mu'ayqib b. Abī Fāṭimah *h*	..	..	..	..	12	? Sh	..	..
— Subayḥ *m* (of Abū Uḥayḥah)	..	..	..	..	..	..	..	16?
— az-Zubayr b. 'Ubaydah	..	..	..	..	..	..	21	..
— Tammām b. 'Ubaydah	..	..	..	..	..	..	22	..
— Muḥammad b. 'Abdallāh b. Jaḥsh	..	..	..	..	..	..	24	..
Pagans								
Ḥanẓalah b. Abī Sufyān b. Ḥarb b. Umayyah	..	..	..	..	..	..	..	PK
'Ubaydah b. Sa'id b. al-'Āṣ b. Umayyah	..	..	..	..	..	..	..	PK
al-'Āṣ b. Sa'id b. al-'Āṣ b. Umayyah	..	..	..	..	..	..	..	PK
'Uqbah b. Abī Mu'ayṭ b. Abī 'Amr b. Umayyah	..	..	..	..	..	..	..	PK
'Utbah b. Rabī'ah b. 'Abd Shams	..	..	..	..	..	..	..	PK
Shaybah b. Rabī'ah b. 'Abd Shams	..	..	..	..	..	..	..	PK
al-Walīd b. 'Utbah b. Rabī'ah	..	..	..	..	..	..	..	PK
'Amr b. Abī Sufyān b. Ḥarb b. Umayyah	..	..	..	..	..	..	..	PP
al-Ḥārith b. Abī Wajzah b. Abī 'Amr	..	..	..	..	..	..	..	PP
Abu 'l-'Āṣ b. ar-Rabī' b. 'Abd al-'Uzzā	..	..	..	..	..	..	..	PP
Abu 'l-'Āṣ b. Nawfal b. 'Abd Shams	..	..	..	..	..	..	..	PP
+ 8 confederates + 4 clients								
Abū Sufyān b. Ḥarb	..	..	..	..	..	..	..	..

	M's tribe	*Age*	*E*	*AA*	*AB*	*R*	*H*	*B*
MAKHZŪM								
Muslims								
Abū Salamah b. 'Abd al-Asad b. Hilāl	Hāshim	..	2	8	•	14	1	50
al-Arqam b. 'Abd Manāf b. Asad	Khuzā'ah	26–34	3	..	..	..	..	52
Shammās b. 'Uthmān b. ash-Sharīd	'Abd Shams	..	..	..	35	16	..	51
— 'Ammār b. Yāsir *h* (of Abū Hudhayfah) . .	..	56?	44	..	90	19	..	53
— Mu'attib b. 'Awf *h/Khuzā'ah*	..	21	..	..	41	20	..	54
'Ayyāsh b. Abī Rabī'ah b. al-Mughīrah . . .	Tamīm	..	18	..	40	18	..	..
Salamah b. Hishām b. al-Mughīrah	Rabī'ah	..	..	..	39	17	..	..
al-Walīd b. al-Walīd b. al-Mughīrah	Bajīlah	..	..	..	..	..	..	..
Hāshim b. Abī Hudhayfah b. al-Mughīrah . . .	Makhzūm	..	..	..	38	X	..	..
Habbār b. Sufyān b. 'Abd al-Asad b. Hilāl . . .	'Āmir	..	..	..	36	X	..	..
'Abdallāh b. Sufyān b. 'Abd al-Asad	'Āmir	..	..	..	37	X	..	..
+ 2 confederates								
Pagans								
Abū Jahl ('Amr) b. Hishām b. al-Mughīrah . . .	Tamīm	..	..	..	..	..	..	PK
al-'Āṣ b. Hishām b. al-Mughīrah	..	..	..	..	..	..	..	PK
Khālid b. Hishām b. al-Mughīrah	..	..	..	..	..	..	..	PP
Mas'ūd b. Abī Umayyah b. al-Mughīrah . . .	..	..	..	..	..	..	..	PK
Abū Qays b. al-Walīd b. al-Mughīrah . . .	..	..	..	..	..	..	..	PK
Abū Qays b. al-Fākih b. al-Mughīrah . . .	..	..	..	..	..	..	..	PK
Ḥudhayfah b. Abī Ḥudhayfah b. al-Mughīrah . .	..	..	..	..	..	..	..	PK
Hishām b. Abī Ḥudhayfah b. al-Mughīrah . . .	..	..	..	..	..	..	..	PK
Umayyah b. Abī Ḥudhayfah b. al-Mughīrah . . .	..	..	..	..	..	..	..	PP
'Uthmān b. 'Abdallāh b. al-Mughīrah . . .	..	..	..	..	..	..	..	PP
Rifā'ah b. Abī Rifā'ah b. 'Ā'idh b. 'Abdallah . . .	..	..	..	..	..	..	..	PK
al-Mundhir b. Abī Rifā'ah b. 'Ā'idh b. 'Abdallah . .	..	..	..	..	..	..	..	PK
'Abdallāh b. al-Mundhir b. Abī Rifā'ah b. 'Ā'idh b. 'Abdallah	..	..	..	..	..	..	..	PK
uhayr b. Abī Rifā'ah b. 'Ā'idh b. 'Abdallah . . .	..	..	..	..	..	..	..	PK
s-Sā'ib b. Abī Rifā'ah b. 'Ā'idh b. 'Abdallah . . .	..	..	..	..	..	..	..	PK
Abu 'l-Mundhir b. Abī Rifā'ah b. 'Ābid (? = 'Ā'idh) b. 'Abdallah	..	..	..	..	..	..	..	PP
Ṣayfī b. Abī Rifā'ah b. 'Ābid (? = 'Ā'idh) b. 'Abdallah .	..	..	..	..	..	..	..	PP
as-Sā'ib b. Abi 's-Sā'ib b. 'Ābid (? = 'Ā'idh) b. 'Abdallah	..	..	..	..	..	..	..	PK

	M's tribe	*Age*	*E*	*AA*	*AB*	*R*	*H*	*B*
MAKHZŪM: *Pagans* (*contd.*)								
Abū 'Aṭā 'Abdallāh b. as-Sā'ib b. 'Ābid (? = 'Ā'idh) b. 'Abdallah	..	..	..	..	..	..	..	PP
al-Aswad b. 'Abd al-Asad b. Hilāl b. 'Ābid	..	..	..	..	..	..	..	PK
Ḥājib b. as-Sā'ib b. 'Uwaymir b. 'Amr b. 'Ābid	..	..	..	..	..	..	..	PK
'Uwaymir b. as-Sā'ib b. 'Uwaymir b. 'Amr b. 'Ābid	..	..	..	..	..	..	..	PK
'Ā'idh b. as-Sā'ib b. 'Uwaymir b. 'Amr b. 'Ābid	..	..	..	..	..	..	..	PK
al-Muṭṭalib b. Ḥantab b. al-Ḥārith b. 'Ubayd	..	..	..	..	..	..	..	PP
Qays b. as-Sā'ib ?	..	..	..	..	..	..	..	PP
+8 confederates at Badr								
'Abdallāh b. Abī Rabī'ah b. al-Mughīrah	..	..	..	..	..	..	..	..
al-Ḥārith b. Hishām b. al-Mughīrah	..	..	..	..	..	..	..	..
Hishām b. al-Walīd b. al-Mughīrah	..	..	..	..	..	..	..	..
Zuhayr b. Abī Umayyah b. al-Mughīrah	..	..	..	..	..	..	..	..
al-Walīd b. al-Mughīrah	..	..	..	..	..	..	..	PP?
SAHM								
Muslims								
Khunays b. Ḥudhāfah b. Qays b. 'Adī	Sahm	..	20	..	57	25	37	74
'Abdallāh b. Ḥudhāfah b. Qays b. 'Adī	Kinānah	..	..	..	62	X	..	..
(Abū) Qays b. Ḥudhāfah b. Qays b. 'Adī	Kinānah	..	..	..	60	X	..	..
Hishām b. al-'Āṣ b. Wā'il	Makhzūm	..	..	..	59	26	..	..
Abū Qays b. al-Ḥārith	Ḥadramawt	..	..	..	61	X	..	..
'Abdallāh b. al-Ḥārith	Kinānah	..	..	..	58	d	..	..
as-Sā'ib b. al-Ḥārith	Kinānah	..	..	..	68	X	..	..
al-Ḥajjāj b. al-Ḥārith (or al-Ḥārith)	Kinānah	..	..	..	?63	X	..	? P
Tamīm b. al-Ḥārith (or Bishr or Numayr)	Ṣa'ṣa'ah	..	..	..	65	X	..	..
Sa'īd b. al-Ḥārith	Jumaḥ	..	..	..	67	X	..	..
Ma'bad b. al-Ḥārith (or Ma'mar)	Jumaḥ	..	(? 30)	..	64	X	..	..
— Sa'īd b. 'Amr *h/Tamīm*	Ṣa'ṣa'ah	..	..	..	66	X	..	..
'Umayr b. Ri'āb b. Ḥudhāfah	Jumaḥ	..	..	..	69	X	..	..
— Maḥmiyah b. Jaz'	Ḥimyar	..	..	..	70	Sh	..	..
— Nāfi' b. Budayl	..	..	..	..	..	..	..	..
Pagans								
Munabbih b. al-Ḥajjāj b. 'Āmir	..	..	..	..	..	..	..	PK
Nubayh b. al.-Ḥajjāj b. 'Āmir	..	..	..	..	..	..	..	PK
al-'Āṣ b. Munabbih b. al-Ḥajjāj b. 'Āmir	..	..	..	..	..	..	..	PK
Abu 'l-'Āṣ b. Qays b. 'Adī b. Su'ayd	..	..	..	..	..	..	..	PK
'Āṣim b. Abī 'Awf b. Ḍubayrah b. Su'ayd	..	..	..	..	..	..	..	PK
'Āmir b. Abī 'Awf b. Ḍubayrah	..	..	..	..	..	..	..	PK
Abū Wadā'ah b. Ḍubayrah	..	..	..	..	..	..	..	PP
al-Ḥārith b. Munabbih b. al-Ḥajjāj	..	..	..	..	..	..	..	PK
Farwah b. Qays b. 'Adī b. Ḥudhāfah	..	..	..	..	..	..	..	PP

	M's tribe	Age	E	AA	AB	R	H	B
SAHM: *Pagans (contd.)*								
Ḥanẓalah b. Qubaysh b. Ḥudhāfah	..	..	..	..	..	..	..	PP
al-Ḥajjāj b. al-Ḥārith b. Qays b. ʻAdī b. Saʻd . .	..	..	..	..	..	..	..	PP
— Aslam (m. of Nubayh) .	..	..	..	..	..	..	..	PP
al-ʻĀṣ b. Wāʼil b. Hāshim b. Suʻayd	..	..	..	..	..	..	..	..
ʻAmr b. al-ʻĀṣ b. Wāʼil. .	..	..	..	..	..	..	..	..
al-Ḥārith b. Qays b. ʻAdī b. Saʻd	..	..	..	..	..	..	..	..
JUMAḤ								
Muslims								
ʻUthmān b. Maẓʻūn b. Ḥabīb b. Wahb	Jumaḥ	..	4	10	•	21	..	69
ʻAbdallāh b. Maẓʻūn b. Ḥabīb b. Wahb	Jumaḥ	30	6	..	44	24	..	72
Qudāmah b. Maẓʻūn b. Ḥabīb b. Wahb	Jumaḥ	32	5	..	43	23	..	71
as-Sāʼib b. ʻUthmān b. Maẓʻūn	Sulaym (her m. ʻAbd Shams)	19–27	31	..	42	22	..	70
Maʻmar b. al-Ḥārith b. Maʻmar b. Ḥabīb . . .	Jumaḥ	..	30	..	..	..	..	73
Ḥāṭib b. al-Ḥārith b. Maʻmar b. Ḥabīb . . .	Jumaḥ	? d.	26	..	45	d.	..	..
Khaṭṭāb b. al-Ḥārith b. Maʻmar b. Ḥabīb . . .	Jumaḥ	? d.	28	..	49	d.	..	..
Muḥammad b. Ḥāṭib . .	..	..	..	..	47	(Sh)	..	..
al-Ḥārith b. Ḥāṭib . .	..	..	..	..	48	(Sh)	..	..
ʻUmayr b. Wahb b. Khalaf b. Wahb	Sahm	..	..	..	..	..	..	P
Sufyān b. Maʻmar b. Ḥabīb b. Wahb	Yaman	..	..	..	51	X	..	..
Jābir b. Sufyān . . .	..	..	..	..	52	X	..	..
Junādah b. Sufyān . .	..	..	..	..	53	X	..	..
Nubayh b. ʻUthmān b. Rabīʻah	..	..	..	..	?56	Sh	..	..
Pagans								
Umayyah b. Khalaf b. Wahb	..	..	..	..	..	..	..	PK
ʻAlī b. Umayyah b. Khalaf b. Wahb	..	..	..	..	..	..	..	PK
ʻAmr b. Ubayy b. Khalaf b. Wahb	..	..	..	..	..	..	..	PP
ʻAbdallāh b. Ubayy b. Khalaf b. Wahb	..	..	..	..	..	..	..	PP
ʻAws b. Miʻyar . . .	..	..	..	..	..	..	..	PK
ʻAmr b. ʻAbdallāh b. ʻUthmān b. Wuhayb . . .	..	..	..	..	..	..	..	PP
Wahb b. ʻUmayr b. Wahb b. Khalaf b. Wahb	..	..	..	..	..	..	..	PP
Rabīʻah b. Darrāj b. al-ʻAnbas + 5 clients, &c.	..	..	..	..	..	..	..	PP
Ubayy b. Khalaf b. Wahb	..	..	..	..	..	..	..	..
ʻABD AD-DĀR								
Muslims								
Muṣʻab b. ʻUmayr b. Hāshim.	ʻĀmir	37+	..	6	•	8	65	35
Abu ʼr-Rūm b. ʻUmayr b. Hāshim	? Greek	..	..	..	?24	X	..	..
Suwaybit b. Saʻd b. Ḥarmalah	Khuzāʻah	..	..	..	19	9	59	36
Firās b. an-Naḍr b. al-Ḥārith.	Tamīm	..	..	..	25	X	..	..
Jahm b. Qays	(by marriage) al-Muṭṭalib	..	..	..	20	Sh	..	..
Khuzaymah b. Jahm b. Qays .	..	..	..	..	23	Sh	..	..

	M's tribe	*Age*	*E*	*AA*	*AB*	*R*	*H*	*B*
'ABD AD-DĀR: *Muslims (contd.)*								
'Amr b. Jahm b. Qays . . +1 client	..	..	..	..	22	Sh	..	..
Pagans								
an-Naḍr b. al-Ḥārith . .	..	..	..	..	..	..	..	PK
'Abd al-'Azīz b. 'Umayr b. Hāshim . . . . . +3 confederates +2 clients	..	..	..	..	..	..	..	PP
'ABD								
Muslim								
Ṭulayb b. 'Umayr . .	Hāshim	22	..	..	18	10	60	88

EXCURSUS F

The Traditions from 'Urwah

THE material derived from 'Urwah b. az-Zubayr for the Meccan period of Muḥammad's life is of considerable importance, especially the fragments of his letter to 'Abd al-Malik preserved by aṭ-Ṭabarī.[1] It is therefore worth while paying particular attention to the question of 'Urwah's reliability as a source. In what follows it will be assumed that what is alleged to come from 'Urwah really is material which he handed on. It will also be assumed, however, that he normally did not mention where he got his material, and that where a prior authority is named the name has been inserted conjecturally by a later person; the conjecture may very well be correct, but there must always be an element of uncertainty about it.

'Urwah was the son of az-Zubayr b. al-'Awwām, one of the earliest Muslims and a close friend of Abū Bakr. 'Urwah's mother was the latter's daughter Asmā', so that 'Ā'ishah was his maternal aunt. He was a full brother of 'Abdallāh, the counter-caliph of the Second Civil War. He was apparently a supporter of his brother's party, but on 'Abdallāh's death he is said to have made his way with extreme haste to the Umayyad caliph 'Abd al-Malik, and on behalf of their mother to have begged his brother's body for burial. This was granted. He was reconciled to Umayyad rule, and lived quietly in Medina. The date given for his death varies from 93 to 101, the favourite being 94.

'Urwah is said to have been the first to bring together scattered materials for the biography of Muḥammad. The diversity of the points in al-Wāqidī (*ap.* Wellhausen) transmitted from him or through him confirms that he must have attempted something of this sort. On the other hand the material from him in Ibn Hishām is largely material concerning the families with which he was connected. Thus there is material involving his maternal grandfather, Abū Bakr: 205, 245 f., 327, 333, 650 (in praise of Abū Bakr's freedman, 'Āmir b. Fuhayrah), 731 f., 1016; cf. WW, 167. There is one passage about his father (809), and some involve other members of the clan of Asad or persons connected with it.[2]

[1] *Ann.* i. 1180 f., 1224 f.

[2] Cf. WW, 189, 376.

Among the latter must be numbered 'Abdallāh b. Mas'ūd, who at an early period had been made 'brother' of az-Zubayr by Muḥammad, and who in his will left his property to az-Zubayr and 'Abdallāh b. az-Zubayr. Zayd b. Ḥārithah may also have been reckoned as connected with the clan of Asad as he had once been slave of Khadījah and perhaps also of her cousin, Ḥakīm b. Ḥizām; he had also been married for a time to 'Urwah's paternal aunt, Hind bint al-'Awwām.[1] Whatever the reason, 'Urwah was interested in Zayd and his son, Usāmah.[2] Aṭ-Ṭabarī gives 'Urwah as one of the authorities for holding that Zayd was the first male Muslim (and *not* his own grandfather Abū Bakr).[3]

All this marks him as belonging to a certain political milieu in the Islamic state—the party in power during Muḥammad's lifetime under the 'triumvirate' of Abū Bakr, 'Umar, and Abū 'Ubaydah; then the party of 'Ā'ishah, Ṭalḥah, and az-Zubayr, which in 36 A.H. opposed both 'Alī and Mu'āwiyah; then the party that was responsible for the rising against the Umayyads from about 62 to 72. (The three groups are not identical but there is some continuity between them.) It is therefore not surprising to find that among the material he transmitted is some which puts the clan of Umayyah and others responsible for opposing Muḥammad and Abū Bakr in a bad light; e.g. Muḥammad's complaint of his treatment by B. 'Abd Manāf;[4] lists of opponents;[5] the rudeness of Abū Jahl and his eagerness for fighting.[6]

The matter, however, is not quite so simple as this. The old groupings were tending to break down, and 'Abd al-Malik doubtless did all that he could to reconcile a man like 'Urwah. Thus we learn from Ibn Sa'd[7] that among 'Urwah's wives were a granddaughter of Abū 'l-Bakhtarī of his own clan of Asad, a granddaughter of the caliph 'Umar (of 'Adī), a woman from the clan of Umayyah and another from that of Makhzūm. We are, unfortunately, not told the dates of these marriages. If that with the woman of Umayyah was prior to the civil war, it would explain how he had the entrée to 'Abd al-Malik. In the material, too, we note a passage in praise of 'Utbah b. Rabī'ah of 'Abd Shams;[8] but this might be countered by the fact that 'Utbah, though of 'Abd Shams, was not of Umayyah b. 'Abd Shams.

[1] IS, iii. 1. 30. 27.
[2] Cf. IH, 791 ff., 1006; WW, 238, 433 f., 437.
[3] *Ann.* i. 1167.
[4] IH, 277 = Ṭab. 1199.
[5] IH, 271 f., 436.
[6] IH, 428; WW, 51 f.
[7] v. 132 f.
[8] WW, 50 ff.

These facts appear to indicate that, while ʿUrwah was certainly not a rabid opponent of the Umayyads, his sympathies had for long been with the opposition—though they may have altered somewhat after 72. Moreover his family tradition, which must have influenced his account of events, must have been hostile to the Umayyads. There is therefore some justification for suspecting that his letter to ʿAbd al-Malik, though genuine, is not impartial. This suspicion is reinforced by the fact that some of the transmitters of the letter moved in Qadarī circles, which were anti-Umayyad; Abān b. Yazīd held the doctrine of Qadar or free-will, and so did ʿAbd al-Wārith b. Saʿīd, the father of ʿAbd aṣ-Ṣamad.[1]

In view of this it is not unreasonable to think that, for example, the letter to ʿAbd al-Malik lays too much emphasis on the need to escape from persecution as motive for the Abyssinian expedition; such persecution as there was would be largely the work of Umayyah and the other clans which had been the traditional enemies of the group round Abū Bakr, az-Zubayr, and their families. Even if the policy of Abū Bakr and his friends had much to do with the migration to Abyssinia, family and clan tradition would not draw attention to this not-specially-creditable fact, while an obvious way of discrediting rivals lay to hand.

[1] Ibn Ḥajar, *Tahdhīb*, i, no. 175, vi, no. 923.

EXCURSUS G

The Various Lists

In order to understand the nature of the first list (*AA*) of those who went to Abyssinia, we must consider two other lists, that of those who returned from Abyssinia (*R*), which Caetani[1] repeats, with numbers, from Ibn Hishām,[2] and that of those who made the *hijrah* to Medina with Muḥammad (*H*), which I use in the form given by Caetani.[3]

In connexion with *R* the point to notice is that all those who both went to Abyssinia and fought as Muslims at Badr are in the list of those who 'returned' to Mecca. There are two exceptions to this, ʿIyāḍ b. Zuhayr (al-Ḥārith b. Fihr) and Shujāʿ b. Wahb (ʿAbd Shams), and of these the latter does not occur in Ibn Hishām's list of emigrants, and so could not be expected to 'return'. On the other hand all who 'returned' fought at Badr with the exception of four: Sakrān (ʿĀmir), who died before Muḥammad's *hijrah*, and three young men whose relatives were the leaders of the opposition to Muḥammad, Salamah b. Hishām and ʿAyyāsh b. Abī Rabīʿah (both of Makhzūm) and Hishām b. al-ʿĀṣ (Sahm), about whom a story is told of how they yielded to family pressure. Thus *R* is essentially the list of those who were both at Abyssinia and at Badr.

It is more difficult to explain *H*, for it does not contain the names of all those who went to Medina before the battle of Badr, and who appear in the list of *muhājirūn* who were at Badr. When the two lists are compared, *H* is found to omit 3 from ʿAbd Shams, 2 from Asad, 7 from Zuhrah (out of a total at Badr of 8), 2 from Taym, 4 from Makhzūm (out of 5), 1 from ʿAdī, 5 from Jumaḥ (out of 5), 6 from ʿĀmir (out of 7), 7 from al-Ḥarith (out of 7). This is very puzzling. Is it merely an accident that these names are omitted? Or is there some purpose behind it? For example, did the people omitted from *H* not count as having made the *hijrah*, from having made it much earlier or much later than the main party? It was said that some made the *hijrah* between the two ʿAqabahs;[4] but this may be merely a later attempt to explain

[1] *Ann.* i, p. 283.
[2] 241 ff.
[3] *Ann.* i, pp. 361 f.; cf. Excursus E.
[4] Ibid., p. 364, n. 3.

the discrepancy. ʿUthmān b. Maẓʿūn is said to have gone to Medina and shut the family house in Mecca, although he is omitted from *H*. Thus it seems most likely that *H* is simply incomplete.

Of *AA* the first thing we can say is that all in it are also in *R*. It is tempting to suppose that *AA* is a list of those who were in Abyssinia who were also reckoned as having made the *hijrah* to Medina; but, although most of those who were both at Abyssinia and at Badr and are omitted from *H* are also omitted from *AA*, the evidence is not strong. The detailed figures are:

those on *AA*, *R* and *H* . . .	8
,, ,, ,, ,, but not *H* . . .	4 (one doubtful)
,, ,, *AB*, *R* and also *H* . . .	4
,, ,, ,, ,, and not *H* . . .	14

Although this evidence is weak, the hypothesis is perhaps still tenable (for want of a better one) that *AA* is, as has been suggested, a list of those who had made two *hijrahs*. We may then further suppose that it was based on a very incomplete list of those who made the *hijrah* to Medina, a list that was as incomplete as *H*, yet by no means identical with it. But, as the Muslims say, God knows best.

EXCURSUS H

The Return of the Emigrants

THE list of those who 'returned' (and fought at Badr), *R*, has already been considered. But this accounts for only about half of the emigrants to Abyssinia. What information have we about the date of return of the others?

In Ibn Hishām, 781–8, we have several lists which are intended to complete the picture. The first of these (*Sh.*) is a list of those who accompanied Jaʿfar b. Abī Ṭālib in the 'two ships' and who joined Muḥammad at Khaybar in 7 A.H. This appears to be quite straightforward so far as the 16 adult males are concerned, and that is all we need consider here. Then on p. 787 there are the names of the 7 men who died in Abyssinia. These names are included in the previous list of 34 names of men who did not join Muḥammad at Mecca, who were not at Badr, and who did not return in the 'two ships'. This is simply a list in which have been lumped together all those who were in Abyssinia about whose return nothing definite is known. The list of the 27 who returned alive may for convenience be called *X*.

Out of these 27, for 22 there are no details which would enable us to say anything about their return, though some of them are said to have taken part in the battle of aṭ-Ṭā'if and later events. For all we know some of them may have remained in Abyssinia after Jaʿfar left. Of four it is definitely stated that they were present at Uḥud: Qays b. ʿAbdallāh (confederate of ʿAbd Shams), Abū 'r-Rum b. ʿUmayr (ʿAbd ad-Dār), Abū Qays b. al-Ḥārith (Sahm) and Salīṭ b. ʿĀmir (ʿĀmir). These must either have gone straight from Abyssinia to Medina or, as is perhaps more likely, have first returned to their relatives in Mecca and then somehow made their way from Mecca to Medina. Finally, there is al-Ḥajjāj b. al-Ḥārith b. Qays or al-Ḥārith b. al-Ḥārith. If these two are to be identified, there is the interesting situation that al-Ḥajjāj was taken prisoner at Badr fighting *against* the Muslims. Ibn Hishām mentions only al-Ḥārith in *AB* and *X*, and al-Ḥajjāj as prisoner, but Ibn Saʿd[1] says al-Ḥajjāj was on the second *hijrah* to Abyssinia and does not mention al-Ḥārith. Ibn Ḥajar[2] mentions that several

[1] iv. i. 144.

[2] *Iṣābah*, i, no. 1608.

authorities, including Ibn Isḥāq, spoke of him going to Abyssinia; he also remarks that some said he did not become a Muslim until after he had been taken prisoner at Badr. Thus it would seem that Ibn Hishām has tacitly corrected Ibn Isḥāq's list (*AB*) at this point, doubtless arguing that, if he was taken prisoner at Badr, he could not have gone as a Muslim to Abyssinia. But is this necessarily impossible? Could he not have been 'seduced' even after his *hijrah*? And does not this supposition help to explain some of the confusion in the sources (for nothing is said about al-Ḥārith that is not also said about al-Ḥajjāj)?

The figures are so shadowy and the evidence so tenuous that it would be unwise to lay much stress upon it. Yet it is important as reminding us of the possibility that some of the emigrants to Abyssinia, even perhaps of those who fought at Uḥud for Muḥammad, had for a time left his party and returned to the camp of his opponents. To later Muslim scholars such tergiversation was almost—though, as Ibn Ḥajar shows, not quite—unthinkable, and in all honesty they have probably covered up most traces of it, if such there were. Yet the case of al-Ḥajjāj b. al-Ḥārith as-Sahmi remains suggestive. And the fact that Yazīd b. Zamʿah (Asad) and as-Sā'ib b. al-Ḥārith (Sahm) are reported as having been present at aṭ-Tā'if but not at anything earlier is an almost certain indication that they were in Mecca with the pagans until its surrender to Muhammad.

INDEX

Names which occur only in the table on p. 7 or in Excursus E have not been included. 'B.' after a name is short for Banū, 'sons of', and indicates a tribe or clan. The article *al-*, *ad-*, &c., is disregarded in the alphabetical ordering.